Community Learning

Co ... *lloedd*

SPYING FOR HI

Newport
CITY COUNCIL

Gwilym Williams

SPYING FOR HITLER
THE WELSH DOUBLE-CROSS

JOHN HUMPHRIES

UNIVERSITY OF WALES PRESS
CARDIFF
2012

www.uwp.co.uk

British Library Cataloguing-in-Publication Data
A catalogue record for this book is available from the British Library.

ISBN 978-0-7083-2520-9
e-ISBN 978-0-7083-2521-6

The right of John Humphries to be identified as author of this work has been asserted in accordance with sections 77, 78 and 79 of the Copyright, Designs and Patents Act 1988.

Designed and typeset by Chris Bell, cbdesign
Printed and bound by CPI Group (UK) Ltd, Croydon, CR0 4YY

CONTENTS

Foreword   vii

Index to persons in narrative   ix

List of illustrations   xiii

Introduction   1

1   Operation Crowhurst   9

2   Wales Ready!   27

3   The Interrogation   35

4   If the Invader Comes   47

5   Double-Cross, Philately and Submarines   71

6   The Cuban Connection   83

7   Key to the Diplomatic Bag   93

8   The Confession   125

9   Inside Alcazar's Spanish Spy Ring   163

10   The Malta Convoy and Sinking of *Ark Royal*   179

11   The Man from Brazil   199

12   The Aftermath   213

Conclusion   221

Notes   227

Select Bibliography   245

Index   247

FOREWORD

THIS ACCOUNT OF THE RECRUITMENT and grooming by MI5 of Gwilym Williams as a fanatical Welsh nationalist to infiltrate German Military Intelligence (the Abwehr) during the Second World War has been compiled largely from a close reading of declassified British Security Service files at The National Archives, in particular TNA, KV 2/468 (October 1939–August 1942). Other information came from the operational *Diaries* of the Abwehr captured by the Americans at the end of the war. The author is grateful to James Muir for assisting with translations. West Glamorgan Archives provided valuable information about Williams's police career until his retirement in 1939. The *Western Mail* possesses one of the few surviving photographs of Williams.

The story of Arthur Owens's espionage activities both before the war and during 1939–42 is covered in files TNA, KV2/444-453, in particular KV 2/446, KV 2/450, KV 2/451. 'Snow' (Owens's alias) is also mentioned in KV 4/283 dealing primarily with the use of camouflage for protecting military installations from saboteurs.

The voyage of the *Josephine* and landing of three Cuban saboteurs in Wales is described in detail in KV 2/546. Examples of suspected Fifth Column activity in Britain during the war years are contained in KV 6/50 and NF 1/257. The confessions of German agents interrogated at Camp 020 are found in KV 4/99, but for the detailed questioning of the Spanish spy Luis Calvo see also KV 2/468.

Besides providing an exceptional insight into the day-to-day running of MI5's counter espionage branch, the Guy Liddell Diaries, Volumes 1-6 in TNA, KV 4/185 to KV 4/190, record the movements of Williams and Snow through this clandestine world.

What is missing is the folder containing the identity of MI5's other agent in Wales, codenamed 'WW'. That this person existed is clear from several references in the Williams file.

Although neither the Owens nor Williams files are complete, they have largely escaped redaction, which has more to do with the passage of time than anything else. After almost seventy years buried in the archives, not only is the cast dead but any residual risk to security has evaporated.

John Humphries
Tredunnoc, Gwent
March 2012

INDEX TO PERSONS IN NARRATIVE

Anton, Natasha	Luis Calvo's Russian mistress
Bade, Lily	Arthur Owens's mistress
Blunt, Anthony	MI5 officer and Soviet spy
Brugada	Diplomat, member of Spanish spy ring
Burton, Maurice	Owens's MI5 radio operator
Burgess, Guy	BBC producer and Soviet spy
Brooman-White, Richard	MI5 officer running Celtic Movements section
Biscuit	MI5 double agent Sam Mcarthy
Calvo, Luis	Falangist journalist, member of Spanish Embassy spy ring
Canaris, Wilhelm	Head of Abwehr, German Military Intelligence
Caroli, Gosta	Double-Cross agent code-named 'Summer' by British
Celery	Double-Cross agent Walter Dicketts
Cottenham, Lord	MI5, travel/documents section
Christensen	Name used by Starziczny to enter Brazil
De Velasco, Alcazar	Falangist Press Attaché at Spanish Embassy and leader of spy ring
Del Pozo, Miguel	Falangist journalist, member Spanish spy ring
Daniel, J. E. Professor	President Plaid Cymru 1940
Davies, Revd G. M. L	Jailed Welsh conscientious objector
Duarte	Code name for Dobbler, Abwehr agent Lisbon
Evertsen, Cornelius	Dutch master of the *Josephine*

Ford, Major   MI5 liaison officer South Wales
Frederico   Code name for Abwehr agent Madrid
GW   Code name for Double-Cross agent
                               Gwilym Williams
Gwyer, John   MI5 officer
Harris, Mrs   Del Pozo's mistress
Hechevarria, Pedro   Cuban saboteur landed in Wales
Hinchley-Cooke, Edward   MI5 officer
Lewis, Saunders   Founder, former president Plaid Cymru
Liddell, Guy   MI5, controller B Branch, counter-
                               espionage
Lloyd George, David   Liberal Prime Minister World War I
Marriott, John   MI5 officer, secretary Twenty
                               Committee
Masterman, John   Chairman Twenty Committee,
                               Double-Cross System
Owens, Arthur Graham   Agent 'Snow' in Double-Cross System,
                               'Johnny' in Abwehr
Owens, Jessie   Arthur Owens's first wife
Owens, Patricia   Arthur Owens's daugher, the movie star
Owens, Robert   Arthur Owens's son
Pablo   Code name for Abwehr agent Madrid
Pasoz-Dias, Nicholas   Cuban saboteur landed in Wales
Petrie, Sir David   MI5, Director-General, 1940–5
Philby, Kim   MI6, desk officer, Iberian Peninsula,
                               and Soviet spy
Dr Rantzau   see Ritter
Robertson, T. A., Major   Controller, Double-Cross System
Ritter, Nikolaus, Major   Abwehr controller, counter-espionage,
                               Hamburg
Robles, Silvio Ruiz   Cuban saboteur landed in Wales
Rothschild, Lord   MI5, head counter-sabotage section
Samuel, Wynne   organiser, South Wales, Plaid Cymru
Segundo   Porter, Spanish Embassy
Snow   see Arthur Owens
Starziczny, Josef   Abwehr agent Rio de Janeiro

Stephens, Robin, Lt-Col   Commandant, Camp 020 interrogation
centre
Stewart, Samuel   Shipping line agent suspected by MI5
Tate   MI5 double agent Wulf Schmidt,
Leonhardt to Abwehr
Trautmann, Werner   Abwehr radio controller, Hamburg
Tricycle   MI5 code name for Double-Cross
agent Dusko Popov
White, Dick   MI5 officer, deputy controller B Branch
White, Hilda   Arthur Owens's second wife
Williams, Gwilym   *see* GW
WW   Code name for unidentified MI5 agent
in Swansea

LIST OF ILLUSTRATIONS

Frontispiece   Gwilym Williams (*Western Mail*)

Illustrations between pages 160–161

1   Inside the exploding fountain pen (TNA)

2   Fountain pen and holder assembled for use (TNA)

3   Torch and batteries Snow and Williams brought back to London after meeting with Abwehr agents in Antwerp (TNA)

4   Torch batteries with time clock and detonators concealed inside (TNA)

5   Penmaen, where a German U-boat tried to land explosives

6   Talcum powder tin, shaving soap and sprinkler (TNA)

7   X-ray photograph of talcum powder tin containing time clock and detonators, and exploding shaving soap (TNA)

8   The fishing boat *Josephine* at Fishguard after being boarded by the Royal Navy (TNA)

9   The master of the Josephine, Cornelius Evertson (TNA)

10   One of the three Cuban saboteurs, Silvio Ruiz Robles

11   One of the three Cuban saboteurs, Pedro Hechevarria

12   One of the three Cuban saboteurs, Nicholas Pasoz-Diaz

13   Cray Reservoir near Brecon, which German agents planned to poison

14   After the Swansea Blitz: the old Grammar School opposite Williams's home in Mount Pleasant (*South Wales Evening Post*)

To Eliana, for enduring my obsessive curiosity

INTRODUCTION

THE SUSPICION THAT SOME WELSH NATIONALISTS were Nazi collaborators cast a shadow at the end of the Second World War over a political movement ostracised for declaring its neutrality and for advocating conscientious objection. Vague rumours persisted about pro-German sympathisers – a visiting university lecturer at Cardiff and a German factory manager – recruiting disaffected nationalists as Nazi agents.[1]

'Bards under the bed' was a phrase coined by critics mindful of the nine months Saunders Lewis, founder and leader of Plaid Cymru, and two others, the Rev Lewis Valentine and D. J. Williams, had served in prison in 1936 after setting fire to buildings on the site of the RAF Bombing School at Penyberth on the Llŷn Peninsula. But instead of this dramatic gesture in defence of one of the 'essential homes of Welsh culture, idiom and literature' becoming a template for further direct action, nationalism was seen by some to have retreated into its cultural shell until a new defining moment, Tryweryn, the protest over the drowning in 1966 of the village of Capel Celyn to build a reservoir for Liverpool. Whereas both events had genuine public support, sandwiched between the two the neutral/pacifist stance the party adopted when Britain declared war in September 1939 provoked condemnation, especially in the more anglicised parts of Wales.[2]

Most nationalists chose to fight in 1939, but those like Lewis who did take a stand against the 'English war' were criticised for refusing to resist Hitler and Mussolini, for tolerating anti-Semitism, and for supporting Franco. Lewis was considered by political opponents to have a track record. Was he not passionate about creating a

'Welsh Wales' in which the language was the sole medium of education from elementary school to university? Did he not subscribe to the de-industrialisation of South Wales and a return to the land after a decade during which half a million people left Wales to escape withering economic and social distress on a scale that persuaded the Government to propose transferring the entire population of Merthyr to the more prosperous Midlands?[3] By refusing to distinguish between Lewis's cultural nationalism and the racist nationalism of Hitler's National Socialist Party, his most bitter critics sought to label him a fascist for once having expressed admiration for Hitler's efforts to create a German homeland.

The Welsh nationalist case for neutrality, as propounded by Saunders Lewis, was that the Second World War was an English war and an extension of the first; and that Wales as a nation had the right to decide independently its attitude to the conflict and to reject conscription into another country's armed forces. Lewis believed the only proof that Wales existed was if some of its people acted as though it did.

Plaid Cymru's official position on the imminent outbreak of hostilities was made absolutely clear by Lewis when, in his final address as president, he spoke at a public meeting in Bangor on the eve of the 1939 National Eisteddfod in Denbigh. His speech followed Plaid's Summer School, which Lewis said, 'revealed a remarkable unanimity in all ranks'. In its account, the *Western Mail* reported the Plaid president as saying that Welsh nationalism knew its mind and knew its principles and that there was no further possibility of hesitation and indecision. In agreeing a revolutionary doctrine, the party, said Lewis, was not appealing to violence. It simply meant that Welsh nationalists possessed a body of principles that would change fundamentally the whole character of the social, political and economic life of Wales. According to the *Western Mail*, Saunders Lewis's final words as president were:

> Today it is our duty as Welsh nationalists to oppose to the demands of a militaristic, totalitarian English state the rights of the Welsh nation. This demands courage, it demands the will to suffer and imperil livelihood and to face uncertainty

and poverty. It demands that the conscript youth of Wales shall conscientiously object to the demands of English militarism on their lives. The Imperial Government of a nation has no right morally to take Welsh youth and compel it to maintain the power of the English state on the Continent of Europe. Power politics is the path chosen by the English Government. It is for England itself to decide whether that is right and just, but it is for Wales to say that power politics has no claim on Welsh loyalty or on Welsh service.[4]

Although Welsh nationalism was initially thought to be a valid ground for repudiating military service, only fourteen gave it as their reason for conscientious objection, and of these six were briefly jailed. Most nationalists pleaded religious grounds, including Gwynfor Evans, who after the war would become the longest serving president of Plaid Cymru. Of the 156 persons from Wales interned as potentially dangerous aliens, most were either nationals of Germany, Italy, and Austria, or their immediate descendants.[5]

Government anxiety about anti-war sentiment in Wales was fuelled by the War Cabinet's failure to recognise the particular position of Wales as a distinct nation rather than simply part of a larger geographical area at war. This, according to Clement Attlee, the deputy Prime Minister, provided 'powder and shot for the extreme Welsh nationalists who are mischievous and tend to be against the war effort'. Such was the political concern that after meeting Welsh MPs Attlee asked the Cabinet to issue a directive to all government departments to the effect that the Welsh should be adequately represented on all committees, advisory councils and similar bodies. Welsh-speaking servicemen were to be posted to Welsh units and, unless security considerations made it undesirable, they should be allowed to send and receive letters in Welsh. By then, however, Attlee's 'mischievous' nationalists had already been driven underground by suspicion and hostility, reduced to meeting in private and out of sight.[6]

Occasionally, public hostility burst into the open. A Plaid Cymru meeting at Fishguard at which the Revd Lewis Valentine repeated the party's demand for Dominion Status within the Commonwealth was abandoned when confronted by a hostile crowd and shouts of 'Yes, and the Dominions are helping the Mother Country in her hour of need, but you are only trying to hinder her'. Pro- and anti-war students clashed at the University College of Wales, Aberystwyth, the former tearing down pacifist posters. Professor J. E. Daniel, who succeeded Saunders Lewis as President, was forced to defend the party's position in the *Western Mail* which accused Plaid of 'uttering the most pestilential trash' and its members of seeking exemption on the grounds that the war was wholly foreign to Wales and not 'chemically pure, 100 per cent Cymric'. In spite of this onslaught Daniel stood firm, reiterating that the war was a clash of imperialisms from which Wales like other small nations had nothing to gain but everything to lose:

> It [the party] has from the beginning advocated, and continues to advocate, a negotiated peace as the best solution of the European dilemma. It does not accept the popular English view that this war is a crusade of light against darkness. It does not admit the right of England to conscript Welshmen into her army or regard it as the duty of Wales to help London to beat Berlin.
>
> But now that English policy has placed Wales in the firing line and exposed her to the dangers both from German attack and blockade and from a panic rush of English refugees numbered in their millions, no party which places the interests and protection of Wales in the forefront of its policy, can, without foreswearing itself, remain passive.[7]

The neutrality stance caused profound divisions within a party that in 1939 had barely 2,000 members and minimal electoral appeal. By contrast, the Labour Party with nearly half the parliamentary seats and 45 per cent of the vote was championing the manifold aspirations of a working class, some of who also speculated whether a German victory might be best for a country still reeling from the catastrophe of the Great Depression. The Government's response to the absence of the wild patriotic fervour that had accompanied the call to arms in 1914 was to promote the conflict as 'The People's War'.[8]

As it happened, it would be war and the demand for armaments that changed the economic landscape of Wales.

Although the clout of political nationalism was trifling, native loyalty remained deeply embedded in the Welsh psyche. Coupled with social hardship and defeatist talk, this was seen as potentially explosive by those needing to unite the country behind a conflict many still thought unnecessary. The fear that Germany might seek to exploit disaffection by recruiting collaborators from among an alienated population was not unprecedented. Had it not been the case among the German-speaking populations of Austria and Czechoslovakia's Sudetenland before annexation? Was not German propaganda aimed at cultivating links with the Breton nationalists by promising self-determination and the restoration of their language in return for collaborating against a French government that had systematically suppressed Breton?[9]

Such concerns literally exploded on Britain's doorstep on the eve of war when between January and July 1939 IRA saboteurs launched a bombing campaign in London, Birmingham and Manchester against civil, economic and military targets. An Irish couple, regular visitors to Wales, were carrying a briefcase stuffed with explosives, detonators and fuses when arrested at Goodrich in Pembrokeshire while the discovery that Jim O'Donovan, mastermind of the London bombings, had visited Germany that year to buy explosives convinced MI5 Irish nationalists would enter the war as Fifth Columnists. But the Irish were divided, the majority supporting the Allies, and the Garda rounding up IRA activists before war was even declared. When it was, the government of Eamon de Valera risked compromising his country's neutrality by allowing a large measure of discreet co-operation between the Irish and British intelligence services in combatting German espionage.[10]

That German military intelligence (the Abwehr) was casting around to forge links with nationalist groups was confirmed to MI5 by its double agent, the Welshman Arthur Graham Owens (alias 'Snow'), when he was instructed by the Abwehr to identify a Welsh nationalist fanatic to mastermind a campaign of sabotage in Britain.[11] From that moment, the security service saw an opportunity to exploit the exaggerated view the Nazis had of Welsh anti-English sentiment.

After all, MI5 also regarded nationalism as fertile ground for potential collaborators, and for that reason had planted an agent in Wales as early as 1938 to keep an eye on the 'mischievous' Welsh.[12] Rather than allow the Abwehr find a genuine traitor MI5 would deliver one groomed to play the role of Welsh nationalist extremist, his mission to open a channel for strategic deception for Britain to supply false information undermining the German war effort. The man chosen for the role was retired Swansea police inspector Gwilym Williams (alias GW).[13] His controller was Major T. A. Robertson, head of B1A, otherwise the Double-Cross System, a recently-formed section within MI5's counter-espionage branch focussed on 'turning' captured enemy spies by inviting them to choose between becoming British double agents or execution. Owens, having spied for Germany before the war, was the Double-Cross System's first recruit. Williams became the second.

Exactly what part Williams and Owens played in the espionage war remained a secret for more than sixty years, other than the occasional leak behind fanciful accounts of supposed Welsh treachery. At the end of the war the automatic response of the security services – MI5 responsible for counter-espionage at home and its younger sister MI6 for matters beyond the twelve-mile limit – was to lock away their secrets forever, thereby inhibiting accounts of the Second World War by denying access to a missing dimension.[14] MI5 and MI6 insiders were left with no other way of circumventing the Official Secrets Act but to camouflage their experiences as fiction.

But the security services were unable to bury their secrets entirely because they had no control over what other countries did. When records from German and Italian archives began appearing, a comparison with concurrent British responses pointed to the existence of missing links such as the code breakers at Bletchley Park and the Double-Cross System, both of which had enabled Britain to stay several jumps ahead of the enemy.[15]

If MI5 was to protect the identities of agents, past, present and future, careful management was necessary to divert interest away from the innermost secrets such as Ultra, the intelligence obtained from breaking high-level Enigma-encrypted enemy radio traffic. The strategic deception practised by the Double-Cross System and the

120 agents who followed Owens and Williams sat in that deep well of intelligence shielded by the security services as the Second World War ended and the Cold War began to employ the same tactics.[16]

Even though the secret service saw that its safeguards were being eroded by public pressure for greater scrutiny, it would still be several decades before documents about the espionage war were released and then only on condition reference to specific methods and resources was omitted. Redaction, the exercise of the censor's blue pencil, continued to obliterate the most sensitive material sometimes to the extent that what finally emerged was neutered, almost worthless.

The curtain was first raised not by a historian but by a novelist, Duff Cooper, formerly Minister of Information in Churchill's Government. His novel *Operation Heartbreak* in 1950 told the story of Operation Mincemeat and the discovery of a body on a Spanish beach carrying documents suggesting that Greece was the intended location for the Allies second front not Sicily, as was the case. This opened the door for Ewen Montagu's history of *The Man Who Never Was* in 1953.

The insider least expected to breach the veil of secrecy was John Masterman, an Oxford don, and chairman of the Twenty Committee, the final arbiter of what information Double-Cross agents could reveal to deceive the Germans. At the end of the war Masterman returned to Christ College, Oxford, to teach history but before he did so he was asked to produce a short account of the Double-Cross System strictly for MI5 internal consumption. The original document remained classified until 1999, but no sooner was Masterman back in academia than he expanded his personal memoir into *The Double-Cross System,* published in 1972 despite the vigorous efforts of MI5 to suppress it. Fearing that publication would trigger a stampede to the publishers by other insiders, the security service pressed for Masterman's prosecution. The final decision landed on the desk of the then Foreign Secretary Sir Alec Douglas-Home who was taught history by Masterman at Christ College, and recalled later:

> Let me tell you an extraordinary thing about J. C. [Masterman] … you won't believe this, but when I was Foreign Secretary they tried to make me lock him up. They

actually tried to make me lock him up. It was that book of his. Both MI5 and MI6 were determined to stop his publishing it. MI5 pushed it up to the Home Secretary, and he pushed it over to me. I squashed it pretty quickly, I can tell you. Lock up the best amateur spin bowler in England? They must have been out of their minds.[17]

Masterman's book coincided with the publication of one in the United States. In *The Game of the Foxes* (Bantam: New York 1973) the Hungarian-born American author, Ladislas Farago, dealt with the much wider subject of Second World War espionage. His cloak and dagger account, partly reconstruction, drew heavily on a hoard of captured German documents found in a dusty metal locker in the National Archives in Washington DC in 1967, including the so-called Abwehr *Diaries*. These contained an entry by Nikolaus Ritter (alias Dr Rantzau), head of counter-espionage at the Abwehr's Hamburg *Ast* (station), to the effect that he paid 'Williams, a leader of the Welsh nationalists' the equivalent of almost £100,000 (at 2011 values) in Reichsmarks to fund a campaign of sabotage.

Faced with the drip-drip of revelation, the security services turned for a solution to what some might see as the final deception of the Second World War – official histories written on condition the most sensitive information was omitted!

Not until the declassification of files relating to Owens (alias Snow) and Williams (alias GW) has it become possible to piece together an authentic account of Wales's contribution to MI5's strategic deception operations during the Second World War. More recently, the wartime diaries of Guy Liddell, head of B Division responsible for counter-espionage, have also entered the public domain. An intriguing record of the day-to-day operations of the secret service, they testify to the resourcefulness and courage of the Welsh agents in infiltrating German military intelligence. The rumours of nationalist collaboration were almost certainly fed by the very secrecy surrounding the clandestine activities of these two men.

ONE OPERATION CROWHURST

WHEN INSPECTOR GWILYM WILLIAMS retired shortly before the outbreak of the Second World War his only claim to fame after twenty-nine years in the Swansea Constabulary was a commendation for stopping a runaway horse. That was until September 1939 when MI5's counter-espionage branch sent him to Belgium to infiltrate German military intelligence (the Abwehr) by posing as a Welsh nationalist fanatic and leader of a group of extremists prepared to collaborate in sabotaging the British war effort. Williams avoided politics even after retiring for fear that to become involved would breach the terms and conditions affecting his pension. But he did agree to join Plaid Cymru on the instructions of his MI5 controller in order to reinforce a cover story that would thrust him into the cockpit of the espionage war between Britain and Germany.[1]

Apart from a career as a policeman, Williams had no obvious qualifications for his new role as one of the founding members of MI5's Double-Cross System, the section inside counter-espionage's B Branch for turning captured enemy spies into British double agents. Before setting out on his mission the only coaching Williams received was in memorising the names of prominent members of the Welsh nationalist party until able to recite them like a catechism. His cover story for offering his services to the Abwehr was that it was too good a chance to miss: that his Welsh nationalist friends had been waiting years for such an opportunity. If asked who had sent him Williams was to say he was replacing 'WW', the code name for an agent the Germans believed they had inside Plaid Cymru, unaware that the man was in fact a British MI5 officer. He was to tell his interrogators that no one apart from WW knew of his visit to Brussels. If faced with any awkward questions from Abwehr officers MI5 advised Williams to create some additional thinking time to reply by asking 'What?' or 'I beg your pardon?' so that the question had to be repeated. This was the only training Williams received for the first exercise in strategic deception undertaken by MI5 following the outbreak of war.[2]

On leaving the police force Williams had become a private inquiry agent investigating divorce cases not very different to his own after his first wife was caught by police colleagues fornicating with a soldier in a shop doorway late at night. It was the First World War and Williams was serving in France with the Military Foot Police, otherwise known as the 'Redcaps', sometimes portrayed with pistol in hand forcing shell-shocked 'Tommies' back to the trenches. Demobbed in 1919, his marriage in ruins, Williams had a variety of lodgings before marrying divorcée Mrs Winifred Amelia Thomas in 1932 and moving into 43 Mount Pleasant, an elegant semi-detached house on one of those steep roads climbing out of Swansea Bay like the fingers of an upraised hand. His first wife Catherine spent the rest of her life as an evangelist for the Baptist Church, living in a caravan in the grounds of a school.[3]

Born in Morriston, Swansea in 1887, Williams at 5 feet 10 inches was not a tall man in a force where many police officers stood well over six feet. His great passion was long distance swimming, and he was often seen ploughing the six miles across the bay from the pier to Mumbles Head, and back, before reporting for duty.

He drank too much on occasions and was reprimanded for being drunk on duty and deserting his beat, and was twice accused of assaulting residents. One householder complained that P.C. 92 punched him when he opened his front door after Williams rattled the knob while patrolling his beat, his superintendent later discovering him drunk and fast asleep in uniform on a sofa in the kitchen at his lodgings. The aggrieved householder dropped the complaint, suddenly discovering his bloodied and swollen face was sustained by slipping off the kerb! The only other apparent blot on Williams's police record followed a confrontation with staff from an Italian café late at night. Grabbing one by the scruff of the neck, P.C. 92 called him an 'Italian bastard' before pushing him backwards down a flight of steps. A formal complaint was made but not pursued.

Pounding the beat on cold, damp nights left its mark and Williams retired with bronchial problems, but not on a full pension, the Swansea chief constable refusing to count his two years service in the Salford Constabulary before transferring to Swansea. Whether or not money was short, soon after leaving the force Williams began his new career as a licensed private detective. At least his recruitment by MI5 would mean no more grubby divorce work.[4]

Operation Crowhurst, the plot to infiltrate a British agent masquerading as a Welsh extremist into German military intelligence, was an audacious attempt by MI5 to manipulate Hitler's belief that nationalist sentiment in Wales, Scotland and Ireland might be harnessed in support of German invasion plans. Hitler had encouraged his intelligence service to cultivate links with the Welsh as part of a scheme to persuade the former Liberal Prime Minister Lloyd George to sue for peace. The Führer had been greatly impressed by the 'Welsh Wizard' when they met three years before the outbreak of war at Hitler's mountain retreat at Berchtesgaden in September 1936. The two men spent several hours together, Lloyd George afterwards describing the Nazi leader as the 'George Washington of Germany' and applauding him for the public works programme that lifted Germany out of the Great Depression. Hitler was, according to some accounts, mesmerised by Lloyd George, and unable to take his eyes off the man credited with winning the First World War. They talked mostly about the Communist threat, which Hitler said was the principal reason for German rearmament. An elated Lloyd George afterwards described Hitler as 'indeed a great man … a born leader'.[5] On his return to England he wrote effusively in the *Daily Express* of his admiration for the Führer, 'a magnetic, dynamic personality with a single-minded purpose' who had no desire to attack any country in Europe. Not unnaturally this endorsement was disquieting for those who regarded Hitler as the greatest threat to peace.[6]

'Hitler had done great things for his country,' Lloyd George told A. J. Cummings, Editor of the *News Chronicle*. 'He is unquestionably a great leader. There is not the slightest doubt that the workers and particularly the younger generation are absolutely devoted to him.

He has affected a remarkable improvement in the working conditions of both men and women. Of that there can be no manner of doubt. And they appreciate it. They look upon him as a Monarch.[7]

Lloyd George was also critical of the British government for 'bullying' Saunders Lewis and his two accomplices by jailing them for setting fire to the RAF bombing school on the Llŷn Peninsula in 1936, reinforcing Hitler's conviction that this was someone with whom he could do business – and Welsh nationalism something to subvert.[8]

In early 1940 an American intelligence agent after infiltrating the staff of Admiral Wilhelm Canaris, the German intelligence chief, eavesdropped on a conversation between Hitler and Dr Robert Ley, head of the Nazi trade union movement Deutsche Arbeitsfront. During this the Führer spoke of the need for a secret understanding with Lloyd George, and personally urged the speeding up of contacts with Welsh nationalists opposed to the war in the hope of destabilising the Churchill government. That Lloyd George might be persuaded to lend his name to the peace movement is also mentioned by the German Foreign Minister Joachim von Ribbentrop in the *Documents on German Foreign Policy* captured at the end of the war.[9]

The man charged by Hitler with subverting Welsh nationalism was Major Nikolaus Ritter (alias Dr Rantzau), head of German counter-espionage at the Abwehr's Hamburg *Ast*. In return Rantzau was authorised to promise self-government to Wales as part of a German peace treaty with England.[10]

Rantzau was the Abwehr's rising star for his part in the German espionage ring that stole blueprints of a top secret aircraft bomb-aiming device, the Norden Bombsight. One of the most closely-guarded secrets of the American armaments industry, the aerial sighting device enabled bombardiers to focus on targets more accurately. After a German immigrant working in the Manhattan factory manufacturing the bombsight obtained copies of the blueprints, Rantzau smuggled them out of America wrapped inside an umbrella.[11] Aged about fifty, six feet tall with broad shoulders, fair hair, and grey eyes set in a round florid face, Rantzau was regarded by some of his associates as 'common' because of his fondness for telling dirty stories. Physically his most distinguishing feature was a gold tooth slightly protruding from the top right side of his mouth. Having spent a large part of his life in the United States, Rantzau spoke perfect English with a strong American accent. He used several aliases but preferred 'The Doctor' which was how he was known to his agents and British adversaries.

In the United States Rantzau failed as a textile manufacturer, but married a rich American, and raised two children before returning to join the Nazi Party, and divorce his wife. By 1938 he was married to his secretary, a woman twenty years his junior, the couple living in one of the more fashionable parts of Hamburg. Known as the 'Baroness' at the Hamburg Opera House where she had a private box, Frau Rantzau spoke perfect English but was unattractive with thin features and a pointed nose, and 'exceedingly tight with money' when paying her husband's agents, according to the most important of those, Arthur Graham Owens.

Born in Pontardawe in 1899 but a naturalised Canadian, Owens began spying for the British, then switched to the Germans but by the outbreak of war was back on side as a double agent after his wife informed on him to MI5. Unaware of Owens's latest defection Rantzau had instructed him to deliver a potential Welsh nationalist collaborator for interrogation by the Abwehr in Brussels.[12]

Owens was 'Snow' to the British Secret Service for whom he started spying during business trips to the Continent until late 1936 when Rantzau offered 'Johnny' (his Abwehr code name) a better deal. An unashamed mercenary, Owens was nonetheless a professional familiar with all the paraphernalia of espionage – secret codes, passwords ('Ginger' for 'Operation Crowhurst'), secret inks, exploding fountain pens, and booby-trapped cigarette lighters.

While claiming to be 42, he had by all accounts the physique of a man ten years older, this attributed by a doctor to a lifetime of heavy drinking and smoking. His MI5 file is even less flattering, describing a typically Welsh 'underfed Cardiff type, very short, bony face, ill-shaped ears, almost transparent, disproportionately small for size of man', with the disconcerting habit of only inserting his false teeth when he ate. He spoke 'uneducated English' with a Welsh accent, and usually wore a brown felt hat and a shifty look. Beneath thick dark brown hair parted on the left, was a pale, cleanly shaven face, thin lips and short, pointed nose. According to both British and German intelligence, he was 'very partial to women'. Jumpy and excitable, his mind touched with the eccentricities of a Walter Mitty, Owens preferred to be known as 'Heinrich Sorau' when working and socialising with Abwehr agents.[13]

But what he lacked in appearance was redressed first by the generosity of Britain's MI5 and afterwards by Germany's Abwehr in funding a passion for trawling the clubs of pre-war Soho. Lily Bade, born in West Ham of German parents, was his latest catch, the young mistress six inches taller than 'Uncle Arthur' – her pet name for Owens who stood just five feet three inches in his socks.[14]

After serving his engineering apprenticeship with a company at Clydach, he had married Jessie Ferrett in Bristol in September 1919 and moved to Mumbles, Swansea. Not long after their son Robert was born the following year the family migrated to British Columbia settling eventually in Toronto where Owens with money inherited from his father opened a battery business. When that ran out, the family, now including a daughter Patricia, returned to Britain in 1934 by which time Owens, according to MI5 was a naturalised Canadian.[15]

Back in London and with the support of a wealthy Canadian backer he started Owens Battery Equipment with customers in Germany, Holland and Belgium. At first the bits and pieces of technical information picked up on business trips to the continent he gave freely to MI5 until deciding it was time to be paid for his trouble. This was agreed and a veteran intelligence officer Col. Peel appointed as his handler. Having had unfortunate experiences of Irish nationalists, Peel took an instant dislike to the cocky Welsh nationalist. As a young army intelligence lieutenant Peel was a member of the 'Cairo Gang', a group of British Intelligence agents sent to Dublin during the Anglo-Irish war to spy on the IRA. So named because they met in Dublin's Café Cairo, most of the group were assassinated by the IRA on 21 November 1920 in a revenge killing for the Croke Park massacre when the Royal Irish Constabulary fired indiscriminately into a Gaelic football crowd. Peel, one of the few 'Cairo Gang' survivors, regarded Owens with disdain, a shifty Welshman without a patriotic bone in his small body.[16] His condescending attitude only fuelled Owens's intense dislike for the English, this manifesting itself in a display of Welsh nationalism rooted in the dubious grievance that the English had cheated his family of thousands of pounds by stealing its design for a shell to shoot down Zeppelins. His inherent dislike of the English, together with a persistent shortage of money were the reasons Owens gave for transferring his services to the Germans after deciding MI6 was not paying enough.[17]

The opportunity to switch sides arose during a business trip to Belgium and a meeting with Abwehr agent Conrad Pieper at the impressive Metropole Hotel on the Place de Brouckere, Brussels, the swankiest in the city, the lobby all polished oak beneath ornate chandeliers, and Owens's preferred working environment.[18] It was late 1936 and Germany had already reclaimed the Rhineland to resolve one of the chronic issues of German reparations, its resolution neither unexpected nor particularly disconcerting for those who regarded the Rhineland as Germany's natural backyard. An accommodating British Government chose to do nothing until Belgium and France were threatened. Even after the next domino fell – the occupation and annexation of Austria by Germany in March 1938 – the general outlook for Europe remained benign and any difficulties seemed negotiable. The British public's increasing distaste for Nazism did not always chime with the Churchillian conviction that conflict was inevitable. Others saw the threat but believed a strong and independent Germany freed from the ruinous injustices of the Versailles Treaty remained the best hope for a lasting peace. The journey along the path of appeasement culminated in the signing of the Munich Agreement by Chamberlain in September 1938, ceding to Germany the Sudetenland, the territory in western Czechoslovakia occupied by ethnic Germans the majority of who willingly surrendered their autonomy to rejoin the Fatherland.

When Owens met Pieper at the Metropole Hotel in Brussels the consequence of this chain of events was still a smudge on the horizon. Since it was in the nature of pre-war espionage for freelances to follow the money the Welshman accepted an expenses paid trip to another swish establishment, the Hotel Vier Jahreszeiten on the Alster in Hamburg as the guest of the Abwehr. The deal 'Johnny' did with Rantzau was £20 for each piece of intelligence (£1,003 at 2011 values), and £50 (£2,520) if especially valuable. Before long, Agent 3504 (the 3500 series denoting Hamburg Station, 4 his serial number) was earning so much that he set up a subsidiary company in Hamburg as a conduit for laundering Reichsmarks.[19]

Owens's greatest value to the Abwehr was the free access his Admiralty contracts gave to sensitive naval and aviation establishments such as Farnborough and Hendon. It was 'Johnny' who, reputedly, first alerted the Germans to the development of radar by supplying the location of a mysterious line of aerials erected along the south coast. Owens probably had no idea what purpose these served but the information confirmed German aerial reconnaissance reports and pre-war sightings by Zeppelins. But as Hitler ramped up his war machine there were other targets, not least of all any scandal about Churchill and Foreign Secretary Anthony Eden. Owens did provide information on pro-Nazi members of the Houses of Parliament and the activities of the British Communist Party.[20] In addition to his payments-by-results arrangement, the little man claimed lavish expenses to support an extensive network of fourteen sub-agents most of whom existed only in his imagination.

The intelligence Owens delivered was rated by Rantzau of 'the greatest value to Germany' if only because at the outbreak of war the Welshman was considered the Abwehr's Number One agent in Britain. Not everyone agreed, one MI5 agent observing, 'If this isn't a bluff, which seems likely, then they are pretty badly off'.[21] Rantzau had attempted to insert others into Britain with instructions to contact Owens but on arrival most had disappeared mysteriously because by then the Welshman had been rumbled and switched sides again. One of the early arrivals was a seaman, Walter Simon, whose instructions included recruiting Welsh nationalists as potential saboteurs although there is no evidence he ever did.[22] At least three of those who followed him were promptly delivered to MI5 by Owens for recycling as British double agents, the Welshman having convinced both MI5 and the Abwehr he was their man. One code-named 'Cato' by Rantzau was captured and turned into the British double agent 'Garbo' who in 1944 would feed German High Command phoney intelligence persuading Hitler that the planned location for the Allied landing was the Pas de Calais, not Normandy. Garbo also convinced the Abwehr there was a 'network' of German agents run from Swansea by a retired merchant seaman.[23] This, and the later activities of Williams in particular, propelled Swansea into a prominent place in the espionage world.

Owens was no James Bond but like the cinema persona he enjoyed the company of women. Before Lily came along he took his wife Jessie to Hamburg to be tempted into spying for Rantzau. After wining and dining the couple the German spymaster blamed his failure to convert Mrs Owens to the Nazi cause on an apparent 'lack of affection' between husband and wife.[24]

Although most of Owens's sub-agents were fictitious, he put real effort into recruitment. On a visit to Hamburg two months before the outbreak of war he and Lily took along an unemployed Glaswegian office clerk. The Scot, R. Myner, of 12 Parklands, Surbiton, Surrey, was expecting a business trip during which he would make some useful contacts.[25]

The three met at Victoria Coach Station in London on 16 July 1939, Myner assuming Lily was the Welshman's wife. For security reasons, Owens travelled alone, joining the others in Brussels to continue the journey to Hamburg and rooms at the Berliner Hof Hotel. There he gave Lily a twenty Reichsmark note and suggested that she and Myner 'took a walk' while he spoke with several Germans, none of whom had the slightest interest in buying batteries. Returning from their walk they met Rantzau at a tea garden, the Doctor welcoming the Welshman like a brother. During the next two days Myner was introduced to several possible 'business contacts' before being sent home by ferry via Flushing and Harwich to London.[26]

The real purpose of the Hamburg visit was for the head of the station's radio section, Major Werner Trautman, to instruct Owens in using a two-way radio transmitter. Before the outbreak of war Owens's main channel to Rantzau was through personal contact or by letter written either in secret ink or code. Almost impossible to spot by the British censor, the letter was the most secure and cheapest way for passing intelligence too bulky to be transmitted. Remarkably two of the techniques used by Owens and Gwilym Williams dated from Roman times, the first of these a jargon code designed to conceal the real message within an innocuous exchange of information between the writer and recipient. The formula for the second technique – secret ink – was first described by Pliny the Elder in his *Natural History*. The most important characteristic of a quality ink was that it withstood heat, cold and sunlight, and be indecipherable unless treated with an equally secret chemical reagent. The inks were distributed as capsules, the agent releasing the liquid by piercing the capsule with a pin and then writing on a clean sheet of paper. Identifying suspicious mail, including letters from Spain, a known supporter of the Axis powers, was a major problem for British security. On one occasion the censor pulled out a letter from an English nun written in secret ink to a priest in Ireland only to discover it was a love letter and highly pornographic. Eventually, the Germans had an ink that used blood as the active ingredient, the agent needing only to prick his finger.

The Abwehr also developed a technologically superior method for communicating with agents: the Dot.[27] The reduction of one hundred words of text to the size of a full stop, however, required large and expensive micro-photographic equipment in place at either end of the process, and for this reason reducing documents to the size of postage stamps continued to be most widely used.

Technically, the Abwehr was advanced but as a force for espionage it was in an even worse state than MI5 at the start of the war. Hitler was on the offensive and intelligence gathering had a lower priority than in Britain where it was essential for defence. Instead, Hitler poured energy and money into armaments to impose his will upon other countries, starving the Abwehr of support to mount serious espionage campaigns. Admiral Wilhelm Canaris, Rantzau's boss, planted agents here and there but never in the highest circles of foreign governments. Consequently, the Abwehr grew lazy, and dependent on freelances such as Owens to fill the vaccum left by neglect.

British intelligence gathering in the thirties was not much better, focussed as it was on watching for Communist subversion and Sir Oswald Mosley's Blackshirts, and with no proper conception of the Nazi threat the secret service was overtaken by events in 1939. Recruitment was still mainly from ex-officer ranks with little investigation into background if the recruit had the right family name.[28] Kim Philby, one of the Cambridge Soviet spies, was recruited into MI6 on the basis of a telephone call! Another potential recruit, Richard Llewellyn (Lloyd), the author of the best-selling *How Green Was My Valley*, was not so successful after offering his services to Guy Liddell, head of MI5's B Branch and his deputy Dick White over lunch at their club. The author of the book that won an Oscar for Best Film at the Academy Awards in Los Angeles in 1941 was then serving in the Welsh Guards, a posting which he said required him to think only two hours a day. 'He has had an extraordinary career,' wrote Liddell, 'and is now a writer of one of the best novels written in three years … but now finds himself in the Welsh Guards like a fish out of water … both Dick and I liked him but he may be rather difficult to fit into the organisation'.[29] White admitted later that most of those employed by MI5 at the beginning of war were 'sleep-walking'. What made the difference between British and German intelligence gathering was that Britain's defensive posture compelled MI5 and MI6 to build up intelligence to warn of enemy designs. As an example, the establishment of an Operational Intelligence Centre helped the Admiralty predict U-boat movements vital for protecting North Atlantic convoys. But the espionage infrastructure was not always so conventional. For a time an astrologer was employed to read the horoscopes of Hitler and Mussolini in the hope of discovering their intentions.[30]

The Abwehr's operations in Britain, Spain, Portugal and the Americas were run from a former merchant's mansion at Kupferreder 45 in open countryside in the north-east of Hamburg. The radio controller Major Trautman had his receiving antennas across the road in a field and his transmitting array a mile away, operated by remote control. His radio men worked four-hour shifts listening intently for the call signs of agents and also the code that acted as a security check against possible enemy interception. For Owens it was 'congratulations'. All agents had specific transmission times, but circumstances could prevent them making contact for weeks, maybe months. Besides transmitter operations Hamburg trained agents in building and repairing radios, using Morse, invisible inks, microdots and microphotography, aircraft recognition, and how to move around enemy territory inconspicuously.[31]

After a week's training, Owens took Lily to Berlin on a tour of the *bierkellers* and sleazy nightclubs, accompanied by Rantzau who not only enjoyed the Welshman's company but regarded it part of his role to build a strong bond between controller and agent. Without this mutual sense of responsibility and affection there was always the risk the agent, once out of sight, and his pockets full of Abwehr dollars or sterling, might desert to the other side, or at best provide the minimum intelligence necessary to remain active. There were abuses, incidences of agents absconding with the cash or diverting funds to support lavish lifestyles. Rantzau's personal connection to Owens was especially strong since the Welshman was his first agent when promoted to head of the Hamburg *Ast*'s counter-espionage branch on 1 January 1937. But even he thought Owens was obsessed with 'booze and dames' while Lily was 'on the side of the money'.[32]

During his absence in the fleshpots of Hamburg and Berlin, Owens's predisposition for playing away came massively unstuck when Mrs Owens blew the whistle on her cheating husband. On 18 August 1939 she informed the Special Branch at Scotland Yard that he was a German agent. She had not done so earlier on account of the children, but now he was implicating other family members in his spying racket. As proof, Mrs Owens handed detectives a receipt for an anti-aircraft shell Owens bought from a man later convicted of stealing it from the Woolwich Arsenal.[33]

Owens had in fact been under Special Branch surveillance for some time after MI5 intercepted letters from him addressed to 'Central Post Office, Box 629, Hamburg', a known Abwehr cover address. When questioned he convinced MI5 that he was attempting to penetrate German military intelligence on its behalf and, with Chamberlain's government pursuing a policy of appeasement and Hitler temporarily forbidding the Abwehr to conduct espionage activities in Britain, no action was taken against him.[34] Owens continued his 'business' trips to Hamburg without interference other than Special Branch recording his movements in and out of the Dover ferry terminal. In fact, Special Branch surveillance was so lax he collected a radio transmitter left by an Abwehr courier in a suitcase in the luggage department at Victoria Station without arousing suspicion. But by the outbreak of war scrutiny was far tighter, not only of his movements but of his love life, too. Without a steady relationship the habitual womaniser was likely to scuttle back to Soho on the prowl with all the attendant risks. The danger signs were unmistakeable for B Branch controller Guy Liddell who on being told that Owens was 'feeling his oats again after a long period of quiescence' ordered his telephone tapped.[35]

Rantzau's confidence in the little man did not waver even though he guessed MI5 probably suspected Owens. He had provided Germany with a wealth of valuable intelligence: the locations of British barrage balloon installations, details of the air raid warning system, Royal Navy tactics for attacking U-boats, and the whereabouts of RAF warehouses stuffed with Rolls-Royce aeroplane engines. Owens was also a good listener, eavesdropping on conversations between RAF officers based at St Athan, near Cardiff. The concentration of oil storage tanks at Skewen which he drew to the attention of the Abwehr became one of the Luftwaffe's main targets during its three-night blitz on Swansea in February 1941.[36] But espionage was never a one-way street, Owens spreading intelligence around like confetti. MI5 was told about the location of Germany's main submarine bases at Cuxhaven and Miel, that the U-boats had a range of 9,000 miles, each armed with sixteen torpedoes, and that Hitler was supplying Russia with shells and oil through Rotterdam. Especially important to MI5 was that Owens provided it with details of the Abwehr's organisational set-up, about which the security service knew remarkably little at the outbreak of war.[37]

Evicted by his wife from the family home at Grosvenor Court, Morden, Surrey, he dismantled his transmitter and moved it and Lily into the back room of the house rented by the Scot, Myner. They had barely settled in when one afternoon Lily hurried home to warn Myner, 'Three men have taken Arthur away at Waterloo'. Owens had left a package in the bathroom. Would he bury it in the garden? He did. A few hours later Special Branch dug up the radio transmitter.[38]

By arrangement officers had met Owens at Waterloo Station to detain him under Regulation 18B of the Defence Regulations. The date, 4 September 1939, was significant. Characteristically, the

Welshman had surrendered to police the day after war was declared, switching sides yet again by offering to work exclusively for British intelligence. The arresting officer thought MI5 was making a big mistake in using a 'most untrustworthy individual whose activities should be curtailed immediately with the outbreak of hostilities.'

'This individual,' the officer said, 'was originally employed by our Foreign Intelligence Section. It was subsequently discovered he had betrayed our trust and gone over to the German espionage service operating against this country, and that he is in fact double crossing. On his own admission he is still in the pay of the Germans and makes frequent journeys to Germany, no doubt taking with him any information he can get hold of'.[39]

Reincarnated as Snow – a partial anagram of Owens – the Welshman was released into the custody of Major Robertson, and the Double-Cross System which had plans for the confiscated radio transmitter. But first he had to prove his usefulness by contacting Rantzau by radio from his cell at Wandsworth. The first attempt failed because of a technical hitch. The second was also unsuccessful, the Germans not responding to Snow's coded message, 'All ready … Have repaired radio … Send instructions … Now waiting reply'. Robertson returned to Wandsworth early the next morning for Snow to try again, but still no reply from Hamburg. By now Robertson suspected Snow was deliberately sabotaging his own transmissions but after reminding him what Britain did to spies who failed to co-operate Snow successfully contacted the Abwehr.[40]

On another occasion, Snow was sitting in his cell at Wandsworth, the transmitter rigged up, the door ajar when the warder on duty outside interrupted. Would Major Robertson object if another prisoner was permitted to pass along the landing? Snow blanched, and trembling with fear whispered to Robertson, 'Don't let them see me – whatever happens, don't let them see me'. Immediately closing the cell door Robertson asked why he was so afraid. That morning, said Snow, he was cornered by a man he had known in Germany and warned not to talk to 'the intelligence cops'. Snow was capable of producing a lie for every situation but in this instance Special Branch thought it knew his assailant to be a man recently detained on arriving in Britain.[41]

After proving himself useful, Snow was released from prison and installed with Lily in a top floor flat furnished by MI5 in Kingston-upon-Thames. The transmitter aerials were concealed in the roof space and MI5's radio officer Maurice Burton was there if needed to imitate Snow's Morse style, the so-called 'fist' which is as distinctive as handwriting.

The Double-Cross System took the view that it was worth putting a man like Snow in personal contact with the enemy even if suspect. The longer the war lasted the more accurate the agency's background knowledge became, and the less the mistrust mattered. Assuming British intelligence prevented an agent from giving away vital material Snow was not really in a position to cause much harm. Even if he attempted a double-cross this still gave MI5 something to check against other sources. Intelligence was as much about psychological profiling as secret codes, secret inks and exploding fountain pens. A dishonest agent while lying about important matters was likely to tell the truth about unimportant ones. And what the agent considered unimportant could very well be the missing piece in a jigsaw the British were already working upon.[42]

Besides transmitting intelligence about the military build-up in Britain, Snow was also expected to use his Abwehr radio to send nightly weather forecasts to assist the Luftwaffe target London and other major cities and towns. When the blitz began access to Snow's radio for transmitting fake weather reports to confuse the German pilots proved a godsend. A trial run took place on the night of 23 September 1939. There were separate codes for the height of the clouds (H2, 1,000 yards), total cloud cover (XTC), visibility (V1, 500 yards), wind speed (W9, representing 0–50 mph), rain, fog or snow, the temperature in Fahrenheit not Centigrade. Snow's call sign was 'BRZ' and Hamburg's 'OEA'. If the Germans asked for more detailed forecasts for a particular town then he was to reply, 'Weather is not good'. Snow settled behind his transmitter, Burton monitoring his transmission. After entering his call sign BRZ, Snow waited two hours before Hamburg replied requesting the wind direction in London to which Snow tapped out 'XVN.XHC.XWC.XFRT.XTC'. In English that read 'wind south east', whereas in fact it was blowing from the north east.[43]

Sitting alongside Snow during transmissions was Col. Edward Hinchley-Cooke, a German-speaking MI5 officer assigned to pump him for information. Hinchley-Cooke was particularly interested in one reply from Hamburg asking Snow to provide 'military and general news urgently'. That, said Snow, referred to a plan to land explosives by U-boat somewhere between Penmaen on Oxwich Bay and Worm's Head at Rhossili to sabotage munitions dumps and the steelworks at Briton Ferry. If this failed the explosives would be brought ashore at Linney Head, near Castlemartin in Pembrokeshire to attack the military installations and oil tanks in the Pembroke Dock and Milford Haven area.

The conversation then turned to Operation Crowhurst. Whoever went with him to Brussels must be a Welsh-speaking nationalist activist, Snow insisted. It would also help if he spoke German. He didn't himself, and much might be missed if they were unable to eavesdrop on the chatter between the Germans.

'He has got to look, speak and act like a Welshman and at least have a smattering of the language,' said Snow. 'The Germans don't understand Welsh; I've tried it on them. But they know what it sounds like and won't be easily taken in.'

'What kind of military information do the Germans want?' Hinchley-Cooke asked.

'As much as possible about troop movements, especially around the coast, but also the troops being sent abroad.'

'Why this specifically?' Hinchley-Cook asked again.

'If the Doctor can show that the majority of troops have left Britain then the Germans can drop paratroopers dressed in British uniforms. He doesn't believe they stand much chance of surviving but the Doctor spent a lot of time in America. He's a showman and knows this would have an immense effect on our morale.'

It was late September 1939. The British Expeditionary Force was pinned down along the Maginot Line hundreds of miles from home; fears of an invasion were widespread. The expectation that the enemy would drop out of the sky was reinforced by a Home Office directive advising any member of the public who spotted a parachutist descending not to advance closer than 250 yards, the supposed range of enemy weapons. As for Hamburg's request for 'general information' Snow took this to refer to poisoning reservoirs.

'I've been asked for some months to identify the positions of all reservoirs in the country, especially those around London,' he explained.

'But why?' Hinchley-Cooke asked.

'It would be their last weapon, and if all else fails they will target our reservoirs, dropping bombs packed with bacteria,' added Snow.[44]

TWO WALES READY!

SNOW WAS THE FIRST TO ALERT MI5 to the fact that the Abwehr was attempting to establish links with Welsh nationalists. When he came under increased pressure to deliver a potential collaborator to Rantzau at their next meeting in Belgium, MI5 saw an opportunity to exploit the situation by planting a British double agent inside the Abwehr. Since the Secret Service did not have a nationalist collaborator it decided to invent one. But Gwilym Williams was not MI5's first choice for the part of Welsh 'traitor'. This was intended to be WW, MI5's agent inside Plaid Cymru. Also employed as an immigration officer at Swansea Docks, the agent who is only ever referred to in Secret Service records as WW or 'The Welsh Agent', was responsible for boarding ships docking at South Wales ports to clear the crews through immigration controls.[1] As such, WW was ideally placed to spot enemy agents attempting to enter Britain disguised as seamen, vessels from neutral Spain and Portugal especially suspect. Although most enemy agents landed by parachute, or rowed ashore by dinghy from a U-boat or fishing trawler, surveillance by the Immigration Service led to the arrest of at least one German agent, named De Jaegar arriving at Newport from Lisbon.[2]

WW had had a working relationship with Gwilym Williams extending over many years. In addition to speaking Welsh, Williams had learned enough French and German during the Great War to act as court interpreter for Swansea magistrates in cases involving the deportation by the Immigration Service of foreign seamen who jumped ship or overstayed their welcome.

At the last moment Major T. A. Robertson, head of MI5's Double-Cross System, pulled WW out of Operation Crowhurst when it was discovered he was unlikely 'to be allowed to travel abroad especially at the present moment'.[3] One possible explanation is that as an immigration officer dealing regularly with foreign consuls WW had become known to German intelligence sources. WW also suspected that an enemy agent masquerading as a bookseller had called at his home in Swansea to check him out. In the circumstances, he was told to lie low, carrying on with his usual work as an immigration officer 'as though nothing had happened, at the same time making contacts with the Welsh nationalist Party'.[4] Meanwhile, Snow was sent to Swansea for a briefing from WW on Welsh nationalism. Returning to London afterwards he radioed Hamburg from the back room of his flat at Kingston-upon-Thames 'Wales ready', the signal that the Welsh nationalist saboteur was on his way, Snow believing at the time this was WW.

Robertson had precious little time to find a replacement able to convince Rantzau of the existence of a Welsh Fifth Column waiting to sabotage military installations and munitions factories. Only six weeks earlier Britain had declared war after Hitler tore up Prime Minister Neville Chamberlain's piece of paper promising 'peace in our time' by marching into Poland. Beneath the gathering storm clouds, both the Netherlands and Belgium expected any day to feel the weight of German armour rushing through the Ardennes to crush their fragile neutrality. Whoever replaced WW would be racing against time to avoid being trapped in the Belgian capital by the enemy's rapid advance. MI5's first thought was to send a trained officer who 'looked like a Welshman'. But the agency had no one suitable who also spoke Welsh, essential according to Snow if the deception was to succeed.

The solution came from WW himself. Writing to Robertson on 11 October 1939, on office notepaper headed 'Immigration Service, Victoria House, Swansea', he proposed his friend and retired police inspector Gwilym Williams for the vacant part in Operation Crowhurst:

Referring to our conversation yesterday evening, I saw Mr [Gwilym Williams] last night. He is an ex-inspector of the Swansea Police Force, is fifty years of age, and during the latter period of his service was the station inspector at Swansea Central Police Station. He speaks fluent Welsh, and was also interpreter at Swansea Police Court.

I have known him for over fifteen years, and during that time he has acted with me on innumerable occasions in connection with Aliens at this port.

I do not know the extent of his knowledge in connection with the subject you are interested in but I can assure you he will satisfy you as to his ability and technique to approach the problem in the way you require.

I am enclosing the passport application form together with the photographs you requested.[5]

Within forty-eight hours of receiving the letter Robertson was interviewing Gwilym Williams at his London club, noting afterwards in his file:

I saw [Mr Williams] today and put the proposition to him. At the present moment he is not a member of the Welsh nationalist Party [but] on his return to Swansea will make it his business to attend their meetings and become *au fait* with their customs and so on. He can talk Welsh and struck me as being an extremely determined type of individual, and I should imagine he would serve our purpose admirably.

I also said that if by any chance he came across any indications that the Germans had already tried to penetrate the Welsh nationalist Party he was to let me know through Mr [redacted]. I also said that he was to make a note of any out of pocket expenses he incurred, and let me know through the same channel.[6]

The retired Swansea police inspector would henceforth be known within MI5 as 'GW'. Not for him an exotic code name like Garbo, Tricycle, Tate, Sweet William, or Peppermint, the aliases hiding the identities of some of his associates in the Double-Cross System.

But there was another problem. Rantzau was still expecting to interrogate WW as the disaffected Welsh nationalist to run the Abwehr's 'Welsh nationalist bombing scheme'.

'I have contacted a gentleman in South Wales,' Snow had said at their last meeting in Brussels. 'Just an ordinary sort of man, not very flush with money, who is in touch with the head of the Welsh nationalist organisation.'

'Reliable?' asked Rantzau.

'Definitely … no need to worry about that,' said Snow handing the German WW's name and address.

'Good,' said Rantzau. 'We must meet in Brussels in two or three weeks at the Savoy Hotel.'[7] Snow would need to be at his most inventive to convince Rantzau of the credibility and reliability of his new companion – a retired police inspector! That he was able to pull it off testifies to the confidence Rantzau continued to have in a man he knew was a consummate liar but who he firmly believed remained a loyal German agent even after suspecting Snow was rumbled by the British. What he never guessed was that Snow had become the cornerstone on which MI5 was building the Double-Cross System for strategic deception – and that soon Rantzau would be persuaded to recruit as a 'Welsh collaborator' Williams, another crucial brick in the edifice.

The final briefing for Operation Crowhurst involved Mark Everard Pepys, 6th Earl of Cottenham. A motoring enthusiast and once a member of the Sunbeam Racing Car Team, war had changed everything for Lord Cottenham who now made travel arrangements for MI5 agents embarking on missions. Snow, Williams and WW were to meet him and Major Robertson at his flat in fashionable Dolphin Square, Pimlico, an oasis of tranquillity in the centre of the capital. That WW attended although no longer directly involved in Operation Crowhurst is a measure of the trust and confidence MI5 had in someone who was a well-established agent of the security service in Wales. For his 52-year-old replacement this was no assignment for the faint hearted. With Britain's links to mainland Europe likely to be severed at any moment, one slip could cost Williams his life.

Arriving by train from Swansea, Williams and WW met Snow by arrangement beneath the lions in Trafalgar Square shortly before their appointment with Cottenham at ten o'clock on the morning of 16 October 1939. A taxi dropped them directly opposite the magnificent triple-arched entrance to Dolphin Square. The home of gentlemen, diplomats and admirals, Dolphin Square was a city of a thousand flats under a single roof, grouped around a quiet inner courtyard of landscaped gardens and lawns. Once inside only the muffled sound of traffic and the clatter of the occasional mower giving a manicured lawn its morning shave disturbed the peace. 'Highly desirable' was how estate agents described Dolphin Square with its back to the city and face to the river. The owners and tenants stubbornly called them flats, but some were the size of townhouses, a world away from the Swansea bedsits familiar to Williams.

The outwards facing rampart of Dolphin Square rose like the Great Wall of China on their right as the three Welshmen sought out the entrance to Drake House where Cottenham lived at Number 912. Dolphin Square comprised a number of individual residential blocks each with a nautical name and separate entrance. The Fascist leader Oswald Mosley lived in one around the corner facing the Thames until interned with his wife in Holloway for the duration of the war.

The Brussels rendezvous was only a few days away when his lordship answered the doorbell. Leading the way inside Cottenham explained that Robertson was joining them later. Cottenham began by establishing exactly what Williams had been told about Operation Crowhurst, the risks involved, and whether he was prepared to pose as a Welsh fanatic and potential collaborator. Williams replied, 'Yes, sir, I will go and I will do my best'. On Robertson's arrival there followed a lengthy discussion about the emphasis he should put on his nationalist ambitions for Wales and his bitterness towards the English, not forgetting to tell Rantzau that there were others of similar mind eager to help if the Germans provided the tools.[8]

The briefing over, Robertson returned to his office, leaving Cottenham to arrange Belgian visas. That afternoon, he met Williams at the Bonnington Hotel in Southampton Row, handing him travel documents and three envelopes, containing £20 each for himself and Owens, the other, £10 for WW. Asked where Owens went after their meeting that morning Williams said he disappeared into a small

Italian shop to make a 'telephone call to the War Office for instructions'. Cottenham was surprised but said nothing immediately. Since the pair had known each other for barely a few days, the plan was for Owens and Williams to get better acquainted by spending the last evening together in a public house at Kingston-upon-Thames.But drawing Williams aside, Cottenham asked him to report on his compatriot's behaviour before they left for Belgium the next day. Owens would never be wholly trusted by MI5.[9]

Probably to impress his companions Owens hired a chauffeur-driven Daimler to drive himself, Williams and WW to Kingston where his 27-year-old blonde mistress Lily was waiting to join them. WW sat in front of the Daimler beside the chauffeur separated by a glass partition from his companions who chatted quietly in the back about their assignment.

'The first person you'll meet is the Doctor. He's in charge of their secret service organisation for the western area – that's England and as far as America,' whispered Owens. 'Don't forget to dwell on your intensely pro-Welsh convictions, and show them you have pro-German sympathies. Make a great deal of the fact that as a Private Enquiry Agent you travel widely in Wales and see the working conditions of the people and how they are exploited by measures decided upon in a parliament largely composed of Englishmen.'

Williams should expect to be questioned about the locations of munitions factories, oil refineries, steelworks, and the shipping using the ports.

'What do I say to this?' Williams asked.

There was no harm, said Owens, in revealing details of various factories the existence of which was common knowledge, such as the I.C.I. works at Landore, and the new munitions factory under construction at Bridgend.

Williams was to suggest Oxwich Bay as a suitable place for a U-boat to land explosives because the Germans already had it in mind. If Operation Crowhurst went well he should thank the Germans heartily for offering to help his compatriots in their struggle for freedom.[10]

That evening, the three men accompanied by Lily went first to the Castle Hotel in Richmond for drinks, then on to a second public house, where they were joined by another couple, the group remaining there for several hours drinking and dancing. Owens drank heavily all evening, whisky with beer chasers according to Williams, although it seemed not to affect his judgement. When Williams was dancing with her girlfriend, Lily leaned across the table and whispered to WW, 'Mr Williams is a grand man!'

Afterwards, back at the flat Owens transmitted a fake weather report to Hamburg monitored by an MI5 radio officer Maurice Burton and afterwards demonstrated how to operate the transmitter off batteries before tuning in to some rapid Morse coming from Berlin.

'Do you read Morse?' Williams asked him.

'Yes, but they send it very slowly for my benefit,' was the reply.[11]

Operation Crowhurst began the following evening. Williams and Owens were to catch the boat train for Folkestone while WW returned to Wales. If questioned by Belgian immigration the cover story was that they were travelling to a business appointment with a Canadian due to sail from Rotterdam to Toronto aboard the *Nieuw Amsterdam*. Before leaving his hotel Williams wrote to his wife explaining that he was detained in London on business, which she assumed meant court work. An MI5 agent was assigned to deal with any telephone calls Mrs Williams made to the Bonnington Hotel.[12]

THREE THE INTERROGATION

NEITHER OF THE TWO MEN MEETING under the clock at London's Victoria Station on the evening of 19 October 1939 exchanged a flicker of recognition until they were sitting comfortably on the boat train to Folkestone for the seven o'clock cross-channel ferry to Ostend, and on to Brussels. Abwehr agents would be waiting to collect them from the Savoy Hotel on the Rue Saint-Lazare in Brussels for a series of interrogations probing GW's claim to be a Welsh nationalist extremist and potential collaborator. The retired police inspector about to be thrust into the frontline of the espionage war might never have taken the risk had he known more about his companion in Operation Crowhurst.[1]

Much of the truth about Snow, alias Johnny, and on other occasions Wilson, Graham, and finally White (the name he took to the grave) will remain buried beneath a mountain of subterfuge. His stock in trade was deception and lies, his tools his wits and natural cunning in support of a complicated lifestyle filled with booze and women. In the last resort loyal only to himself, Snow was never wholly trusted either by the British or Germans, leaving Gwilym Williams dangerously exposed to the aberrations of an individual some thought at the very least psychologically erratic.[2]

The crossing to Ostend was uneventful apart from the late autumn gale burying the boat beneath mountains of spray. From Ostend the train was virtually empty, but on arriving at Brussels an hour later it was engulfed by refugees wrenching open carriage doors and clambering aboard for the return trip. Many were Jews desperate to stay one step ahead of the German advance, some having fled

Austria in 1938 when the Germans walked in. None believed the Dutch or Belgians could stop Hitler.

Standing amongst the heaving mass of humanity GW saw his first Nazi. SS officers were free to walk the streets of the Belgian capital because the Government and monarchy opted for a policy of 'maximum administrative collaboration', the ruling elite adopting an anti-semitic culture that required Jews to wear yellow stars – with the exception of Brussels whose authorities refused to enforce the order. Collaboration, many Belgians believed, was the only way to safeguard their country's precious neutrality.[3]

It was late evening when GW and Snow checked into the Hotel Savoy. No one was waiting, nor were there any messages. Neither were there any the next morning. All they could do was wait for Rantzau to make contact.

GW met the Doctor for the first time that afternoon, 21 October 1939. Returning to the hotel from another walk around the block, Snow was greeted with a warm smile by a man waiting at the reception desk. Rantzau asked the pair to accompany him to Antwerp, less than an hour's train ride away, where he left them drinking beer in the station saloon until some time later a man approached through the fog of cigarette smoke. As tall as Rantzau but dark and more slightly built, he wore thick glasses and spoke bad English. Major Brasser, Chief of Air Intelligence at Abwehr headquarters in Berlin, had a particular interest in the Doctor's latest recruit as a potential source of information for the Luftwaffe.[4]

Brasser led the Welshmen across the station forecourt to a woman standing on the pavement beside the taxi rank. She was Lisa Kruger, until the outbreak of war a moderately successful Abwehr agent in Britain extracting information from unsuspecting officials at the Royal Aircraft Experimental Establishment at Farnborough. A tall woman aged about 38, and wife of another of Rantzau's agents, Kruger asked GW and Snow to deliver a message to some 'good friends' of hers in Oswald Mosley's British Union of Fascists. By the time their taxi arrived Frau Kruger had disappeared into the night having taken a close look at GW for future reference.[5]

The taxi wound its way through Antwerp's maze of frustratingly identical streets reaching down to the banks of the River Scheldt.

Around and around they drove, bumping over tramlines and into streets named after saints, convents and monks, remnants of the city's Roman Catholic legacy, and finally through the red light district – the Schipperskwartier or Rosse Buurt between Sint Paulusstraat and Brouwersvliet. Young women flaunted themselves in the large bay windows of the brothels, the red light above the side entrance flicking on and off depending on the briskness of the trade from a motley crowd strolling along the pavements like window shoppers. After touring the back streets the taxi eventually dropped them outside a large block of offices on the waterfront opposite the Canadian Pacific Railway Wharf. GW made a mental note to locate it on a map for MI5. Entering the building quickly through a side door, an elevator was waiting to whisk them up to the second floor and a large suite of offices overlooking the Scheldt.[6]

A stiff Bavarian type of average height greeted GW at the door with a vigorous handshake. Kapitaenleutnant 'Charley' Witzke spoke excellent English and as head of the sabotage section at the Abwehr's Hamburg *Ast* would be GW's controller if he survived the interrogation. But first there were sandwiches, beer, and polite conversation during which it became evident Witzke was familiar with the Bristol Channel having served aboard freighters trading between South Wales and Hamburg. Introduced as the 'Commander', Witzke would run the interrogation which began immediately Snow, Rantzau and Brasser left the room to spend a large part of the next three days in some other part of the building. What they talked about and what they were planning Snow refused to say. Occasionally, Rantzau and Brasser reappeared to ask more pointed questions about GW's links to the leaders of the Welsh nationalist movement, the party's objectives, and how it planned to achieve these.

'Until now,' explained GW, 'we have only adopted pacific methods such as the distribution of leaflets and the publishing of a book setting out the various resources of Wales indicating the country's ability to be self-supporting. We are now anxious to obtain the assistance of Germany to gain our ends, and for this we will assist in every possible way. For us, we've been waiting for this the kind of chance for years'.[7]

The probing went on and on, at times so intense that GW didn't know whether he 'stood on his head or feet'. Like a mantra, he repeated the names of prominent nationalists as proof of his credentials, and whenever an awkward question was thrown, stalled for time to produce a credible reply. Oddly enough at no point was he asked why a former police officer was prepared to betray his country! Apparently satisfied with GW's nationalist credentials, Rantzau and Brasser left Witzke to discuss the detailed planning of a sabotage campaign while they resumed their conversation with Snow.

'You can best render assistance to Germany,' said Witzke, 'by destroying dockyards, ships, sheds used for the storage of stores and cotton, electricity generating stations, aerodromes and munitions factories'. Nor was GW's group of saboteurs to confine themselves to targets in Wales. Military and civil installations were to be attacked in Bristol, Manchester, Liverpool, and Glasgow. As a reward for collaboration, the independence of Wales would be guaranteed in any peace treaty Germany negotiated with England, promised the Commander.[8]

'Sabotage – what with?' GW asked. 'There's no way we can find the materials to do all of this. It's impossible to get hands on this in England at present.'

'No problem,' said Witzke. 'We'll supply everything.'

A discussion followed about the best way to deliver explosives and detonators to Wales, the generally preferred route by submarine either into Oxwich Bay on the Gower, or from a U-boat waiting ten miles off shore for a fishing trawler to unload the cargo. The other suggestion was by parachute, GW pointing to a spot on a map of the Black Mountains as a possible drop zone. The location and method by which explosives would be delivered was postponed until the following month when GW was in Hamburg for instruction in Morse code and to collect his radio transmitter.[9]

The next morning Snow was more nervous than usual and insisted on buying a revolver before they met the Germans again that evening in Antwerp. If the Abwehr was wise to them, they might need to defend themselves, he told GW. A gunsmith agreed to sell them a weapon if they could get a permit, which Snow explained to the Commissaire de Police was for 'shooting rats'. With the revolver and twenty-five rounds of ammunition in his jacket pocket the little man was still unable to relax. There was another problem, he said for no apparent reason – women, in particular women agents sent to trap him. 'Never work with women,' the notorious womaniser whispered. 'Too dangerous!' The next moment he was planning to steal a Spitfire and fly it to Germany. Worth £50,000 and a job for life, he said. How he admired 'a race that got things done!'

'And the Doctor, he is very impressed with you,' he told GW as they waited in the hotel lobby for the car to collect them for the next stage of the interrogation. 'But be careful. When we get back to England don't speak to anyone until I contact you again. Phones are being tapped, letters opened,' he warned.[10]

Witzke sat behind a desk studying a sheet of paper when GW entered the office on the Antwerp waterfront that evening. The windows were shuttered and as was now the custom Snow left the room before the Commander resumed the cross-examination. He had a list, Witzke told GW, of information they would expect to receive from their new Welsh nationalist allies:

1. Types of searchlights used.
2. What protection did balloon barrages have against lightning strikes?
3. The reason for the suspension of air raids on German targets, and if these are resumed what would be the main targets?
4. Details of the engines used in the new Short Bros. fighters; how many had been produced, and where were they based?
5. Was Fairey Engineering building the new torpedo plane on the Hamble, and where were they being used?
6. Were the headquarters of 22nd Army Group at Farnborough or Weybridge?
7. Which army groups were defending Jersey and Guernsey?
8. Was the 600th Auxiliary Flight Squadron at Manston or Hendon?
9. The location of mobilisation centres.
10. RAF radio navigation frequencies and the apparatus being used.
11. Which RAF pursuit and reconnaissance squadrons, and anti-aircraft units were stationed in France?

12. What were the main British ports for supplying its forces in France?
13. The strength of the various sections of the British Expeditionary Force.
14. Which British ports were being used to unload supplies from the United States?
15. The locations of airfields, and the numbers of planes operating from each.
16. Information about munitions factories at Speke, Liverpool, and elsewhere.

Could the Welsh nationalist movement deliver, Witzke asked? From the very outset GW insisted that his group was small and primarily interested in sabotage, not espionage. 'Off hand,' he told Witzke, 'there are 500–600 [nationalist] members in South Wales and of these twenty or thirty can be depended upon to carry out any necessary work provided the risk is not too great. I can't say exactly what the total membership of the movement is, but I believe it is stronger in the north than the south.'[11]

GW asked how they were expected to carry out sabotage in England when the group's membership was restricted to Wales.

'By getting these men to find employment in other cities and to carry out the work whenever the opportunity presents itself,' replied Witzke. 'Once they've finished they move on to jobs elsewhere. We'll compensate them for everything.

'We are anxious for this senseless war to end,' he continued. 'We want nothing more than peace with England and France. We would appreciate acts of sabotage by the Welsh to bring an end to this unnecessary war, which serves no useful purpose for Germany, England, or France. And the way to bring it to a quick conclusion is to cripple England internally, to make her listen to sense and reason without slaughtering the youth of these countries.

'The sinking of the occasional ship will not stop the war. England has abundant means of transport available. But internal disruption by means of sabotage at places of vital interest will be of immense value to us in bringing those in England who are responsible, to such a state of mind as will cause them to listen to reason.'

As for Poland – the immediate reason for Britain's declaration of war – Germany intended, said Witzke, giving Russia 200,000 square miles, 80,000 for the Poles, 60,000 for the Jews, while retaining 100,000 for itself.[12]

After several more hours of interrogation – and propaganda – the meeting was adjourned. The next day Snow was collected by taxi from the hotel by Major Brasser, leaving GW alone for the entire morning. On his return Snow mentioned nothing about his dealings with the Germans, except to inform GW his interrogation was to continue. That evening they were driven out of the centre of Brussels to a leafy suburb and a large detached house built of heavy grey granite, the home of the owner of the Antwerp offices.

The house was lavishly furnished but as far as GW could see the only occupant was a female German servant who led the way into a large first-floor dining room where Witzke was waiting. GW spent another hour discussing various ways of delivering explosives to his Welsh nationalist cell. Again, the final decision was postponed until they met in Hamburg the following month. In the meantime, GW was told by Witzke to identify secure hiding places for the explosives once they were landed and for his group to augment these stockpiles by raiding dynamite stores at Welsh collieries. 'Nationalists' were also to be used to spread anti-war propaganda.[13]

The final task the Abwehr commander set GW was to make a direct, personal approach to the former Liberal leader Lloyd George with a view to encouraging him to influence 'Welshmen against joining the forces of England'. True to his assumed character, GW responded to the Lloyd George proposition by suggesting Germany reciprocated by providing preferential treatment for Welsh POWs. 'This will help with the propaganda at home because the POWs are bound to mention this in their letters,' he explained.[14]

Apparently convinced GW was genuine, the Abwehr told him to obtain a visa to travel to Holland the following month. There he was to collect a fake American passport before crossing into Germany for further instructions at Hamburg *Ast*. In the meantime, he was to pose as a stamp collector, one in a chain of philatelists transmitting intelligence to Hamburg. The so-called philatelists were all cover addresses for a stamp exchange passing micro-photographic copies of secret documents hidden behind postage stamps to the Abwehr. GW's contact in the chain was 'Mme. de Ridder, No. 22 Avenue Helene, Anvers, Belgium'. Until he was given the codes necessary to become a link himself he was to communicate with Mme. de Ridder by concealing intelligence intended for Rantzau in the fifth paragraph of his letters.[15]

Before leaving Brussels, Rantzau would give Snow two micro-letters to deliver to 'Charlie', an Abwehr agent based in Manchester. Charlie was a British-born German named Kiener with a brother Hans and other relatives living in Nuremburg. By threatening his family, Charlie, a photographer, was forced by German military intelligence to provide the expertise and specialist equipment necessary to reduce documents photographically but in November 1939 he surrendered to police in Manchester and confessed. As was the custom, the choice offered by MI5 was: work for us or we'll drop the SS a copy of your confession. Charlie became another Double-Cross agent working under MI5 control.[16]

On his return to London Snow told Robertson about the micro-letters but instead of delivering them to Charlie as instructed by MI5 he sent his Scottish friend Myner to Manchester, accompanied by Lily. Checking into the Queen's Hotel as 'Mr and Mrs Thomas Graham' the pair met Charlie by arrangement in the bar to hand over the micro-letters containing instructions to take photographs of Liverpool and Speke aerodromes. After miniaturisation the photographs were to be hidden behind postage stamps on a letter addressed to 'Thomas Graham, c/o British Columbia House, Regent Street, London', a dead-letter box used by Snow. MI5 was furious. Asked to explain why he had not done the job himself, Snow replied nonchalantly, 'I didn't fancy the journey'.[17]

On the final day of interrogation in Belgium, GW, Snow and Witzke took a taxi to a shop in a cobbled square a short distance from the hotel. Witzke rang the bell at the end of a narrow passageway. A bolt was released but when the door swung open there was no one to be seen, only a lift waiting to take them up to a first-floor apartment. The kitchen of the apartment had been loaned to Witzke by a Flemish nationalist for the purposes of a demonstration.

Removing his jacket, Witzke the sabotage expert stepped across to the kitchen table. 'You must take a careful note of what I say,' he instructed. 'If you don't then you might kill yourself although this is still the safest and most effective way to make a bomb. There are other methods and these will be demonstrated in a laboratory when you visit Germany in three weeks.' GW took notes as Witzke ran through the list of ingredients like a recipe.

'Take three parts of potassium chlorate and one part sugar. Grind the two to a powder separately; then thoroughly mix without causing friction. For this use either a large bottle or stone jar.' Picking up a bottle from the table Witzke tipped in the two ingredients, gently shaking before emptying the mixture into a cardboard shoebox. From a kitchen cupboard the German took an empty medicine bottle, and dropped the cork-stopper into a small saucepan partly filled with paraffin wax, then lit the stove.

'Boiling the cork in wax excludes all the air,' he explained. While waiting for this, Witzke poured a small quantity of undiluted sulphuric acid into the medicine bottle before replacing the boiled cork after piercing the centre several times with a sowing needle to allow the acid to filter through.

'Now this is the most difficult part,' he said picking up a small oval piece of waxed paper and sticking it across the head of the cork. 'This will kill you if you don't take care.' The paper was waxed apart from a tiny section immediately above the point at which the cork was pierced. 'Experiment with different thickness of paper,' he advised GW. The thickness controlled the rate at which the acid escaped from the bottle through the holes in the cork, determining the time a saboteur gave himself to escape after the neck of the medicine bottle was inserted into the explosive mixture in the shoebox.

Demonstration over, they adjourned to a local tavern for a few beers and to say their farewells. Leaning across the table Witzke gave GW £50, adding, 'Only a fanatic works for nothing. This is for your trouble. If you need more, call upon our friend [Snow]. He is authorised to give you what you need.' To fund sabotage operations the Germans were, according to Snow, depositing a large sum of money in his Canadian bank account. If this was true, GW never saw a penny.

The interrogation was over, although GW was warned to expect a visit from a German agent already operating in Britain. The agent would call at his house in Mount Pleasant, Swansea, identifying himself by showing a photograph and asking, 'Are you Mr Williams?' The reply to this was, 'Yes. Do you deal in pictures?'

The manner in which GW dealt with the questions impressed Snow, or so it seemed at first. Whatever traps the Germans set appeared to have been avoided. GW's vehement dislike and distrust of the English and his commitment to achieving a self-governing Wales had struck home. If Hitler wanted nationalists to prepare the way for an invasion then GW was his man.

By 9 p.m. on 24 October 1939 GW and Snow were on the train to Ostend, arriving in Folkestone by 1.30 a.m. As a precaution, the pair parted company before reaching London Victoria. GW was back in Swansea by 11 a.m. the next morning. After a week of interrogation by the Abwehr the retired police inspector returned home as Abwehr agent A.3551, recruited as a saboteur and Fifth Columnist, and paid by Snow, agent A.3504.[18]

Guy Liddell, head of MI5's B Division, was pleased with the success of Operation Crowhurst, noting in his diary:

> Snow and his Welsh friend appear to have had an interesting time in Brussels where they had long discussions with various Germans. The idea is that they should both be employed in blowing up factories and works of importance in this country, for which ample funds are to be made available. There is a suggestion that explosives should be sent by submarine and landed somewhere off the Welsh coast. Snow was offered £50,000 for anybody who would fly one of our latest craft to Germany.[19]

But that was not all. Snow had returned from Brussels with two small blocks of wood in which detonators were concealed.[20] Rantzau also gave him £470 and a letter postmarked Bournemouth containing his 'salary'. The money trail led to Mrs Mathilde Kraft, the Abwehr's paymaster in Britain who was eventually arrested after exchanging large sterling notes in Selfridges in London for smaller denominations with which to pay Snow.[21] The notes were the first German forgeries to appear in Britain.

A year *after* Rantzau's first meeting with Williams the Abwehr counter-espionage chief noted in its Logbook of Counter-Intelligence (Section II) that he had authorised the payment of 20,000 Reichsmarks in local currency to 'Williams, the leader of the Welsh nationalists' to fund a sabotage campaign. The payment to Williams was being delivered by an IRA member code-named 'Margarete' employed as a courier for the Abwehr between Madrid and London. The German intelligence logbook entitled 'Operations against England undertaken by the Section in association with members of the Irish Republican Army' was among a cache of German intelligence documents known as the Abwehr *Diaries* captured by the Americans at the end of the war. Another entry code-named 'Whale' refers to a plan in November 1940 to land a radio operator, V-Mann Lehrer, from a trawler to establish closer links with Welsh nationalists. Whether the Abwehr radio operator ever reached Wales is not known, only that his departure from Brest on 11 November 1940 was delayed by bad weather.[22]

FOUR IF THE INVADER COMES

WILLIAMS AND SNOW RETURNED to a country where the spectre of invasion was never far away. Even during the Phoney War between September 1939 and D-Day in June 1940, when air raids were few and there was no enemy on the beaches, the nation was alert to the possibility of sabotage by Fifth Columnists, especially in the aftermath of an IRA bombing campaign in London and other major English cities in the months immediately prior to the declaration of war. MI5's priority was to ensure that Irish nationalists did not enter the war as Fifth Columnists and that the thousands of German and Italian aliens in Britain were rounded up, interrogated and interned. The possibility of Fifth Column activity was reinforced by intercepted radio traffic that revealed the Abwehr was attempting to recruit saboteurs in Anglesey. The German High Command was also preparing 'Operation Green', its plan to land 5,000 troops in Ireland to cross into Wales in support of Hitler's main invasion force 'Sea Lion'.[1]

Parliament had been recalled from its summer recess the week before Prime Minister Neville Chamberlain declared war on 3 September 1939 to pass the Emergency Powers (Defence) Act interning aliens of 'hostile origin or association' and persons concerned in 'acts prejudicial to the public safety' under Regulation 18B. Although there was a right of appeal, Regulation 18B automatically suspended habeas corpus.

The description of a group of people plotting to undermine a nation from within as Fifth Columnists was relatively new at the outbreak of the Second World War having first entered the revolutionary lexicon during the Spanish Civil War when in November 1936 the armies of the nationalist Spanish generals Franco and Mola were approaching Madrid. At Franco's headquarters were a number of German and Italian staff officers. One Nazi officer, having impressed on Franco the importance of having supporters in Madrid who could rise up at the right moment, referred to them as a Fifth Column, the other four being columns of troops converging on the capital. Later in a statement to foreign correspondents, General Mola adopted the phrase and said, 'We have four columns of troops marching on Madrid and in the city we have a fifth column,' its aim being to undermine the morale of the defenders.

At first, the round-up of aliens was slow due in part to a dispute between the Home Secretary Sir John Anderson, and MI5. The latter, mindful of the Fifth Column potential of aliens wedded to a foreign power, wanted immediate wholesale internment accompanied by tighter control of refugees flooding in from the occupied territories of mainland Europe. As for Sir Oswald Mosley and his British Union of Fascists, MI5 knew they were being funded by Berlin to spread Nazi propaganda, and wanted them arrested immediately. The Home Secretary, however, was strongly opposed to locking up British subjects unless a cast-iron case could be made that they would actively assist the enemy in the event of an invasion. Had not the BUF, he reminded MI5, appealed to the patriotism of members in its party newspaper, *Action*, adding that he thought it a mistake to imprison Mosley and his supporters who would be 'extremely bitter after the war when democracy would be going through its severest trials'. Guy Liddell, head of counter-espionage, was privy to this exchange. At the time he held his tongue, but noted later in his diary, 'I longed to say that if someone did not get a move on there would be no democracy, no England and no Empire, and that this was almost a matter of days [away] … The possibility of a serious invasion of this country would seem to be no more than a vague suggestion in Anderson's mind.' While conceding that the Germans had no real grip on British fascists, there were undoubtedly links between the two, and Liddell wanted the most prominent members locked away for the duration of the war. MI5 had much the same view of British communists.[2]

Anderson regarded large-scale internment as not only impracticable but likely to create hotbeds of intrigue, camps becoming recruitment centres for Nazis and controlled by the Gestapo. Until the military was able to police the camps adequately the Home Secretary preferred to leave it to the appeals tribunals to decide ultimately who was interned. Both the Joint Intelligence Committee and MI5 thought his confidence in the appeals tribunals grossly misplaced, MI5 describing them as 'farcical' and Britain's immigration restrictions as so lax that the country was saddled with a large number of undesirables about whom the Security Services knew very little. But the Home Secretary did ask the colonies to take their quota of German, Austrian and Italian internees. Help came from Canada who accepted 6,000, Newfoundland 1,000, Jamaica up to 100,000, while Australia was prepared to take an unlimited number. Within twelve months there were almost 20,000 men and women in camps in Britain, the most dangerous of B Category internees held in Dartmoor but the majority on the Isle of Man. Much to the concern of the security services the tribunals released more than 5,000 on appeal, largely on medical grounds, including 100 members of the British Union of Fascists.[3]

This still left 13,000 known resident aliens at large in Britain and with MI5 having also to contend with the huge influx of refugees it was vetting 50,000 suspects a month. Unable to discharge its main intelligence function the agency recommended that shipping aliens abroad was a greater priority for the war effort than the arrangements then being made to evacuate one million children from Britain's main urban centres.

The round-up of aliens in Wales did not start much before 13 May 1940 when German troops and armour attacked along a forty-mile front between Forbach and the Vosges mountains. In a dawn raid the Cardiff Constabulary descended on 'Little Berlin', a part of Whitchurch that was home to 130 residents of German or Austrian ancestry. Such was the concentration of aliens in this area that the early morning bus was known to locals as the 'Berlin Special'. Roused from their beds, all those aged between 16 and 60 were taken first to the Law Courts and then to a reporting centre for processing after which some were interned until the end of the war. The following month the net was extended to more than 260 Italians after Mussolini declared war against Britain and France and police were forced to use truncheons to break up anti-fascist demonstrations outside an Italian fish and chip shop in Swansea. Soon afterwards all enemy aliens naturalised since 1932 were ordered to surrender to police maps, guide books, train timetables, in fact anything that might be useful to an invader.[4]

The country was 'rotten with Fifth Columnists of the infamous IRA' according to the *Western Mail*, reminding its readers that the Nazis made no secret they believed Ireland was Britain's vulnerable heel from where they could overrun first Wales then England. The most trivial incidents assumed sinister proportions even amongst those in high places fancying themselves as amateur detectives sniffing out subversives.[5] Nor was the War Cabinet immune, Winston Churchill wasting many man-hours by insisting on an investigation into the 'bow and arrow' he was shown in an aerial photograph taken by an RAF reconnaissance plane. The arrow pointed from a church towards an Ordnance Factory alongside which appeared the outline of a large white bow on the ground in the middle of a conifer plantation on the estate of the newspaper magnate Lord Iliffe. A wildly excited Cabinet Office felt vindicated when told that a piece of paper found by MI5 at the church revealed that one of the congregation was also a member of the pacifist, anti-war Peace Pledge Union known to have been infiltrated by Fascists. On investigation the head of the 'arrow' proved to be a car park outside the church, and the tail the drive leading up to the entrance. The 'bow' appeared white because of the chalky ground used since 1923 as a feeding area for his lordship's pheasants. Embarrassed by the revelation, the local RAF squadron felled the surrounding trees to hide the offending space.[6] Not long afterwards the War Cabinet caused another security alert after a general left his copy of secret deliberations on a table in his suite at the Hyde Park Hotel. Seeing the file stamped 'Top Secret' a chambermaid hid it under a cushion for safety before reporting the discovery to the floor waiter who told the head waiter, an innocent Italian. Before long Special Branch officers were crawling all over the Italian's apartment.

Not least in the spate of ridiculous inquiries distracting MI5 was an investigation of a public telephone kiosk from which a man was heard to issue instructions to another male person to go to a house with a red flowerpot outside, knock four times and give the password. The suspicious call was from a scoutmaster to a member of his troop he was training in exercising powers of observation. The agency, however, did refuse to comply when asked to vet applications for membership of the Girl Guides from the daughters of aliens![7]

Curious signs chalked on telegraph posts in various parts of the country were another distraction. It nonetheless fell to Anthony Blunt, the Soviet spy embedded in M15, to explain the mysterious telegraph post graffiti. Following his evacuation from France, Blunt – one of the infamous Cambridge Spy Ring that included Kim Philby, Guy Burgess and Donald Maclean (Foreign Office) – joined MI5. At the end of his first day in post he sent his controller Guy Liddell a note summarising the events occupying the day. There was a letter from a lady pointing to the danger of sentries being poisoned by ice-creams sold by Italians; then a report on a colonel who made some indiscreet statements; a complaint about an engineer and conscientious objector training army personnel; an investigation into a Scottish hotel owner with 'German blood' who proved to be of pure Scottish descent and had never left the country; and finally the strange markings chalked on telegraph posts. These, Blunt discovered, were messages left by courting couples and common practice among the working class! Even so the Government issued a regulation prohibiting the use of telegraph posts for such purposes. Liddell's response was that reports of this nature were 'obviously junk … and if some could be strangled at birth it might save a great deal of time'.[8]

That the country was jumping at shadows was hardly surprising after secret documents obtained by the British Embassy in Belgrade revealed that the Luftwaffe was preparing to drop an estimated 100,000 tons of bombs on British cities, 12,000 parachutists were expected to land on the east coast, and 70,000 German troops were waiting to come ashore between Deal and the Isle of Wight.[9] In the circumstances the lights were switched off for the next five years and Britain held its collective breath.

When a solitary air attack on ships in the Firth of Forth was all that occurred many wondered whether predictions of an imminent German invasion were exaggerated, the blackout too harsh, and food rationing unnecessary. From the declaration of war in September

1939 until the main German offensive nine months later not much happened. The British Expeditionary Force remained dug in along the Maginot Line, which the French thought impregnable, while the British War Cabinet and intelligence services tried to second-guess Hitler. As a precaution, tens of thousands of children were evacuated from the south-east and the Midlands to the relative safety of Wales, the first arriving on Sunday 19 May 1940, 7,100 to dispersal centres in schools and churches in Glamorgan and another 2,900 to Monmouthshire. After hot drinks and medical examinations the evacuees were handed over to billeting officers for placing in homes across the valleys. The following month troop trains arrived in Cardiff packed with soldiers snatched from the jaws of death at Dunkirk. That this influx of evacuees was disconcerting is evident from the reaction of the *Western Mail* in promoting a scheme to evacuate Welsh children to Canada in collaboration with North American Welsh societies.

But as the fear of imminent invasion receded from the collective consciousness, the English evacuees began returning home. A quarter of the 1,311 children billeted with families in the Cardiff Rural District Council area returned to the cities as complacency spread.[10]

Britain seemed more secure than in the previous September. But the security services still believed Hitler would invade, his forces stationed along the French coast a constant reminder of this while he waited for Spain to join the Axis, seize Gibraltar, and drive the British fleet from the Mediterranean to secure Germany's Middle East oil supplies. After Dunkirk Germany intensified the air attack on British cities and stepped up the U-boat campaign in the North Atlantic in an attempt to break morale and starve the country into surrender. Boffins at the Ministry for Home Security calculated that the Luftwaffe needed to drop 300 tons of bombs on a city like Bristol, Cardiff, or Southampton for three successive nights, then five tons for ten consecutive days followed by another 300 tons a night for two more days before morale collapsed.

The complacency of the Phoney War was gradually replaced by defeatism, a hidden enemy sapping at public morale after the Germans forced British troops out of Norway, then occupied Denmark without a shot being fired in early April 1940. The next month Luxembourg, the Netherlands and Belgium surrendered in quick succession, Churchill replaced Chamberlain, and as France fell 335,000 British, French and Belgium troops were plucked to safety off the beaches at Dunkirk. But for the Royal Navy Britain was defenceless, the retreat from France leaving the British Army with only 12,000 Bren guns and fewer than 600,000 rifles.[11] The Local Defence Volunteers (Home Guard) was mobilised to fight the invader.

Rumour fed upon rumour spreading like a virulent disease to infect people who by becoming part of the rumour mill were blindly supporting Fifth Columnists if, indeed, any existed. That they did was given some credulity by an entry on 30 May 1940 in his diary by the newly appointed Commander-in-Chief, Home Forces, General Sir Edmund [later Field Marshal Lord] Ironside, who wrote:

> Fifth Column reports coming in from everywhere … a man with an armband on and a swastika pulled up near an important aerodrome in the Southern Command. Important telegraph poles marked, suspicious men moving at night all over the country … I put piquets [*sic*] on all over the place tonight. Perhaps we shall catch some swine.[12]

Not everyone believed in the existence of a Fifth Column outside a public imagination fuelled by accounts of what happened in occupied Europe ahead of the German advance. Those at MI5 who dismissed its existence based their assessment on Germany's pre-war effort, which was wholly directed at keeping Britain out of the war while estimating the country's capacity for rapid industrial mobilisation if there was one. Not until they reached the Low Countries did Hitler and the German High Command realise on taking stock of the position that they had not the resources in place for an effective Fifth Column, the Abwehr having failed to make the effort to establish a deep-seated espionage organisation prior to the war.[13] For such reasons Hitler regarded his intelligence service as ineffective and the head of the Luftwaffe Hermann Goering preferred to run his own. Despite this, Lord Swinton, who had assumed Cabinet responsibility for MI5 and MI6 took the precaution of creating a 'thinking committee' to weed out all those most likely to engage in subversive activities: enemy aliens, right-wingers, dual nationals, allied nationals and the IRA. When the Dutch Foreign Minister after escaping to Britain blamed his country's capitulation on German parachutists dressed in a variety of disguises, monks and nuns, nurses and tram-car conductors, reports of burly men in habits acting suspiciously poured in to MI5.

After France fell and it was reported that the French Government was moving to North Africa, the rumour spread like wildfire that the British Government was preparing to flee to Canada. Some suggested that a 'Shadow' Cabinet had already relocated to the other side of the Atlantic. According to another rumour, the King and Queen were packing their bags, while the young Princesses had been sent abroad.

Defeatism in advance of an imminent invasion was an explosive mixture Churchill sought to defuse with one of the most inspirational speeches of the Second World War:

> We are told that Herr Hitler has a plan for invading the British Isles. This has often been thought of before … we shall defend our island whatever the cost may be. We shall fight on the beaches, we shall fight on the landing grounds, we shall fight in the fields and in the streets, we shall fight in the hills; we shall never surrender.

Whereas Churchill's broadcasts did much to sustain morale during the dark days of 1940, from Dunkirk through the Battle of Britain and the blitz, they would have been rather less convincing had his listeners known of another entry in General Ironside's diary. Three days after the 'fight them on the beaches' speech the man responsible for Home Defence was arranging for his diaries to be sent from his family home in Norfolk to Canada to prevent them falling into enemy hands if Germany invaded, a battle he feared Hitler might win.[14]

Defeatism was fuelled by the view insinuating its way into public opinion that the British would not be any worse off under Hitler if it were true that their own leaders were preparing to flee the country. 'If Hitler were here it would not affect you and me,' said some. 'If Hitler ruled England it would only mean that I would pay my taxes to him instead of to the King,' suggested others.[15] After the resignation of Chamberlain the British public continued to believe peace hung on the Führer's every word. Until the shooting started the German leader was widely regarded as not so much an enemy but as a hothead, albeit an unpleasant one, who could still be managed if the proper policies were pursued. Appeasement took a long time dying.

The official response to fatalism was to invoke support for 'The People's War'. But unlike the First World War, when two million volunteered in the first two years, this latest appeal for self-sacrifice lacked conviction. Although at the outbreak of war, unemployment was at its lowest for ten years, Wales remained a country of intractable social divisions, huge swathes of it still industrial desert. Divisions about whether to fight or not were not confined to the nationalist movement. Politicians of all complexions, as well as religious leaders, were not convinced that war was inevitable, that a deal could not be done with Hitler. The nonconformist chapels, still a powerful influence on Welsh religious, cultural and social life, were perceived in the more anglicised South Wales valleys as cells of rabid nationalism and Plaid Cymru sneered at as a party of 'preachers and teachers' for actively encouraging conscientious objection. Nationalism and pacifism were synonymous for critics of neutrality and the anti-war sentiments broadcast from chapel pulpits, the *Western Mail* for one endeavouring to defeat what it evidently saw as the enemy within by unleashing on the pusillanimous Welsh the Revd Dr E. Griffith-Jones, a former chairman of the Congregational Union of England and Wales. A man who boasted of not having a drop of English blood in his veins, Dr Griffith-Jones had recently retired to Wales after spending almost all his life ministering to the English across the border. From the platform given him by the *Western Mail*, he lambasted renegade clergymen for their cowardice, describing their pacifist spirit as the country's greatest national peril for 'its crass and selfish acceptance of all the privileges and securities of civilisation while shirking the duty of defending them … That there is something seriously the matter with Wales is manifest to such as have the eyes to see and ears to hear what is being said by certain of our Welsh ministers'. Appealing to fellow ministers to answer the call, he said the trouble with Wales was that while the rest of the Empire had made up its mind, 'Wales was still hesitant about its duty'. In an interview with the newspaper's parliamentary columnist, 'The Junior Member for Treorchy' – the pen name for a Conservative Member of Parliament – he ascribed the trouble to a 'rabid species of pacifism with which so many of our Welsh ministers have become infected'. Another London-Welsh clergyman, the Revd J. D. Jones, saw no difference between pacifism and nationalism when in fact they should have been draggers drawn. 'For the life of me,' he added, 'I cannot understand why all classes in Wales should not regard England in the same light as do the Scottish people … why are the Welsh clergy not praying for the gallant sons of Wales in battle?'

Because of the secretive nature of the anti-war undercurrent in Wales it is difficult to be certain of its pervasiveness, except that judging from the addresses of those seeking conscientious objection it was more prevalent in rural Wales where the influence of the chapel and nationalism was greatest. The validity of the very vocal observations of the two London-Welsh clergymen, and claims by a newspaper that failed to quote the sources for its allegations must remain questionable. Nevertheless, the frequency with which these concerns surfaced during the Phoney War helped convince Nazi Germany it could manipulate what it perceived as a strong anti-war sentiment in a nation struggling against a common enemy, the English.

With the memory of the lost generation still fresh, many, like the Peace Pledge Union and its Welsh affiliate Heddychwyr Cymru, whose first secretary was the future leader of Plaid Cymru, Gwynfor Evans, discouraged another rush to the colours. The PPU supported appeasement, accepted Hitler's claim to the Sudetenland as legitimate, and promoted conscientious objection. In 1937 after merging with the No More War Movement its anti-war pronouncements at times seemed indistinguishable to MI5 from Mosley's British Union of Fascists for which reason it was infiltrated by the Security Service. But Home Secretary Sir John Anderson thought the BUP not dangerous and that to suppress it would create martyrs. Nevertheless, MI5 continued gathering evidence for prosecutions, in particular against one of the PPU's most active members, the Welsh Methodist preacher George Maitland Lloyd Davies for organising mock tribunals to rehearse conscientious objectors in the presentation of their cases. He was not alone, according to the *Western Mail*, which reported that 'Pacifist Homes' had been opened by PPU supporters in Cardiff, Penarth, Carmarthen and the Swansea Valley where on several nights a week young men were coached to become conscientious objectors and instructed in preparing their case for the local tribunal. In Penarth, a six-bedroom house with an acre of land was acquired by two former BBC employees as a refuge and 'self-subsistence community' serving Cardiff and district, and it was not uncommon to see conscientious objectors working in the garden. The newspaper claimed that in the Swansea Valley a non-conformist minister regularly preached that any man who fought in France should be considered a murderer. The Peace Pledge Union even ran a Peace Stall in Cardiff Central Market distributing pacifist literature entitled *How to register as a conscientious objector*, and *How a conscientious objector should appeal* until the City Council closed it down after the *Western Mail* reported:

> The Peace Pledge Union does not deny that it encourages men to attend conchie classes. There the men are warned of the questions which will probably be put to them by the tribunal members and the appropriate answers are suggested to them. The result is that many objectors have learnt the answers off by heart … Many objectors put forward the Sixth Commandment, Thou Shalt Not Kill, as a ground for their registration but their records on the other nine make interesting reading.
>
> This war finds the enemy at our gate threatening civilisation. The freedom of democracy gives objectors the right to air their views, but they will not lift a finger to help to defeat the Nazi terror.

As of May 1940 the number of men registering under the Military Service Act in Wales as conscientious objectors totalled 1,592, or 1.7 per cent of all those registering in the United Kingdom. The *Western Mail* estimated that three-quarters of these were either Peace Pledge Union members or Welsh nationalists, 'the majority of nationalist conscientious objectors in North Wales'.

According to other accounts only six known members of Plaid Cymru claimed political grounds when registering for exemption from military service but this did not stop the *Western Mail* from campaigning vigorously against what it saw as an abuse of the legislation and from protesting at the use of nationalist witnesses to support such cases. In an editorial it thundered:

> … It was never contemplated from the outset that the tribunals would be used by a political faction as a platform for the dissemination of their propaganda, as they have been used by Welsh nationalists. Such cases amount to an abuse of the tribunals and should have been ruled out of order from the outset. If a man states his objection is purely political that should be the end of the case …

Significantly, the Conservative *Western Mail* addressed Welsh nationalists in the broadest sense, avoiding specific mention of Plaid Cymru for fear of conceding one iota of recognition to it as a credible Welsh political party, a policy that I (as a former editor of that newspaper) know continued well into the 1960s.

Not everyone claiming political grounds for exemption from military service was successful. A Clydach, Swansea man, Reginald Morgan Williams who told the tribunal sitting in Cardiff that 'this is an English war … they have done nothing for Wales … even Scotland has its own Secretary of State' was refused exemption and told to join a Welsh regiment. Others, like Gwynfor Evans, leader of the Peace Pledge Union's Welsh arm, registered successfully on Christian grounds, as did Lloyd George's nephew, William George (27), a Criccieth solicitor, who refused to fight but volunteered for humanitarian work with the Society of Friends. Asked by the tribunal if he thought Britain should resist German invasion, he replied, 'I should prefer resistance of a non-violent character'. Reminded by the tribunal chairman Sir Thomas Artemus Jones that the war was being fought against the 'gospel of brute force' and that a Nazi victory would open a new chapter in the history of civilisation, Mr George replied that it was in such circumstances Christianity was born. His application for exemption was approved.

Exemption on political grounds ceased to be an option in July 1940 after three young Welsh nationalists – Dafydd Williams (21), student from Caernarfon, G. Jones (21), coal miner from Wrexham, and R. J. Evans (23), agricultural worker from Corwen – appealed in Welsh to the London Conscientious Objectors Appellate Tribunal. Williams and Evans had been removed from the exemption register by the local tribunal and Jones had been registered for non-combatant duties. Williams appealed because as a Welshman he considered it wrong to be pressed into the service of England.

His case hinged not on whether his beliefs were reasonable but on whether they were honestly and sincerely held. If they were then he was entitled to exemption under Section 5 of the Act.

'What would you do if Wales was invaded by Germany?' Williams was asked by Sir Arthur Pugh.

'I would fight to resist the invasion,' replied Williams, a student at the University College of Wales, Aberystwyth.

Mr W. E. B. Henderson, for the Minister of Labour, submitted the appeal was not founded on conscience, which must have some connection with what was called the soul. It was really about politics and chauvinism and should be dismissed.

In a reserved judgement, published by the *Western Mail* on 22 July 1940, the Tribunal dismissed Williams's appeal, stating:

The appellant in this case states that he is a Welsh nationalist and he bases his claim to be registered as a conscientious objector entirely on this ground.

The Appeals Tribunal have given careful consideration to this important point and have come to the conclusion that he is not a conscientious objector (a) to being registered in the military service register, or (b) to performing military service, or (c) to performing combatant duties within the meaning of the National Service (Armed Forces) Act 1939.

The *Western Mail* was jubilant, claiming the decision endorsed the protest it had made many months earlier. 'After the belated decision of the Appeal Court short shrift should now be given to any further cases of this kind which have exposed the Welsh people to much undeserved and unenviable notoriety,' it proclaimed.[16]

Churchill appointed Alfred Duff Cooper as Minister of Information to tackle what might become a serious drag on the war effort. A right-wing Conservative diehard, Duff Cooper told Liddell of MI5 over dinner that the old school tie was one of Britain's finest institutions and that educating the working class was a mistake. MI5 could hardly disagree since its preference was to recruit Oxbridge-educated public school types, certainly into the highest echelons of the service. A man convinced of the superiority of the British race, Duff Cooper as Information Minister reminded the British that because they had far more freedom and better conditions than any other country there was no need to change the status quo. Ideologically incompatible with the vast majority, Duff Cooper's opinion was echoed by another propagandist who believed his country superior to all others, Joseph Goebbels. The response from Hitler's Minister of Propaganda was to exploit Britain's social divide and the cultural ones between Wales, Scotland and England.[17]

After failing to keep Britain out of the war Hitler decided to invade, issuing Directive No. 16 in July 1940 instructing the German High Command to prepare 'Operation Sea Lion' for the following September. He prefaced the order by stating: 'As England, in spite of her hopeless military situation, still shows no signs of willingness to come to terms, I have decided to prepare, and if necessary to carry out, a landing operation against her. The aim of this operation is to eliminate the English Motherland as a base from which the war against Germany can be continued, and, if necessary, to occupy the country completely.'

Originally the German High Command planned to invade at a point on the coastline between the Wash and the Thames until Hitler decided a more viable option was between Margate and the Isle of Wight. Before it was postponed indefinitely for Germany to focus on the invasion of the Soviet Union, at least eight different locations would be considered.

In advance of the anticipated invasion Goebbels employed an arsenal of propaganda stations to undermine British morale. Under the umbrella of the 'New British Broadcasting Service' (NBBS), the 'star' of this propaganda blitz was William Joyce, the infamous 'Lord Haw-Haw', an estimated two million tuning in every night for 'a good laugh' at propaganda dressed up as news although afterwards it was not unheard of for some listeners to remark, 'There may be something in what he says'. These 'jitter broadcasts' fed into Fifth Column psychosis affecting military and civil authorities alike, some army units taking matters into their own hands by preparing blacklists of those to be detained or shot when the balloon went up. 'Collar' was the code word one unit had for triggering a round-up. In one instance a unit seized a perfectly inoffensive former officer with a fine record in the First World War and held him and his wife prisoner for seven days without any justification except that they had a foreign sounding name.[18]

Overseas troops exposed for the first time to Goebbels's propaganda machine were no less jumpy and even less impressed with the response of the British security service to suspicious sightings. In the absence of police a Canadian regiment billeted in Oxford turned out in force to look for a parachutist reported to have landed in the vicinity. On hearing of this in London, MI5 and MI6 officers piled into cars and dashed off to Oxford by which time the Canadians had ransacked a farmhouse in a frantic search for the enemy parachutist. Eventually a man was found hiding behind a bush with a bicycle and eating a piece of bread. He claimed to be a Welsh prisoner of war who, having escaped from a POW camp in France, had stowed aboard a German plane from which he baled out the previous night. The security services were told three different stories before the truth emerged that he was an army deserter cycling home to Wales.[19]

Aware that the British felt especially vulnerable to attack by German parachutists the NBBS posed as the BBC with advice for listeners not to molest parachutists who were making 'trial drops' in various parts of the country. In all, Goebbels had forty stations blasting propaganda at different sectors of the community, Radio Caledonia targeting Scottish nationalists, the Christian Peace Movement aimed at pacifists and the anti-war movement, Radio National was anti-Semitic, and Workers' Challenge exploited class differences in Britain. The Irish were also treated to nightly propaganda broadcasts in both English and Irish, the Germans calculating that by supporting the republic's neutrality Britain would be discouraged from invading Eire which some members of the War Cabinet thought necessary to deny the protection of the Irish coastline to U-boats preying upon the North Atlantic convoys.

Reports broadcast by NBBS stations that 100,000 German parachutists had been dropped dressed as British soldiers frightened the public to such an extent that the press and BBC were instructed to publish rebuttals to steady morale. So convincing were the propaganda stations – all supposedly based in the countries they served – that a man arrested for sticking NBBS advertising slips in telephone kiosks believed it to be a pirate station of the pacifist Peace Pledge Union.[20]

Despite MI5's doubts about the existence of a Fifth Column it had to assume that embedded in each propaganda broadcast was an instruction to a subversive or Nazi agent. A radio expert borrowed from the BBC thought he had cracked the code for contacting subversives after noting that in certain broadcasts the names of towns were spelt out, sometimes two or three times, and usually broadcast in groups of three. Plotted on a map they formed a triangle showing at its apex the town due to be bombed the next day, or so the expert believed. Another sinister feature was that some broadcasts were repeated the following day on the excuse that the previous day's transmission was poor, suggesting that there had been a rapid transfer of intelligence between a German agent located in Britain and the Abwehr's Hamburg station.[21] The Ministry of Information routinely ridiculed broadcasts although the source of these was not always immediately apparent. In its debut broadcast Workers' Challenge presented itself as a UK-based station reporting on working class unrest over the war, a subterfuge given credence by the response from its parent station NBBS:

> In the course of our routine activities we quite naturally listen to many radio stations and are always interested to discover a new one. During the last few days we have found the Workers' Challenge Station. It evidently represents an extreme socialist movement. Its speakers are unmistakably of the British working class, and so we may add is their

language. In this respect the station is certainly an innovation. It is interesting to note the extreme violence of the station's propaganda, and although there is a certain kind of humour in the broadcasts, there can be no doubt there is great bitterness behind them. This may be regarded as a reflection of unrest now perceptible throughout the whole of the working class. This dissatisfaction, often bordering on mutiny or revolt requires only such stimulation as 'Workers' Challenge' gives to become an extremely ugly force. 'Workers' Challenge' as it calls itself represents the natural reaction to desertion of the trade unions by their own leaders. Churchill has bought the leaders, but will he be able to buy the men? We think not. We shall not therefore be at all surprised if these true and violent broadcasts will have an effect which they would not secure under normal conditions.[22]

The two stations were complementary and the broadcasts designed to exploit the class divide by driving a wedge between the ruled and rulers, while offering to restore normality with a German solution to the 'red horde' hammering at the gate. Immediately following this particular broadcast, one exasperated senior official at the Ministry of Information complained that the 'voice' of the BBC was out of touch with the British working class. Better, he said bluntly, if the BBC enlisted presenters like the Labour Member of Parliament for Llanelli James Griffiths and the Midland Miners' Association leader George H. Jones to promote 'The People's War'.[23]

Appearing to echo Duff Cooper's ideological mantra, the official said the thrust of British propaganda should be to remind all classes of the need to defend British values '… of the achievements of labour, of their social services, their high standard of living, their tradition in public education, the emancipation of women, their industrial pre-eminence, and that they are a race of pioneers and leaders, [and that] "The People's War" is about preserving these achievements'.[24]

The reality was different. Though Stanley Baldwin's National Government was credited with aiding economic recovery in some parts of Britain, not much was done to assist the communities most devastated by the collapse in the coal, iron and shipbuilding industries. *The Times* reported that in Merthyr, where 25 per cent were still out of work, people were wasting away from lack of nourishment. Edward VIII was so horrified by living conditions in South Wales during his visit in 1936 that he famously commented 'something must be done'. The Baldwin Government had tried by designating the most destitute areas of highest unemployment such as Merthyr and Sunderland as 'Special Areas' in which the Government bought sites and built factories to induce industry to set up new businesses. When that failed it contemplated transferring the entire population of Merthyr to a green field site in the more prosperous Midlands. As it happened it was the war and demand for armaments that revived these industries, not government policies. In the circumstances, the notion of 'The People's War' never achieved real traction.

The possible existence of a Fifth Column, however, did galvanise public awareness, providing the Information Ministry with a platform to attack defeatism and eradicate complacency. Those who asked 'Is it true that …' or 'Have you heard that …' were portrayed as amateur Fifth Columnists. The same people said 'Now that Germany has conquered France I do not see how we can hope to achieve final victory'. In response the Ministry propagated the view that if Germany won then the wealth of the nation would be seized, and the working class reduced to slaves and paupers as in Czechoslovakia and Poland. Whether MI5 believed it or not, the official line was that Hitler had an army of paid, professional collaborators ready to support an invasion. Was it not the case that when Poland was invaded a Fifth Column was waiting to provide the German army with food, petrol and horses? German parachutists were guided to safe landing areas, Polish troop and tank positions revealed to the enemy, and communications between the Polish Army headquarters and its troops cut. Haystacks and hedgerows were set alight to signal to the advancing Germans, and Polish Fifth Columnists sent false orders to troops by secret radios.

In Norway the Fifth Column issued instructions to Norwegian troops not to mobilise, coastal batteries were ordered to cease firing, military communications cut, and munitions factories captured. In Holland, Dutch Nazis delayed their army's response by transmitting false reports to headquarters while directing incoming German parachutists to hidden food dumps.

Although Belgium's resistance lasted less than three weeks, sentries were murdered at their posts by Fifth Columnists, dissension sown in the ranks of the Belgian Army, and German agents and SS permitted to mingle freely in Brussels with troops and refugees ahead of the invasion.

The British Fifth Column was portrayed as a very real threat and instructions issued to MI5, the police, armed forces, Air Raid wardens, and Home Guard on how to identify and deal with subversives. Every British home received a leaflet entitled *If the INVADER comes* explaining what to do:

> RULE 1:
> Do not believe rumours and do not spread them. When you receive an order make sure that it is a true order and not a faked order. Most of you know your policeman and ARP warden by sight, and you can trust them. If you keep your heads you can also tell whether a military officer is really British or only pretending to be so. If in doubt ask the policeman or the ARP warden. Use your common sense.

> RULE 2:
> Keep watch. If you see anything suspicious note it carefully and go at once to the nearest police officer or station, or to the nearest military officer. Do not rush about spreading vague rumours. Go quickly to the nearest authority and give him the facts.

By no means all foreigners were potential German agents. Most hated Hitler and it was wise not to be over-suspicious of strangers, advised the Ministry of Information. 'Be vigilant. Be cautious. Be sensible. Keep your head and use it' was the way to act. Those spreading rumours were criticised for playing the enemy's game because there were 'in this country German agents, maybe British by birth and upbringing, whose object it is to increase fear and uncertainty among the people and by so doing lower their morale'.[25]

Unlike their continental neighbours Britain, apart from a brief skirmish with the French in Wales in the eighteenth century, had not been invaded since 1066. But the British knew what to expect. The Royal Navy might defend the shores but it was from the skies the invaders would come, tens of thousands of German parachutists supported by glider-borne troop carriers as had happened in Holland. No one was therefore surprised when Churchill issued instructions for obstacles to be erected across all large flat fields to prevent enemy gliders landing. The ideal barrier was a line of stout posts partially buried and strong enough to rip off the wing of a glider. An RAF pilot flying out of Weston-super-Mare on a reconnasiance mission could not have been aware of this when he photographed lines across a field near Newquay in Cornwall which a police sergeant discovered were fence posts erected on the instructions of the Air Ministry to prevent enemy aircraft landing.[26]

More lines, on this occasion white ones, were reported on another farm, this time near St Austell, by a reconnaissance aircraft from RAF St Athan. Since the lines formed a cross the immediate thought was this marked the landing place for enemy parachutists. A closer look revealed several piles of lime for liming the fields.[27]

At Leeds the resident MI5 agent was told to investigate a woman known locally as 'Miss Angel', but whose real name was Frances Steigman. Although British born and not having visited Germany for sixteen years, 'Miss Angel' rented out caravans at various locations around the country, which led someone to recall how in Holland a touring circus was used to conceal radio transmitters in holes dug beneath caravans. Appropriately, the investigation of Miss Angel's caravans was referred to Cyril B. Mills, joint owner of the Bertram Mills Circus. As an amateur pilot, Mills had flown over Germany often before the outbreak of war, reporting to MI5 anything of a suspicious nature. Now resident MI5 agent in Oxford – and later MI5's liaison officer with the FBI in New York – Mills knew the German Jew who owned the circus in Holland which gave rise to the story of buried radio transmitters. 'The very fact that a circus is always on the move,' Mills told MI5 in London, 'makes the digging of holes under caravans seem absurd. I can assure you that anyone who did that sort of thing with our show would have been in great trouble for spoiling the grass in the parks!' After a police raid on the caravans found nothing suspicious, the investigation was dropped. Miss Angel was totally innocent and the victim of local gossip.[28]

More difficult to explain was the photograph of a map found in an envelope on Hunter's Bridge, Welwyn Garden City, and marked with crosses, circles and drawings of tiny aircraft. At the top of the photograph in pencil was a radio frequency, 157.43 Mc/s, one not normally associated with clandestine radios. The photograph was a reduction of part of a one-inch Ordnance Survey map and unusually good for an amateur. The use of the symbol 'Mc/s' suggested the frequency was written by a trained operator as amateurs rarely used the 'per second' in any form. The paper and envelope were United States Army issue. The crosses marked on the map indicated important bridges and culverts, the circles searchlight positions, and the drawings of tiny aircraft the sites of real and dummy airfields, and gun positions, all accurate.

Perhaps coincidentally, MI5's sister organisation MI6 used the same radio frequency to contact its agent 'Hans' at Scheveningen, a coastal resort near The Hague in occupied Holland. The map was found at about the time Hans was dropped into the sea just off the beach at Scheveningen. The agent, Peter Tazelaar of the Dutch resistance, swam ashore in a wet suit, wearing a dinner jacket beneath it. Once on the beach he stripped off his wet suit and calmly walked into the seafront casino to keep an appointment.

While the security services suspected that the map and radio frequency were a hoax, a watch was maintained at Welwyn Garden City on the frequency for forty-eight hours. Although nothing was heard, MI5 maintained an interest in the frequency, which it said was of 'importance in another connection'.[29]

There was never any satisfactory explanation for another suspected case of subversive activity. Flight Lieutenant R. M. Walker, head of a department described as dealing with 'odd and suspicious bits of paper found', wrote to Albert Foyer who ran the Plain English Code Section at High Holborn in London enclosing a piece of paper found by a policeman at Combe Florey on the Taunton–Minehead road. It contained a block of typed capital letters arranged in rows across the page in five-letter groups. Walker thought this was a five-letter cipher, similar to that used by Snow for transmitting messages. On the back of the sheet of paper were some indecipherable figures in pencil and resembling wireless signals. The five-letter blocks sometimes made complete words, such as PEACE, NAZIS, BLITZ, RAIDS, PANIC, FIRED or were shortened like HITLE (R), REVOL (VER), SPECI (AL). The block also included a list of distinctly foreign sounding names: RESSK, DUPRE, EISER.

Foyer was baffled but could find no hidden code. Occasionally, the message broke down, suggesting it was a copy and not an original, the cryptologist concluding it was produced by a teleprinter operator, either for practice or amusement. But Foyer could offer no explanation for one especially odd combination of words, BLACK WHITE BOATS, planted in the middle of the block of letters.[30]

In the absence of real, live Fifth Columnists, MI5 invented GW. At that time the agency had about thirty officers and another six engaged on surveillance duties and was ill-prepared for counter-espionage. Training was virtually non-existent, while during the years of appeasement there was a reluctance to move against Germany for fear of undermining Chamberlain's diplomatic efforts. Everything changed when Churchill as First Lord of the Admiralty blamed the sinking of the *Royal Oak* in Scapa Flow in 1940 by a German U-boat on a security breakdown, forcing Admiral Vernon Kell, head of MI5, to resign. In the shake-up that followed, MI5 was placed temporarily under the control of Lord Swinton's Home Defence (Security) Executive until April 1941 when Sir David Petrie became Director-General. Petrie, a rugged Scot who spent most of his professional life as an intelligence officer in India, inherited an agency riven by internal feuds and near collapse. While the staff had grown from thirty to 200, recruitment was haphazard, morale low and the chain of command confusing. A powerfully built man with a steady gaze, square jaw, and military moustache, Petrie was straightforward, firm, and decisive, combining a thorough grasp of practical intelligence work with the skills of an unspectacular but effective manager. His mere presence improved the atmosphere although his manner was rather formal, calling those closest to him by their surnames. Very industrious, he briefed himself with great care before meetings, generally speaking little but to the point, and did much to restore official confidence in his top-secret department.[31]

The appointment of Petrie was a blessing for Guy Liddell who had been moved from the Home Office Directorate of Intelligence to run B Branch (counter-espionage and counter-subversion) which was expanded in the reorganisation to cover Double-Cross agents, radio interception (Radio Security Service) and telephone bugging.

Despite all its difficulties MI5 did have some pre-war successes, the most significant its penetration of the Communist movement in Britain. But not until eighteen months into the war was publication of the party newspaper the *Daily Worker* finally suppressed. In the meantime MI5 did form a unit to collate data on important socio-political movements, their aims, personalities and practical chances of succeeding with their policies. Guy Burgess, another of the Cambridge Four, was appointed to it by Liddell who also approved the recruitment of Kim Philby to the MI6 desk covering Spain and Portugal on account of his knowledge and experience of the Spanish dictator General Franco after covering the Civil War for *The Times*. Philby's opposite number at MI5 was Richard Brooman-White heading the new Celtic Movements section. It was thought that since the Germans had penetrated the Breton nationalists they might try the same thing with Welsh and Scottish nationalists. 'We have a certain amount of information about these various movements and the individuals connected with them but it may be well to develop this side,' observed Liddell.[32] One immediate result was the arrest of Arthur Donaldson, leader of the Scottish National Party, for allegedly planning to form a puppet government if the Germans invaded. Interned under regulation 18B for six weeks Donaldson was never charged.

FIVE DOUBLE-CROSS, PHILATELY AND SUBMARINES

THE DAY AFTER RETURNING TO SWANSEA from Brussels GW ignored Snow's instructions to lie low and immediately telephoned Lord Cottenham at his flat in Dolphin Square. Cottenham was delighted to hear of the success of the mission and rather than wait for the Post Office to deliver GW's report, rushed off to Swansea accompanied by an MI5 officer, Munro, leaving Robertson to debrief Snow in London.

Checking into the Metropole Hotel at 6.40 p.m. on 28 October 1939 Cottenham sent Munro to collect GW from his home, the pair not going directly to his lordship's hotel room but wandering around the town centre for a time until satisfied no one was following.

After complimenting GW, Cottenham wanted to know about Snow's private conversations with the Abwehr agents. GW shook his head. Snow said nothing, except to give the distinct impression he was squeezing the Germans for more money. What GW did not know was that back in London Snow was smearing him, alleging to Robertson that the former Swansea police inspector was a Nazi sympathiser who had confided that he believed the Abwehr agents were 'very fine fellows, and that the Nazi Party had done a tremendous job for the German people, workers in particular, and that he did not feel he was quite playing the game [by posing as a Welsh collaborator]'.[1] For this there is only the word of a man who saw his pre-eminence in the espionage fraternity rivalled, the damning allegation a product of his natural duplicity.

'Are you prepared to go back to Hamburg?' Cottenham asked, mindful that the Doctor expected GW to pick up a radio transmitter when they next met.

GW hesitated momentarily before replying, 'Yes, so long as my wife and daughter will be provided for in the event of my death,' adding that since it was no longer possible to run his private inquiry business, would MI5 pay him?

'Major Robertson will be very pleased with this,' replied Cottenham, indicating the report. 'All I can say is that your services will not be overlooked in any particular.'[2]

After delivering GW's report, with his personal observations attached, Cottenham returned to MI5's transport department. Responsibility for handling GW would in future he shared between Robertson, and Victor, 3rd Baron Rothschild, member of the wealthy banking family. Before the war Rothschild was a brilliant young research scientist at Trinity College Cambridge when the Soviet spies Blunt, Burgess, Philby and Maclean were contemporaries. Having had social contact with all four, Rothschild later became the target for malicious and unsubstantiated attacks. While admitting he was 'left leaning', Rothschild said later he was 'too busy with my scientific work and social life to have any time' for consorting with the most notorious Soviet agents planted in Britain.[3]

Rothschild was an expert on sabotage, his gallantry recognised with the award of the George Medal. As head of the anti-sabotage section his priority was to persuade the Germans to supply GW's Welsh 'nationalist collaborators' with samples of their latest devices and explosives. MI5 duties did not, however, prevent Rothschild from continuing to socialise with the great and the good, among them the prime minister whose cigars he examined for booby traps. After a private dinner party for Churchill and friends in a room at the Savoy one guest noted in his journal afterwards, 'Dinner was excellent and the wine, from the Tring [Rothschild's family estate] cellars, included Pol Roger 1921, the Rothschild Chateau Yquem and a remarkable brandy! There was an extremely good conjuror who appeared at the end of the dinner and whom the PM declared to be the best he had ever seen.'[4]

Robertson and Rothschild advised GW to be patient, to expect to spend a great deal of time waiting for something to happen, and under no circumstances to make a move until the stamp-collector Frau de Ridder was in contact. In the meantime, GW provided regular reports to MI5 about the military build-up in Wales, the nationalist movement, and Welsh attitudes to the war.

As it happened not long after returning from Belgium a letter arrived from Frau de Ridder enclosing two pages of Belgian stamps for his collection. In exchange de Ridder asked for some of the new British 9d, 10d, and 1s. 0d stamps. The Abwehr had opened a communications channel for GW to include in the fifth paragraph of his reply disguised as innocent chatter about stamp collecting a reminder to Rantzau of his promise to supply explosives:

> You will remember that you promised to obtain some special stamps for me to augment my collection, and which you said you would send me as soon as they were available. I would be most pleased to receive them as soon as it is convenient for you to let me have them as I am most anxious to convince you that I am taking up the hobby in real earnest.[5]

When there was no response GW grew impatient. Perhaps Frau de Ridder had not received the letter? Should he write again? 'Sit tight,' said Rothschild, sending GW a battery-driven radio transmitter on which to practice Morse. Snow had promised to give GW lessons but Rothschild thought that laughable as the little man was an 'extremely poor performer'. Having picked up some Morse during the First World War he thought GW would learn better by practising at home in Mount Pleasant.

The immediate consequence of Snow's smears was that Robertson pulled GW out of the next meeting with Rantzau for 'his own personal safety'.[6] Instead, Snow travelled alone to Antwerp (not Hamburg as previously arranged), MI5 risking his defection to the victorious Germans advancing on the Channel ports. But he did return from what at first sight appeared an uneventful mission until MI5 discovered that en route Snow had been joined by Samuel Stewart, a shipping agent for a line operating between Belfast, Dublin and Antwerp. Suspected of acting as a courier for the Abwehr, and operating a clandestine transmitter in Northern Ireland, Stewart's phone was immediately bugged. The phone taps never found the radio but did reveal Stewart was in regular contact with Snow and that their meeting on the boat train from Victoria Station was not coincidental. Detained under regulation 18B, Stewart was released after refusing to change his story while admitting to having had lunch with Snow in Antwerp.[7]

GW knew nothing of Snow's betrayal. When by Christmas 1939 there was no word either from Frau de Ridder he suggested writing a second letter only to be told again by Rothschild to sit tight. It was no fault of his that she had not answered, said Rothschild. Matters, however, were proceeding satisfactorily, and GW was to concentrate on infiltrating the Welsh nationalist movement. GW offered his services to the party's South Wales organiser Wynne Samuel on condition his membership remained confidential in case it was construed by the police authority as contrary to the provisions of the Police Pensions Act, 1921, Section 15, prohibiting membership of political parties. GW did not want to risk the pension it had taken him twenty-nine years to accrue.

One consequence of the neutrality stance was that some nationalists were driven underground for fear of being labelled Fifth Columnists. Membership was disintegrating, the poorly attended meetings held in private houses to avoid unwelcome attention. One of those credited with holding Plaid Cymru together during the difficult war years, Wynne Samuel was also secretary of the Ystalyfera Branch, the largest in the area. A lifelong pacifist and conscientious objector he told the party faithful in 1940, 'We have always decried war. We believe in the method of passive resistance as the only weapon for attaining Dominion Status within the British Commonwealth of Nations.' Such statements culminated in his dismissal by Swansea Town Council.

The attitude of Welsh local authorities to employees registering as conscientious objectors was ambivalent. Some were dismissed immediately, other councils waited until the tribunal ruled. In one area a conscientious objector was compelled to resign while in the neighbouring authority he was able to shelter on full pay behind the benevolent cloak of the council. By August 1940, Swansea had suspended sixteen staff; Cardiff, Pembrokeshire and Cardiganshire had all voted to do so, Merthyr had not taken a decision, while Newport Corporation claimed to have none. Pressure from other staff persuaded Swansea to suspend not only conscientious objectors for the duration of the war but also members of the Peace Pledge Union unless they signed a statement declaring support for the war. Samuel refused and was sacked spending the next few years working on a farm in West Wales while continuing to edit Plaid's English-language monthly *The Welsh Nation*. Using the Ystalyfera branch as his base he spoke at many public meetings and campaigned fearlessly against the transfer of Welsh workers to munitions factories in England. MI5 employed Welsh speakers to report on the anti-war sentiment of their countrymen. Once accepted as a member of Plaid Cymru, GW attended meetings as instructed by his Double-Cross System controllers.[8]

GW was losing patience with both the failure of Frau de Ridder to reply and with Snow for not supplying a list of overseas 'philatelists' with whom Rantzau had asked him to correspond. His suspicions about Snow were further aroused when told that under no circumstances was he to contact him at home in Kingston-upon-Thames. Feeling out of the loop, GW voiced his concerns in a letter to Rothschild:

> With great respect, what can I say if at the next meeting [with the Germans] I should be asked, 'What have you done since our last meeting?' I am sufficiently patriotic to do anything within reason, but I can assure you that I would hesitate to attend another conference with such astute people unless in the meantime I can pay Snow a visit or two so as to go into matters that would be likely to arise at such a conference. I certainly would feel happier if this could be arranged. There are funds available from our 'special friends' under the control of Snow which can be utilized for this purpose … wishing you a Happy New Year.[9]

Two months later he was given the go-ahead to write a second letter to Frau de Ridder. 'How are you?' GW asked. '… It is practically impossible to travel these days … it is quite a long time since I last heard from you. I am glad your country has been able to keep out of the war up to the present'. After mentioning the weather – 1940 was a hard winter – the introduction of summer time and the long, warm evenings, GW arrived at the all-important fifth paragraph asking de Ridder for 'some special stamps for my collection', code for the explosives the Germans had promised but not delivered.[10]

It was a shot in the dark. 'Frau de Ridder' was probably Frau de Ritter the Doctor's wife, and by then back in Hamburg. On the other hand she might be the woman from the previous October, standing on the pavement outside Antwerp station studying his appearance intently. GW waited anxiously for a reply, the opportunities to infiltrate the Abwehr slipping away as the Germans advanced. MI5 was surprised that Frau de Ridder replied at all, if only to say she was leaving Belgium for a long holiday in the United States and had arranged for GW to exchange stamps in future with 'Louis de Mercader, 67 Rue Bosquet, Osborne Residence, Bruxelles'.[11]

By the time M. de Mercader replied inviting GW to Brussels to inspect his stamp collection, the Panzers were pushing through the Ardennes and could be in the Belgian capital within weeks, maybe days. Despite the risk, GW volunteered to go, to seize the last opportunity to open a channel to the Abwehr, replying to M. Mercader:

> You know of course that we have no stamps of our own in Wales as we use the English ones. But there are other things in Wales that are very interesting and of which, I am sure, you will be interested to learn … I trust that in the near future we will have an opportunity of exchanging opinions on the question of stamp collecting and other topics.[12]

The letter never left Britain. The censor returned it with a note attached to the effect that stamp exchanges with the nationals of neutral countries were forbidden![13] By then it was too late, GW's espionage career appearing to peter out days later when the Germans marched into Brussels in May 1940 brushing aside feeble resistance. The link with Rantzau broken, the former police inspector was left to contemplate a return to divorce work. But MI5 still had a job for him: spying on nationalists and reporting on the military build-up, which he did with great thoroughness thanks to the free petrol coupons supplied by the intelligence service for his travels around Wales.

Over and over again GW was reminded of the importance of cultivating the confidence of nationalist leaders. It may be, said his MI5 controller Robertson, that one day [if there was an invasion] the movement would be of considerable interest. Meanwhile, GW was asked to discover which nationalists took a particular interest in listening to the German propaganda channel, the 'New British Broadcasting Service' suspected of transmitting instructions to Fifth Columnists.[14]

Another month passed without much of interest to report until July 1940 when GW was sent to collect Snow from Swansea station, accompanied by 'Biscuit' (alias Sam McCarthy), a reformed petty criminal and the latest Double-Cross agent. The two Welshmen last met in Antwerp the previous October and while the reason given for the surprise visit was to warn GW that Rantzau was sending an Abwehr agent to check him out, he guessed it was he who was being investigated by Snow and Biscuit.

From the station, GW drove them to their hotel beside the sea at Langland Bay and the next morning on to Oxwich Bay, a few miles along the coast and, in particular, the cove at Penmaen GW had identified as suitable for a U-boat to land explosives. Photographs were taken of the cove before the trio drove to Pontardawe – Snow's birthplace – visiting several local public houses before lunch. The first stop in the afternoon was the Tŷ'r Werin public house in Ystalyfera described by GW as a hang-out for local Plaid Cymru members. Biscuit bought a copy of a nationalist pamphlet, *Can Wales Afford Self-Government?*, from the landlord and quizzed locals about nationalist activities. 'Very quiet at the moment,' said the landlord, adding that because of the war and shortage of funds the party had dismissed some of its head office staff. Most of the locals, he said, were anti-war and had the same objectives as Irish nationalists. A local pacifist non-conformist minister, the Revd Iorwerth Jones, was coaching party members on registering as conscientious objectors. Had GW heard what happened to Wynne Samuel, the landlord asked. 'Swansea Corporation sacked him because he is a conscientious objector and he is working on a farm at Aberaeron,' he added.

On their return to Swansea they stopped again at Pontardawe to pick up an unidentified man to join them for an evening meal and drinks at the Metropole Hotel. The very last time GW saw Snow or had any dealings with him whatsoever was the next morning when he dropped him at Swansea station to catch the London train. Thereafter, GW worked independently for the Double-Cross System, no longer part of Snow's imaginary cell of Welsh agents. Leaving the station forecourt, the former police inspector struck up a conversation with Owen ap Owen, a Plaid Cymru activist who believed Fascism and Communism had 'a lot of good points' – and the imprisonment of Welsh people [under the Defence Regulations] without trial by jury was 'worse than dictatorial'.[15]

MI5 could not justly claim to have rebuilt its organisation and reputation until eighteen months into the war. Selling the story of Welsh treachery to the Abwehr as portrayed by GW and Snow was a vital part of that rehabilitation by enabling the Double-Cross System to open its first secure channel for planting bogus information on the German High Command. This stream of fake intelligence persuaded the Abwehr – unaware that every spy it landed was captured, executed or turned into a British double agent – that it was unnecessary to reinforce its British spy ring. Since the majority chose to spy for Britain rather than execution, the Double-Cross System accumulated during the course of the war 120 agents of various nationalities of whom half proved useful. Four or five were picked up as a direct result of Snow's controlled radio traffic. Although agents were rarely cast from the same mould most did expect to be caught eventually, and cracking under interrogation would decide to switch sides to save their necks. Very few had either the loyalty or fanaticism to opt for the firing squad or hangman's noose. Remarkably, among the mass of new wartime regulations rushed into law no specific provision was made for hanging spies. Action could be taken under the existing Prison Act but the Director of Prosecutions warned MI5 that cases could be difficult to prove using this statute while prosecution for high treason was far too cumbersome. If a German agent was arrested before becoming operational, there were no grounds for a charge of high treason without solid evidence about his mission. Moreover, he could always claim that because he had no allegiance to the King it was impossible for him to commit an act of high treason. MI5 wanted a law framed quickly so that if a man was convicted of espionage the judge automatically passed the death sentence as he would in murder cases. The Treachery Act passed by Parliament in May 1940 plugged the loophole. Initially, executions were publicised as a deterrent until MI5 thought it better to keep convicted agents alive for further interrogation.[16]

If anyone acted treacherously then on the balance of evidence it could have been Snow. Before being exposed by his wife and turned into a British double agent, the Welshman had for three years operated as a one-man Abwehr cell, the linchpin for German intelligence in Britain, supplying a mass of information about airfields, RAF squadrons, and troop locations. That Snow was never charged with anything only testifies to his cunning, acute sense of self-preservation and a work ethic that delivered a professional service to both sides, simultaneously if necessary, in return for payment.

Personal contacts and secret writing might have been his pre-war stock in trade but when these were replaced by two-way radio transmitters Snow helped the British code-breakers at Bletchley Park decrypt intelligence service messages transmitted by the Abwehr. Until the Enigma machine, these were encrypted by hand and in September 1939 the Radio Security Service (RSS) picked up one using the same call sign as Snow, OEA. MI5 referred it to the Government Code and Cipher School at Bletchley Park, predecessor to the Government Communications Headquarters at Cheltenham (GCHQ). The code-breakers failed to crack the code but thought the message was being routed from Shanghai to Hamburg. Unconvinced, the Radio Security Service had another go and eventually succeeded in deciphering the message. It had been transmitted by a trawler off the Norwegian coast on the intelligence network used by the German High Command. With this knowledge and that gathered from Snow's nightly transmissions to Hamburg, Oliver Strachey at Bletchley was able from March 1940 to tap into German espionage traffic from Kirkness to Ankara, and later across north and South America. These so-called ISOS messages – an acronym for Intelligence Service Oliver Strachey – were invaluable to the war effort and to the Double-Cross System in converting captured German spies into conduits for supplying fake intelligence.[17]

The British and German security services, at one time or another, received a considerable amount of intelligence from Snow, most of it accurate when checked against other sources. In April 1940 Snow warned that two bombs had been planted aboard the *City of Sydney* in Amsterdam. After being told the ship never touched Amsterdam, Liddell controller of B Branch ignored Snow's tip as spurious, only for the bombs to be discovered when the ship reached its destination in Mauritius.

GW was to prove no less valuable to MI5, in some respects more so, after flashing across the espionage landscape before disappearing as suddenly as he had appeared. Outwardly steady and trustworthy, GW's rectitude was, however, tested by the sight of the large amounts of money sloshing around the espionage world, causing Liddell to describe him at first as 'an unpleasant type who is obviously on the make'. On the other hand the Oxford history professor John Masterman, appointed in January 1941 to chair the Twenty Committee supervising the activities of the Double-Cross System, rated GW a master spy, the Abwehr believing him to be its top British agent, after Snow who had always batted at number one was eliminated.

The Twenty Committee, so named because the Roman numerals XX formed a double cross, met every Thursday in a faceless building near Regent Street for faceless men emerging from the undergrowth of the espionage world. At the outbreak of war, MI5 was a multi-faceted insect living in the shadows, each part jealously guarding its own turf, sometimes more fearful of each other than the enemy. Each sent a representative to the weekly meetings of the Twenty Committee to ensure its own operations were not compromised by the latest scheme dreamed up by Robertson, the Double-Cross controller. The committee's role was to balance rewards against risk by approving the information agents were permitted to pass to the Germans for purposes of strategic deception.

At 49, Masterman was too old for military service but, having escaped the fate of many contemporaries in the Great War by being interned in Germany, volunteered for the Second World War immediately. A tall man of exceptional energy and bulldog determination, Masterman had played hockey for England and cricket for the MCC.

While he could appear ashen and intense while wrestling with a problem, once it was resolved Masterman was a relaxed and amiable companion. But it was his gift for assessing people and their potential that ideally suited him for supervising the intricate operations of agents. While doubting Snow's loyalty although admitting he was 'uniformly successful', GW epitomised his theory that double-cross was a game, a very long game that handsomely rewarded the investment of time and energy if played with patience and consistency. Masterman thought of his adversary Rantzau as impatient and gullible, his judgement warped by egotism, interested only in the credit for recruiting and launching an agent into the field. Having made little attempt to build up an espionage network in Britain until after the invasion of Holland and Belgium the Abwehr's efforts were regarded by Masterman as uninspiring and slipshod. An internal MI5 intelligence review concluded that at the outbreak of war Snow, and later Williams were the only resident agents the Abwehr believed it had in Britain:

> None of the agents who have been apprehended or identified since the war have had any instructions to make contact with any subversive political movement in this country, not even with the BUF ... But the Germans have made an attempt to establish contact with the Welsh nationalists and also with the IRA and, therefore, have not in general concentrated on political movements but on movements which are racial or nationalist in character.
>
> There is no *Kriegsnetz* [spy network] in this country because the Germans relied on the NSDAP [Nazi Party] to keep us out of the war because they themselves were too preoccupied in 1933–7 with internal problems and problems affecting European states ... and lastly their trust in Snow and his notional group of 12 sub-agents.[18]

In the absence of support those agents the Abwehr did eventually send to Britain were soon providing a rich harvest for Robertson, the handsome, tough-minded Scottish controller of the Double-Cross System. Together, he and Masterman made a perfect team.

The Twenty Committee was itself supervised by the W. Board advising on policy matters until it became increasingly involved in day-to-day operations. Churchill headed the chain of command, followed by the Joint Intelligence Committee (JIC), comprising the heads of MI5, MI6, Military Intelligence and the National Intelligence Division (NID). The reorganisation of the security services by Petrie when he was appointed controller of MI5 distinguished clearly between the functions of MI5's B Branch (counter-espionage at home) and MI6's Section V responsible for collating counter-espionage intelligence from overseas stations. But friction between the two existed through the war because Liddell at B Branch had a fundamentally different approach to his opposite number Felix Cowgill running MI6's Section V. Cowgill took the view the security services only needed agents in the field, and that the academics Liddell employed to compile memoranda on the theory of espionage and the psychology of the Abwehr were a total waste of time. Liddell, on the other hand, appreciated the value of 'thinking time' for people of high intellect and academic achievement, allowing them to sit back periodically, take stock, and plan the way forward. Cowgill ran a one-man show at MI6, and was afraid to trust the 'intellectuals' in Liddell's B Branch with his secret sources of information.[19] The Soviet spies Burgess and Blunt were two such 'intellectuals' with who Liddell was especially close, a relationship that ultimately cost him promotion to Director-General at the end of the war.

At the bottom of this command structure were the Double-Cross agents, a mixed bag of nationalities from backgrounds that had little in common with the old school tie. Some ran their own network of sub-agents, others like GW worked alone.

SIX THE CUBAN CONNECTION

AFTER BRITAIN'S LINK TO FRANCE WAS finally severed by the evacuation of 200,000 British and French troops off the beaches at Dunkirk in June 1940, GW waited, no longer expecting to hear again from his stamp-collecting contact in Brussels while Snow continued sending nightly weather forecasts to the Abwehr from the back room of his flat at Kingston-upon-Thames. The Battle of Britain was underway, British ports and airfields were being bombed regularly, and in September 1940 London suffered the worst three nights of the blitz. As Liddell left the Reform Club in Pall Mall at 11.30 p.m. after dining with Anthony Blunt and Guy Burgess, a cluster of incendiary bombs, a 'Molotov breadbasket', fell on the Mall and St James's Park, lighting up the whole area as if by Roman candles. 'All sorts of people were rushing about in dressing gowns with bags of sand,' recalled Liddell. 'When I arrived at the office I found that part of the Registry had been burnt by incendiary bombs and that all the card index had been destroyed. Mercifully, we had it photographed. Some thousand files had also been destroyed.' Not long afterwards B Branch moved most of its staff out of London to a more secure location, Blenheim Palace.[1]

If Snow's weather reports for the Luftwaffe had been accurate bomb damage might have been even more widespread except that the MI5 minders at his shoulder made sure they were not. At the height of the blitz Winston Churchill reputedly issued instructions that the intelligence fed to the Germans should be aimed at diverting the Luftwaffe from strategic targets towards less important areas. When the Labour Home Secretary Herbert Morrison heard this might mean bombing working class residential areas, he exclaimed angrily to Churchill during a Cabinet meeting, 'Who are we to play God?'[2]

One evening towards the end of August 1940 Snow received a transmission from Hamburg about the imminent arrival of three German agents. Their mission was sabotage and they were to contact GW at 42 Mount Pleasant, Swansea. With another opportunity to add to his list of double agents, Robertson hurried to Swansea to assist GW set up a safe house to which the three were to be led before Special Branch swooped. The trap was never sprung because the agents failed to materialise, or so it was thought at the time.[3]

The imminent arrival of the three saboteurs was mentioned in radio traffic on several other nights until Hamburg suddenly announced that only one agent was now being sent to Swansea where he would collect fake ration cards, a supply of petrol coupons, and other documents:

> We intend to drop South African citizen in England or Ireland. Please radio reply to the following questions – is passenger traffic Ireland–England still possible? What papers of identification absolutely necessary for him in Ireland and England? In case he comes to England can he stay with you or friends? Can you get him all papers required?

Snow replied reassuringly, identifying the Quantocks west of Bridgwater in Somerset as a suitable drop zone. When there was no show it was believed the agent had parachuted into the Bristol Channel and drowned. Swansea was beginning to assume the reputation of being an Abwehr staging post for their agents in transit to other parts of Britain.

Another possibility was that the three originally said to be heading for Swansea were Herbert Tributh, Dieter Gartner, both South Africans, and Obed Hussein, an Indian from Antwerp, who landed by boat at Skibbereen, County Cork in July 1940. Hussein, leader of the group, asked the first person they met, 'Do you know anyone from the IRA?' at which point they were promptly handed over to the Garda. Hussein described himself as a bird fancier, but had a suitcase stuffed with bombs. His South African companions had orders to get to England, reputedly to blow up Buckingham Palace with tins labelled French peas but packed with high explosives.[4]

Neutral Eire was unlikely to have been their target because nothing was more certain to propel the Irish into the war on the side of the Allies. The great majority of Irish were anti-German and wanted Britain to win. But unable to forget past injustices, they would never allow British troops to enter the country except by invitation. Neutral but defenceless, President de Valera lived with the constant fear of invasion by Britain or Germany for whom access to the republic's west coast was critical in the battle for control of the North Atlantic shipping lanes. Britain's decision to surrender its Treaty Ports – sovereign bases at Berehaven, Queenstown, and Lough Swilly – in 1938 as part of the Anglo-Irish Trade Agreement to end the damaging trade war between the countries had angered Churchill at the time. Restored to government as the First Lord of the Admiralty a year later Churchill offered to buy back access to Ireland's crucial west coast ports for £50 million! De Valera suspecting that Churchill did not want the ports but the land in the immediate vicinity for air bases told Liddell at a secret meeting in Dublin that the Irish would never tolerate British troops entering the country, believing they would not leave again.

'He [de Valera] deplored the lack of trust between the Irish and the English and that Churchill could clear away the distrust at once by making a public statement that under no circumstances whatsoever would British troops enter Eire except on his [de Valera's] direct invitation,' wrote Liddell later. 'He said that in the case of a German invasion of the south there would undoubtedly be scrapping on the border if the troops from the north attempted to come over the border except on his invitation … he talked at great length on the subject of partition … and said this question must always prevent any real friendliness between the Irish and the English. I asked him what he would do if America came into the war and he said "I can only repeat to you that I am determined to maintain the neutrality of my unprotected country to the very best of my ability".' Liddell left Dublin with the impression that de Valera was 'an extremely worried man in a bad jam but determined not to admit it'.[5]

Ironically, what little defence Ireland had was organised by the local gentry, most of whom were ex-officers and retired civil servants loyal to Britain and supplied with weapons by fiercely patriotic nationalists dipping into their secret caches of arms. The effect was to further lessen the influence of the IRA.

If the dates are disregarded it is very tempting to believe that the South Africans and Indian were the three saboteurs destined for GW's safe house in Swansea because when interrogated they admitted to the Garda they were due to meet a contact to provide the necessary papers for operating in England.

Amidst the flurry of radio traffic there was another theory to explain the missing agent. Might he have been the Swede Goesta Caroli (alias 'Summer')? As a young man, Caroli had tried his hand at most things, finally failing disastrously to set up a business breeding silver foxes on a farm near Uppsala in northern Sweden. He then wandered aimlessly in Europe for some months while attempting, again unsuccessfully, to support himself as an itinerant artist and journalist. It was as such Caroli fell into the hands of the Abwehr in Hamburg and was sent to England to spy in 1939 before the outbreak of war. Posing as the representative of a Swedish newspaper he collected information about the economy and the RAF in the Midlands, mostly gleaned from guidebooks and local newspapers. Returning to Sweden and failing to shake free from German intelligence, he was back in Hamburg in July 1940 being prepared for a second mission to Britain. Caroli was dropped with his radio transmitter by parachute near Denton, Northants, on 6 September 1940 to report on air raid damage in the Midlands. Rantzau was told by Snow that Caroli had injured a leg on landing, had spent ten days in open countryside, and with the weather worsening planned to find shelter by posing as a Swedish refugee. Rantzau vetoed the idea and told Snow to collect the agent, which he did from High Wycombe Railway Station on 17 September. Snow then notionally took Caroli to London, lodged him in his flat, and checked that his false seaman's papers passed scrutiny.

Because Caroli had spent so long in the open, Rantzau was told he was ill, and being nursed by one of Snow's sub-agents, Biscuit. Once 'recovered', Caroli was given new instructions to work the area between London-Colchester-Southend, which he did from fictitious lodgings in Cambridge. The deception was so successful that Snow was sent £200 by Rantzau to pay Caroli! At the end of January 1941 Caroli's transmitter suddenly went off the air, Snow telling the Abwehr its man was under suspicion by the police and had cut and run using the fake seamen's papers provided for that purpose. Snow retrieved the wireless transmitter from the cloakroom at Cambridge Station.

The truth was that within hours of landing Caroli was arrested and turned over to Camp 020 – the high-security interrogation centre for enemy agents – before being released into the custody of Robertson for whom he became agent Summer. Later, he was returned to Camp 020 for further questioning when it became clear the Swede was hiding something. After a failed attempt at suicide, Summer was released again and installed under guard in a house near Hinxton. In the meantime, the Double-Cross section used his transmitter to send misinformation to the Germans, until Summer attempted to escape at the end of January 1941 and was returned to Camp 020 for the duration of the war.[6]

On the balance of evidence the no-show at Swansea can be explained by the voyage of the French fishing smack the *Josephine* sent to land three Cuban saboteurs in Swansea Bay. The Cubans were Silvio Ruiz Robles (40), a former grocer from Havana, Pedro Hechevarria (33), a one-time customs officer in Santiago, and Nicholas Pasoz-Diaz (36). The master of the *Josephine* was Cornelius Evertsen (49), a burly Dutch sea captain from Flushing. The crew was a mixture of nationalities, a Danish engineer, Peter Marcussen Krag, at 26 the youngest member, the others French, Dutch and Spanish.[7]

After the fall of France the Abwehr established a station on the Brittany coast at Brest and a sub-station at Le Touquet. Agents destined for Britain were trained in espionage and sabotage at a villa outside Brest before transferring to Le Touquet for instruction in seamanship, or how to row ashore from a fishing trawler or U-boat. Enemy agents bound for Britain usually set off from Le Touquet but Brest was where they were first sent, boats fitted out, and crews engaged.[8] The Abwehr recruited potential agents by various means, even advertising in local newspapers, offering loans to suitable candidates usually drawn from the civil service and officer classes. Indebted individuals were pulled deeper and deeper into the espionage web with promises of extensions on their loans in return for better quality intelligence. Abwehr scouts trawled through POW camps in the occupied territories recruiting pro-German sympathisers, visited Labour Exchanges, and procured prostitutes to work for German intelligence.[9]

At Brest, Korvettencapitaen Schneiderwind was in charge of operations and his second-in-command was Leutnant 'Charley' Witzke, the Abwehr 'Commander' who interrogated GW in Antwerp in October 1939. Witzke's involvement, his knowledge of the South Wales coast, and his links to GW further supports the theory that the agents heading for Swansea were the three Cuban refugees from the Spanish Civil War who after fleeing to France were destitute and recruited off the streets of Paris by the Abwehr.[10]

All three Cubans had fought with the Republicans, joining the exodus to France after Franco's Nationalists were victorious. Robles worked for a time in a French labour battalion until the Germans disbanded it. He and the other Cubans were offered the choice of working for the Germans, or returning to Spain or Vichy France, neither option particularly appealing. In Spain Robles, Hechevarria, and Pazos-Diaz risked execution as Franco continued mopping up after the Civil War; and in Vichy France they would almost certainly be interned. Without any means of support, and seeing no way to escape from France, the Cubans remembered the Paris address of a fellow refugee from the Spanish Civil War, a Hungarian Ernst Vaida. By now Vaida was prospering, well dressed, flush with money, and after listening to their story gave them 100 francs, arranging to meet later at a café in the Place St-Michel. Over an aperitif he loaned them more money and made an appointment for the following day at Café Scossa in Place Victor-Hugo. There, Vaida introduced them to Leutnant Schimmler, an Abwehr officer in civilian clothes. Schimmler explained he was looking for three men to cross the channel for sabotage work. The Cubans agreed, later claiming they did so only as a means of escaping from France. Each was given 2,000 francs by Schimmler for new clothes and told to meet him the next morning at the Café de l'Université. As they waited a German staff car drew up with Schimmler accompanied by Leutnant 'Charley' Witzke in naval uniform.[11] Given more money and rail tickets, the Cubans travelled overnight to Brest and were lodged in a small hotel by Witzke. The next week was spent at the villa outside the town learning how to build and plant bombs.

On 27 September, with kit bags packed with explosives and detonators, including exploding tins of French peas, the Cubans boarded a trawler and received final instructions from Witzke. They were to land on the west coast of Britain to undertake sabotage in the Bristol area. The Cubans each received £50 sterling to support themselves until finding work in England. On arrival, they were to report to the Cuban Consul in London as refugees from Germany and seek work in factories in the Bristol area. Witzke promised large bonuses and future employment in Nazi Germany if the mission succeeded. No mention seems to have been made of how they would return to France, nor did they ask.[12]

About sixty miles from Brest the trawler was caught in a gale, the engine broke down, and the boat was forced to turn back under sail with three exceedingly seasick Cubans aboard. While Witzke found a new boat, master and crew, the Cubans waited for most of October in their lodgings at 40 Rue Pierre Loti, Brest, their daily allowance increased from 40 to 50 francs. By 23 October the new master, an unemployed Dutch sea captain Cornelius Evertsen found a replacement vessel for the channel crossing, which the Germans renamed the *Josephine.*

Summoned to Witzke's office for a final briefing, Evertsen was told his wife would be sent 500 Reichsmarks at the start of the mission and if the Cubans were landed successfully another 1,000 Reichsmarks. Reminded again of their mission, and given a revolver and clip of bullets each, the Cubans left Brest on 5 November on their second attempt to cross the channel aboard the *Josephine,* her hold full of sabotage materials.

The voyage was a nightmare of high seas, whipped by gale force winds and torrential rain. The Cubans were extremely sea sick, and on the second and third days after leaving Audierne in northwest Brittany threw their sabotage material and revolvers overboard. As the boat neared Swansea Bay, Hechevarria and Pazos-Diaz were too ill to land and Robles refused to do so alone. By now Pazos-Diaz was also suffering from a painful abscess and in need of urgent medical attention. Witzke had marked the proposed landing place in Swansea Bay on the chart before the *Josephine* left Brest, according to Robles. But later at Camp 020 Evertsen insisted the destination was always St Brides Bay on the Pembrokeshire coast.

From Swansea Bay the *Josephine* headed west, hugging the coast, but buffeted by the storm it completely missed St Brides Bay. Evertsen thought he had sighted the southwest coast of Ireland only to discover that the flashing light marked the treacherous Fastnet Rock. The weather worsened, requiring all the Dutchman's seamanship to keep the tiny fishing smack afloat. Altering course to south east by south along the Irish coast, the *Josephine* next came upon the Smalls lighthouse at which point Evertsen turned his storm-battered boat northwards towards the Irish Sea.[13] On 12 November, a week into the voyage, the *Josephine* by now in grave danger of sinking took shelter in Fishguard Harbour where she was boarded by a naval patrol, the crew arrested and the vessel searched. All that was found was a German flag, a Belgian Browning automatic, a clip of ammunition and cartons of English cigarettes.[14]

Evertsen's story was that the Cubans were refugees heading for Dublin, and that one needed urgent medical attention. Later, at Cannon Row Police Station he claimed to have been taken prisoner by the Germans and was put to work in the fields with other refugees. It was then he befriended a Frenchman who repaid him by arranging the boat for him and for the others to escape. When his long and complicated story unravelled under interrogation at Camp 020 Evertsen finally admitted being paid by the Abwehr to land the Cuban saboteurs in Britain.[15]

Since the Cubans threw their weapons and sabotage materials overboard before they got anywhere near the Welsh coast, it was probably true they went along with the Abwehr's scheme as a way of escaping from France. The entire group was held at Camp 020 until the end of the war and then deported, the two Cubans, Robles and Hechevarria, to the United States, the third, Pasoz-Diaz, having died from tuberculosis in Liverpool Prison the year after his arrest.

The accounts of the voyage given by Evertsen and the Cuban Robles differed considerably. The Dutchman claimed it was always his intention to surrender to the Allies and that he had only pretended to co-operate because the Cubans were armed. On the other hand, Robles and his companions said that with the exception of the French and Spanish deckhands, the crew was pro-German, and that Evertsen did all he could to carry out the mission successfully. Twice Evertsen had pointed out the spot on the Welsh coast chosen for the landing but had erased the boat's course from the chart before it was boarded at Fishguard.[16]

Masterman was convinced the Cubans were heading for the safe house in Swansea.[17] Not everyone agreed, even though the Cubans arrived in Wales at about the right time, and were to work in about the right area. Furthermore, speaking little English they were unlikely to succeed in their mission without local assistance. Witzke had also recruited GW in October 1939 and was familiar with the South Wales coastline. If not the Cubans, the final candidate was Josef Starziczny. Soon Starziczny would be running an Abwehr spy ring in Brazil but before this had been chosen by Rantzau to replace the agent drowned in the Bristol Channel. After landing he was to make his way to GW on Mount Pleasant. But Starziczny lost his nerve and pulled out of the mission by feigning illness but would not forget GW, the Abwehr's supposed Swansea contact.[18]

Whatever the explanation, Rantzau's record in delivering agents to Britain suffered another knock with the arrest of the Cubans. The South Africans, Indian, Swede, and Cubans had all disappeared without trace on landing. So had three others – de Deeker, Vera Erikson and Walt – all arrested with false identity papers Snow had helped the Abwehr falsify. Disaster had befallen no fewer than ten agents sent by the German spymaster to England with instructions to contact either Snow or GW. Of all that can go wrong for a spymaster, the loss of a succession of agents before they become operational must have seemed more than coincidental to Rantzau whose confidence in Snow and GW was, nevertheless, unshaken. Knowing nothing about the Double-Cross System, Rantzau not unnaturally cast around for other means of getting his people into Britain. After the Channel Islands were captured Snow was told to buy a motor launch to ferry agents from there to the mainland.

SEVEN KEY TO THE DIPLOMATIC BAG

AFTER HIS LINK WITH FRAU DE RIDDER was severed by the fall of Belgium and then France GW's espionage career seemed at an end despite several false alarms as he waited patiently to be contacted by 'friends from the other side', his euphemism for the enemy. The Cubans got closest to the safe house in Swansea and while others were rumoured to be on their way no one ever arrived. In the meantime, he cultivated contacts in the Welsh nationalist movement, sending Robertson regular reports about nationalist sentiment and the military build-up in Wales. After vetting by Masterman's Twenty Committee at least part of what GW supplied was transmitted to the enemy by Snow as 'intelligence'.

The process was more complicated than appeared, beginning with Robertson and his team at MI5 compiling a reasonably accurate document for transmission. The next step was merging this with that produced by GW from observations during his travels around Wales. Only information in the public domain was fed to the Abwehr on the assumption that if the location of a munitions factory, airfield, indeed, any military establishment was common knowledge then the enemy already knew about it. The Double-Cross System regarded itself as a purveyor of the truth but cooked the books in a deadly game of deception that could easily misfire. The first aim was to persuade the Abwehr by providing a regular supply of plausible intelligence that its espionage organisation in Britain was functioning satisfactorily. From an initially defensive strategy evolved an offensive posture, employing 'turned' enemy agents as channels for planting fake intelligence. GW and Snow were the first to be used for such purposes.[1]

Whereas most of Robertson's agents started life as enemies, GW was home-grown, groomed to pose as a fanatical Welsh nationalist collaborator. In addition to providing the military raw material for deception GW was briefed to spy on nationalist activity and Welsh attitudes as part of the business of persuading the Nazis there was a reservoir of support waiting. For this he bought a car with MI5 help, was given free petrol coupons and ample expenses for travelling around Wales, his eyes wide open, ocassionally questioning unsuspecting locals.

GW had a particular assignment from Lord Rothschild, MI5's counter-sabotage expert. Without intelligence about the latest techniques and explosives employed by enemy saboteurs Rothschild considered British industry dangerously exposed.[2] The medicine bottle slowly leaking sulphuric acid into an explosive mixture demonstrated to GW in Belgium had been superseded by far more sophisticated techniques and incendiary devices about which Britain then knew little.

A new opportunity for GW to penetrate the Abwehr arose on 7 October 1940 when he received a letter from 'Miguel Piernavieja del Pozo, Athenaeum Court, 116 Piccadilly, Mayfair'. The writer introduced himself as a stamp collector friend of M. Louis de Mercador in Brussels, and invited GW to meet him at his apartment in Athenaeum Court in London the following Thursday, 10 October 1940. The letter mentioned that del Pozo had 'met a friend of Mr Kettering in Madrid and would very much like to see GW at the earliest opportunity'. 'Kettering' was the password that Snow and Rantzau used until changed to 'Ketroch'.[3] Before GW was given the go-ahead the security service asked its Madrid agent to verify the password. 'Man with password Kettering is OK … is man of Captain for propaganda and sabotage,' was the reply.

MI5 believed the 'Captain' was the German agent Don Angel Alcazar de Velasco, a mercenary suspected of running a spy ring based upon the Spanish Embassy in London. An ex-bullfighter who fought with the Falangists in the Spanish Civil War, Alcazar was reputedly involved in a failed plot to kidnap the Duke of Windsor during a visit to Portugal, and transport him across the border into Spain as a pawn in a scheme to broker a peace deal between Britain and Germany. Alcazar arrived in London as Press Attaché at the Spanish Embassy in late 1940 and although considered *persona non grata* by MI5, the agency's attempt to deny the Spaniard a visa was overruled by the Foreign Office under instructions not to alienate neutral Spain. On arriving in Britain Alcazar's anti-British, pro-Nazi sentiments provided enough evidence for expulsion but the Foreign Office refused to act, leaving the Spaniard free to build a spy ring serving both German and Japanese intelligence services.[4]

Del Pozo also posed as a Falangist journalist, his cover story that as a member of the Spanish fascist party's youth wing he was sponsored by the British Council to study the Boy Scouts movement. At the outbreak of war the Spanish dictator General Franco declared Spain a non-belligerent country, but provided material support for the Axis powers. MI5 suspected del Pozo's real reason for visiting Britain at the height of the London blitz was espionage and his apartment at Athenaeum Court was bugged from the moment he contacted GW.

Del Pozo was employed by EFE, the Spanish news agency founded by Ramón Serrano Suñer, Franco's brother-in-law, president of the Falangists and Spain's Foreign Minister. The principal advocate for Spain joining the Axis powers, Suñer met Hitler in the south of France during late 1940 in an attempt to engineer such an alliance. If MI5 could prove a direct link between Suñer and del Pozo's espionage activities in Britain then this could be used to destabilise the ruling junta, thereby ensuring Spain stayed out of the war. To this end, del Pozo was treated to a display of anti-aircraft gun fire every night by the ack-ack battery located in Hyde Park across from his apartment in Athenaeum Court, taken to docks packed with warships, shown tanks on the lawn outside Windsor Castle protecting the Royal Family, and visited busy aircraft factories. The VIP treatment was designed to convince del Pozo that Britain was well prepared if Hitler invaded.

After 110 days, the battle for control of the skies over Britain and the English Channel was won by the RAF to whom Churchill paid the immortal tribute that 'never in the field of human conflict was so much owed by so many to so few'. But no sooner was it over and Hitler sent the Luftwaffe to bomb London and Britain's other major cities into submission. On the thirty-third day of the blitz GW left Green Park underground station and crossed Piccadilly to Athenaeum Court with its uninterrupted view over wooded meadows towards Buckingham Palace, and beyond to the Houses of Parliament, Big Ben and the Thames. The Palace Chapel had already been bombed, so had the House of Commons and Tower Bridge. The Luftwaffe came usually at night just after dark, up the River Thames to the docks, the grinding aero engines and wailing sirens driving the population deep underground into the tube stations as the incendiaries rained down, stabbing the city with fountains of fire. Next came the high explosives tearing buildings apart, the night sky red and angry, swept by clouds of pink smoke pouring from the ruined city. Amidst the crackle of flames and shouts of firemen, the city fought back with white-hot bursts from the ack-ack batteries. By the time the blitz ended the following spring 43,000 civilians were dead and 1.4 million homeless.

On the morning GW arrived in London the city was gripped by another scare – mustard gas! A curious substance like a spider's web had landed on a policeman's arm causing blistering. That Hitler might resort to mustard gas as his predecessor the Kaiser had in the First World War was an ever-present fear. At first the substance was thought to have been dropped by enemy aircraft but on investigation proved to be a real spider's web of the sort that commonly forms on the ground under certain conditions in autumn. The evaporation of the dew settling on the web overnight stimulated convection currents, lifting the web into the air, attached to it poison hairs from nettles containing formic acid.[5]

The swarthy individual who opened the door at Number 117 Athenaeum Court asked GW his age, height and occupation, before checking his visitor against the photograph given him by the Abwehr in Madrid, a copy of the one taken by Rantzau in Brussels the previous year.

Evidently satisfied, del Pozo said, 'I have something for you from a friend in Madrid'. He then produced a large sprinkler metal talcum powder tin, adding, 'It's full of pounds for you.'

'What's the friend's name?' GW asked, guessing it was Rantzau.

'I don't know,' replied the Spaniard. Aged about 28, 5 feet 8 inches tall, slightly built, with thick black hair brushed back sharply off his forehead, del Pozo's most distinguishing feature was a tightly-clipped thin black moustache. In his dark lounge suit, white shirt and black tie, a typical Spaniard, thought GW.

Del Pozo wasted no time addressing the purpose of the meeting in good but hesitant English. 'Your friend in Madrid wants you to give him a report of the activities of the Welsh nationalist Party and a list of places in England and Wales where industries are making military materials and aircraft,' said the Spaniard. 'The report must be delivered each week commencing on Tuesday next 15 October at 10 p.m. by a trustworthy man living in London. I send reports twice a week to Madrid.'

The talc tin contained £3,500, the largest amount of money GW had ever seen. At 2011 values it was equivalent to £486,000 using average earnings, or £142,000 measured by the retail price index. Because the notes originated in Spain, GW was to change them immediately to avoid suspicion and then give del Pozo £100 for 'tipping' contacts for information.

After a half hour they agreed to meet again the following Tuesday. With the talc tin in his pocket GW took a taxi from the Athenaeum directly to the Bachelors' Club, reluctantly surrendering the money to a waiting MI5 agent, John Marriott. It was GW's first visit to the club in South Audley Street, Mayfair. There would be many more, his MI5 controllers doing much of their business over lunch or dinner surrounded by the polished ambience of these comfortable inner sanctums where the meals were always good and the cellars full. Not once would GW be invited to stay a moment longer than his business necessitated. The Bachelors' Club, a favourite haunt of Liddell, Robertson and Masterman, was so named because membership was reputedly restricted to 'confirmed bachelors', a euphemism in some quarters for homosexuals at a time when gays were still locked in the closet.[6] After being told of GW's reluctance to part with the talcum powder tin, Liddell noted in his diary, 'GW is very incensed at having the money taken away from him and threatens to resign. Marriott managed to calm him down. He is rather an unpleasant type who is obviously on the make'.[7] Since Liddell never met GW, his assertion that the Welshman was just another mercenary seems rash when judged against the opinions of Masterman and Robertson who came to regard GW as the most effective channel MI5 had for feeding fake intelligence to the enemy.

GW's first contact with del Pozo plunged him into a new world in which acronyms and passwords punctuated furtive conversations in clubs and swish London hotels. Gwilym Williams was always 'GW', Robertson became 'TAR', Masterman 'JC', Rothschild 'R', the controller of MI5 'DG'. The Director of Millitary Intelligence was 'DMI', the Director of Naval Intelligence 'DNI', and head of RAF intelligence 'DOI' (Director of Intelligence). Rantzau, Ritter, and the 'Doctor' were one and the same; Snow was Johnny, alias Owens; the 'Commander' was Abwehr's sabotage expert, and all the others seemed to be 'Doctors'.

Del Pozo was chatting to four Spaniards in the foyer at Athenaeum Court when GW arrived on Tuesday 15 October 1940 for their second meeting. The Spaniard smiled, evidently pleased with himself, having just returned from Glasgow where by arrangement with the British Council he visited an airfield and toured an aircraft factory, afterwards broadcasting a detailed account to Spain and South America. In order to talk more freely del Pozo led the way across the foyer to the lift and up to his apartment. Almost immediately he asked for £100 for 'tips when I get information'. GW didn't have it, explaining the money was handed to his 'chief' [Snow] because it was too risky for him to change such a large amount. GW promised to have the £100 next time they met.

The conversation was mostly about the best way for GW to deliver his reports to the Spanish Embassy. The Welshman knew no one in London he could trust, while to visit the city every week was impossible since he was awaiting the arrival of some 'friends from the other side', an apparent reference to the Cuban saboteurs. After agreeing to meet in future either at the apartment or Embassy at a time that enabled GW to return to Swansea the same day, del Pozo pulled out a sheet of paper and read from a list someone had evidently prepared for him:

> We are particularly interested in places where aeroplane parts, such as propellers and engines are made.

> We want to know about the arrival of convoys from the
> United States, the time, dates, and ports.
> What types of aircraft are being supplied to England by the
> United States and the shipping lines delivering them?
> The names of regiments stationed in southern England.
> Where bombers used for bombing Germany were based.
> What factories and warehouses the Welsh nationalists will
> sabotage.

A tall order, thought GW. 'We can't organise sabotage,' he said, 'until
"our friends over there" provide the necessary materials by means of
an aeroplane or submarine as they [Rantzau] promised in Antwerp.
Owing to their failure … I have been wasting my time for twelve
months when I could have been making some move.' Del Pozo promised to mention this to the Abwehr in Madrid.

'There's a great deal of risk,' continued GW. 'It's not possible
to obtain the information directly … I can't get near these places.
[The only way] is to obtain information from men employed at these
places and from soldiers in the area … I may have to bribe them as
well.' Del Pozo nodded, and asked, 'How are the people in Wales taking the war?'

'Before the bombing commenced,' replied GW, 'they were mostly
pacifists and many of them defeatists. They are still anti-English but
owing to the indiscriminate bombing in Wales the people seem to
have a greater leaning towards England … it [the bombing] has
got their backs up.' Del Pozo made no comment, except to say that
Segundo, the Embassy porter, would be GW's contact and that the
intelligence would be sent to Spain in the diplomatic bag. For MI5
this was the first real evidence the Spaniards were abusing their diplomatic immunity.[8]

GW handed del Pozo a report about the Welsh nationalist movement. Headed 'Welsh Activity' the document was a potent mix of
fact and fiction designed to use nationalism in the war against Hitler
by building GW's confidence ratings with the Abwehr. Having spent
many years in the United States, Rantzau spoke and read English perfectly and would not be easily fooled by a report claiming the party
had 20,000 members when in fact it had only 2,000:

… A large number take no interest … from a political or Welsh freedom point of view, but all are deeply interested in Welsh culture. For many years the party had put up candidates for parliamentary honours, but none has been successful at the Parliamentary Elections.

In so far as direct action against the English Government is concerned, the only overt act was in 1936 when Professor Saunders Lewis, the Revd Lewis Valentine and Mr D. J. Williams set fire to the bombing school, near Pwllheli in North Wales as a political gesture after many appeals had failed, which were made to the English Government not to establish aerodromes in Wales. These three gentlemen, prominent Welsh nationalist leaders, afterwards gave themselves up to the police. They had a spectacular trial at the Old Bailey and were each sentenced to nine months' imprisonment. The party gained much sympathy and support for their aims by this political gesture, but no one followed the lead given by these ardent supporters of Welsh nationalism. This, no doubt, is due to the fact that the necessary material with which to commit acts of this kind is too difficult to obtain. I have no hesitation in saying that further acts of this nature would be carried out if the necessary materials were available.

Before the outbreak of war the party was not very progressive in its efforts to obtain Welsh freedom, but ever since hostilities began the Party has become strongly pacifist and is continually proclaiming that Wales desires no part of England's war. All possible encouragement and help are given to the young men of Wales to put forward Nationalism as one of the grounds for conscientious objection to military service in the English forces.

At the annual conference of the Welsh nationalist Party at Aberystwyth last August Mr Saunders Lewis, who has resigned the Presidency but still takes a very active interest in the Party's affairs, called upon the Executive to use its utmost endeavours to persuade the English Government to conclude an early armistice so as to avoid further bloodshed.

Mr Lewis's speech on this occasion was well received and supported by the many delegates representing the various branches of the Movement. The Party is now engaged in propaganda to emphasise the need for a free Wales so that peace for this country can be concluded.

In addition to pacifist work the Party is continually making protests to the English authorities concerning the construction of armament factories and aerodromes in Wales. Considerable stress is laid on the fact that the Llŷn Peninsula – where the bombing school is situated – being bombed and, as a result of this bombing, attention is being called to the leaflet, entitled *Aerodromes today – bombing tomorrow*, published by the Party when Saunders Lewis and the others sabotaged the bombing school.

At present much propaganda is being carried out in connection with the evacuation of English schoolchildren into Wales. We in Wales feel considerable indignation because we are swamped with English evacuees. The Party is claiming credit for having always urged that safe areas in Wales should be reserved for the evacuation of children from bombed Welsh districts and they are now sending petitions to the English Government to remove English children from Wales to safe places in England.

Concerning the possibility of an invasion the Party leaders are exercising great caution as to the action they would be likely to take, as they have to be very careful owing to the severe penalties that can be imposed under the Defence Regulations. They emphasise that in the event of an invasion large numbers of English refugees would swarm into Wales and that necessary measures should be considered for countering this menace.

It is obvious that the leaders of the Welsh nationalist Party will not commit themselves as to their attitude should foreign troops land on Welsh soil. Personally I am of opinion that some of the Party members will join the English in resisting but, if tactfully handled, I believe that a large proportion would at least be passive in [*sic*] invading troops.

It may be gathered from the foregoing notes that the attitude of the Party may be defined as passive hostility rather than open resistance to the English.

I have worked very hard in an effort to build up a nucleus of people to render us assistance, but the task has been uphill as, in this connection, the Welsh mentality is so very different from the Irish and the ancient tradition of revolutionary struggle is nearly played out.

However, I feel that given the necessary means I can increase quite considerably the number of my compatriots who would be prepared to render assistance in the cause. In the present juncture I must admit there is little prospect of stirring up any effective resistance of a widespread nature in the Welsh nationalist Movement as a whole. The most that we can reckon upon from the majority of really convinced nationalists is goodwill rather than active support, the remainder appear to be leaning towards England. This is due, in some degree, to intensive propaganda by the English and the present bombing of Welsh towns, both these are bound to affect the weaker and muddle-headed members. It must be realised that as public opinion outside the ranks of Welsh nationalists becomes more bitter against Germany, Party work for our cause, or even from a purely pacifist angle, becomes increasingly difficult, unpopular and dangerous.[9]

The 'Welsh Activity' report had the authenticity of a document that could easily have been pieced together from contemporary newspaper accounts of the divisions within the nationalist movement over the war. Apart from exaggerating public sentiment, all that was new was GW's reminder to the Abwehr about the failure to supply his saboteurs with the necessary materials. This would become a constant refrain.

GW felt under pressure five days later when del Pozo was expecting another intelligence report. The Twenty Committee was taking too long to vet the document. 'Expedite it,' he suggested to Robertson. 'What with travelling and making out these reports I feel rather muddled, so perhaps you will overlook any errors that I may have made in typing them out.'[10]

The strategy was to persuade the Abwehr it had a reservoir of support in Wales controlled by GW. But for the deception to work the intelligence must be credible otherwise GW's cover as a Welsh nationalist fanatic would be blown. Even for someone with the observational skills of an experienced police officer GW was in unknown territory, mindful that in gathering the information for his 'intelligence reports' he could get himself arrested, and blow the entire operation. 'You can quite imagine what a commotion that would cause,' he told Robertson. 'I would, with every respect, emphasise the absolute necessity of supplying me with information to pass on as will maintain the confidence that they now seem to repose in me ... We have no means of ascertaining how this affair will develop, but I can only suggest it's likely to develop favourably for us if we can throw the proverbial sprat to catch a mackerel.'[11] And that was the problem for the Twenty Committee. Service departments were unprepared to go along with the Double-Cross System's schemes until they saw some concrete return for themselves. Nor would they approve the passing of any intelligence that risked getting military units bombed or defences pinpointed by an enemy planning an invasion. Although the Battle of Britain was won and the Joint Intelligence Committee thought Hitler was turning to southeast Europe after German troops moved into Romania as a base for operations against Greece and Turkey, shipping and troop transports continued to assemble in France's Channel ports. From this the JIC deduced that Hitler was either completing arrangements for an invasion, or it was a decoy, the Germans having other plans. The belief that the invasion would be through Ireland and Wales gained some credibility when it was discovered the Germans were attempting to recruit an Irish Brigade from among captured POWs. Despite persevering, they however failed to wean southern Irish POWs off their loyalty to the Crown as members of the British forces. Hitler's next ploy was to offer peace terms to the Vichy French Government: Alsace Lorraine to go to Germany, Italy to take the French coast as far as Nice, Tunisia divided between Italy and Germany, Algiers to remain French, French Morocco split between France and Spain and French colonial troops to join the Italians in attacking the British in Egypt.[12]

Nailing down the information to pass to the Germans was a lengthy and perplexing process. The original draft was often threadbare after being circulated among all interested parties, stripped of authenticity and unlikely to impress del Pozo, let alone Berlin. At other times potentially disastrous consequences were narrowly avoided by deleting information that rather than mislead the Luftwaffe pointed it in the right direction. GW was about to inform the Germans that the Free French Forces, Canadians and Australians were stationed at Camberley, about two miles from Sandhurst, until someone reminded the Twenty Committee that 'as Camberley is full of New Zealanders, I do not feel we are justified in getting them killed'. On the other hand, the Abwehr, by supplying del Pozo with a list of specific questions, revealed the direction of German strategic planning. That was the case when GW was asked to confirm that 'RAF Hullavington was the largest aerodrome in England from which fighter and bomber aircraft set off on sorties to bomb Germany and Italy'. In confirming this GW persuaded the Luftwaffe to bomb what was only a base for the Meteorological Office.[13]

Robertson was very satisfied with the raw material he got from GW. 'The stuff you have sent already seems to me to be first class,' he wrote, adding:

> If you could work on along these lines and see whether you can obtain similar information about other factories in your part of the world to begin with, I should be most grateful. Since you have no information on specific points, I would be glad if you would submit it to me at once for my approval. I will then return it to you as early as possible, so that you can pass the information on to your friend.
>
> I am most anxious that you should not go out of your way to obtain the required information, as it is most essential that you should not attract any attention to yourself. If you see signs of any trouble brewing, please get in touch with Major Ford [MI5's station agent in Cardiff] at once …

I fully agree with you that we should not be too forth-coming with the information we give and that only one or two items should be passed over at each meeting. I shall assist you as much as possible in answering these questions, but I feel it is most important that you should be able to convince our friend from personal experience that it is extremely difficult to get detailed answers to a great many of his questions. Don't forget that rumours are always acceptable. This gives us scope for a great deal of imaginary information. I am trying to get hold of a telephone application form for you to fill in and will let you have this as soon as I can lay my hands on one.[14]

Whereas the rationale was clear the implementation was not without grave risk. In his first report for del Pozo, GW told the Abwehr that the Bristol Aircraft Factory adjoining the Great Western Railway between London and South Wales produced engines for Blenheim bombers and was well-protected by anti-aircraft guns. The factory in fact manufactured thousands of aero-engines for the Blenheims bombing German airfields. Since it is incomprehensible the Double-Cross System set out to deliberately to draw German fire power to Bristol it has to be assumed that since the existence of the aircraft plant was widely known locally, the Luftwaffe knew about it from other sources.

The same might be said about two of Wales's most important Royal Ordnance factories – at Bridgend and Pembrey – details of which GW passed to del Pozo. Just before the outbreak of war the ordnance factory at Pembrey was reopened to manufacture TNT, as it had in the First World War. The new factory at Bridgend produced explosives and other munitions transferred from the Royal Woolwich Arsenal. But it was on this cusp of credibility that GW's reliability rested in the mind of the German spymaster Rantzau.[15]

Before the next rendezvous with del Pozo on 7 November in the foyer of the Cumberland Hotel at Marble Arch, GW made a curious discovery. Del Pozo had landed at Bristol Airport at the end of September 1940 intending to stay no longer than three months as an Alcazar agent. Nevertheless, he soon took a mistress, a Mrs Harris who moved into the apartment in Athenaeum Court. Whenever GW telephoned, Mrs Harris answered employing a variety of accents depending upon who was calling. Sometimes she spoke with a marked foreign accent, or sounded slightly American, Cockney on occasions, switching from that into a comparatively educated but fluent English accent. When speaking to del Pozo on the telephone she appeared to be rather elderly with a poor command of the language, but at other times spoke fluently, quickly, with practically no accent at all.[16]

GW's meeting with del Pozo at the Cumberland almost never happened. On the way to the hotel he picked up a copy of the *Daily Express* to find the Spaniard's name splashed all over it in an account of del Pozo's enthusiastic remarks about Hitler made at a House of Commons lunch given by the BBC for foreign journalists. The chief guest was Lord Halifax, who as Foreign Secretary and supporter of appeasement in Chamberlain's Government believed Hitler acted in Europe's best interests by banning the Communist Party and sending its leaders to concentration camps. Thinking he was among friends, del Pozo echoed these sentiments publicly, only for his indiscretion to be seized upon by the *Daily Express* as further proof Spain was about to join the Axis powers. Spain wasn't. Only if the Italians seized the Balearic Islands would Franco enter the war. Nevertheless, the *Daily Express* demanded the head of the subversive, at the very least his immediate deportation, and the Foreign Office lodged an angry official protest with Madrid. Apologising, Spain claimed del Pozo was imposed upon their Foreign Ministry by an 'outside body'.[17]

'What was the idea of that article?' GW almost screamed at del Pozo in the hotel lobby. 'You're almost certainly being watched now. And so will anyone who contacts you. That includes me, and all those working with me. I can't take the chance of visiting your apartment again. If I'm seen it could mean ten years inside!'

Instinctively, both looked over their shoulders searching the faces in the busy lobby for someone paying them particular attention. Del Pozo was worried, blaming the newspaper for misquoting him and was demanding a correction immediately. For the moment, however, they had best go to the Embassy to talk, and meet Segundo, GW's new contact.

During the ten-minute taxi ride around Hyde Park to 24 Belgravia Square GW made it clear to del Pozo there was no way of gathering more information about munitions factories and airfields because to get any closer needed special permits. Anyhow, he insisted as he did frequently, he and his nationalist friends had volunteered to carry out sabotage not espionage. 'I have accomplices,' said GW, 'doing important jobs, one with the water board, another at a Royal Ordnance Factory. All are bitter, anti-English; all are ready to carry out sabotage, including polluting the water supply to Birmingham with bacteria. But I can't make a move until I am supplied with the means … and the men who do the work will also expect to get paid.'

The Spanish Embassy was one of those grand white-stuccoed terraced houses in Grosvenor Square grouped around a large central, private garden. The property next door, number 23, had been the German Embassy identical in every respect except for the amazing assortment of radio transmitters the Swiss discovered when they took it over after war was declared.

Del Pozo led the way to a discreet tradesmen's entrance. A man aged about 45, of average height, receding hairline, and dressed in a blue serge suit with brass buttons opened the door. Segundo's complexion was like del Pozo's sallow, but when he spoke, and only ever in Spanish, a pair of prominent front teeth seemed to jump in and out of his mouth. After talking briefly to del Pozo, Segundo ushered them into a small room, then disappeared briefly before returning with a letter for GW from 'his friend' in Madrid, another list of questions about Britain's defences.

'We want to know everything of interest concerning the south coast of England,' said del Pozo. 'For example, the positions of all regiments and where they are; what length and breadth of line they occupy; positions of reserves, tanks and big guns. We want details of the coast from Margate to the Isle of Wight, what parts of the coast are steep and flat, and what you can find out about the beaches. We would like you to find out all you can about particulars of battalions, naval bases, aircraft and aerodromes all over England, giving their exact location.'

The Welshman was being sucked into Hitler's invasion planning. 'This would be easier for you to do,' GW replied impatiently. 'You're a foreign journalist. You can move freely around the country.' Del Pozo said nothing. Still shaken by the splash in the *Daily Express* the Spaniard was anxious to cover their tracks. 'Burn everything,' he told GW, 'all my letters. I will not write again, not to you. You must give me the name of someone else. I write to him about meeting, and we meet three days after the date in letter. Next time you bring me money, £100. I gave you plenty.' GW nominated his father-in-law as his Swansea contact.

If Hitler was rolling out the invasion it was essential GW remained embedded in the Spanish spy ring. But GW was worried. 'This man is a sap,' he told Robertson. 'I suggest that the "little man" [Snow] informs our special friends that I consider it too dangerous to work with such a man … who discloses matters for publication that will eventually end in his deportation, if not something more serious … and the imprison-ment of those who co-operate with him clandestinely.'[18]

Until GW obtained access to the Spanish Bag, Snow's radio was the only channel open to MI5. To reinforce the notion that the pair were working together for Germany, GW at his next meeting in the Chancellery of the Spanish Embassy on 29 November 1940 told del Pozo that his 'chief' [Snow] was shortly to visit Madrid for a confer-ence with 'our friends'. Del Pozo's Welsh update from GW described a country where loyalty was crumbling, anti-Jewish sentiment hard-ening, and resentment increasing over the use of Welsh workers as 'slave labour' in munitions factories in England. In the meantime, GW's cell of potential saboteurs was frustrated by the failure to pro-vide 'the necessary material and funds'. If the first 'Welsh Activity' report was an introduction to passive Welsh nationalism, the second was about an inherent and smouldering bitterness:

A prophecy made by the Welsh nationalist Party since the outbreak of war concerning the effect of the war on Wales is already being fulfilled. North and mid-Wales and indeed every part of Wales which is reasonably safe are rapidly being occupied by wealthy and leisurely English folk and Jews who are buying and renting every imaginable kind of dwelling at high rents. As for as can be observed these peo-ple are not grateful to Wales for the hospitality given them.

They regard their sojourn here as a period of necessary boredom and have adopted a sneering tone towards these 'quaint' places and 'quaint' people. Resentment of their presence is fast growing and much more so as Welsh workers are being forced in thousands to seek work in highly dangerous areas of England – the very areas precipitately abandoned by the vulgar English rich. The country responsible for plunging an unwilling Wales into war was England; the power responsible for the denudation of Welsh quarries and mines is England. When Wales's workers are deprived of their homeland; when their contribution to England's conscript army numbers hundreds of thousands; when she cannot even offer the shelter of her quiet countryside to her own mothers and children – the Wales of tomorrow – the only role left for her to play is that of unwilling host to England's cowardly rich.[19]

The Twenty Committee had no problems approving this for transmission via the Spanish diplomatic bag but failed, despite GW's prodding, to provide credible answers to the Abwehr's questions about England's south coast defences. That the coast was lined with beaches and cliffs was hardly a revelation! To compensate for this, GW was permitted to reveal that Britain had a new anti-aircraft shell, to which del Pozo replied, 'Yes, we've heard of it … a new type of larger shell containing smaller ones. When the larger explodes the smaller ones are scattered over a wider area before exploding.' This was most likely a reference to the new proximity fuse. Before this was invented, shells were detonated either by a direct hit, a timer set before it was fired, or an altimeter. The chances of a direct hit on a small moving target were relatively low. But with a proximity fuse the artillery or tank commander had only to calibrate a trajectory that passed close to the target for the detonation to occur, the explosion affecting a wider area. The Spaniard asked GW to get him a plan of the fuse before he returned to Madrid.

Del Pozo was uneasy, anxious to leave the country. Two men had followed him for a week and only by jumping on a London bus did he lose them.

'Could you let me have a big interesting report to take back to Madrid?' said del Pozo.

'Supposing whilst I am endeavouring to carry out acts of sabotage it's necessary for me to suddenly leave the country, can you suggest how I can do so and [with whom] I could get in touch for help?' GW replied.

The Spaniard hesitated until GW repeated the question, at last replying, 'You go to Portugal, then easy for you to get to Spain,' As for himself, he would be on his way home soon.

Del Pozo pulled out the same list of assignments given him in Madrid and read it again, adding another of interest: the visibility of barbed wire entanglements along Britain's south coast beaches at high and low tide – a sure sign Germany's invasion planning was at an advanced stage.

The significance was not lost on GW who asked immediately, 'Only as regards the coast between Margate and the Isle of White?' Del Pozo answered, 'Yes.'[20]

The Double-Cross System was learning a great deal from the questions the Abwehr was asking its Welsh agent, about the anticipated invasion, where it was likely to occur, and the limitations of German intelligence.[21]

By the end of November 1940 the blitz on London finally eased after fifty-one consecutive nights of raids, the ferocity of the Luftwaffe's attack moving to Britain's munitions factories and industrial heartlands. Coventry suffered its worst night on 14 November, the hail of incendiaries starting a fire storm speading to every street in the city centre. After London and Coventry, Liverpool, the largest port on Britain's west coast, was the next most heavily bombed, followed by Birmingham with its industrial complexes producing aircraft, military vehicles, bombs and small arms.

The German bombers flying up the Bristol Channel towards the Midlands were thought to be directed to their targets by a clandestine radio beacon operating somewhere in that area. Bristol, Swansea, Cardiff and Newport, the four most important ports in the area, were all targeted. Cardiff and Bristol were hit on successive nights in January 1941. The next month Swansea town centre was destroyed by three nights of bombing in the worst of the blitz on Wales.

Del Pozo's brief included reporting on the extent of the damage to Britain's military and public infrastructure. Free to travel, the Spaniard was, nevertheless, chaperoned so successfully that he missed the worst-hit areas, telling his controllers in Madrid that not only was Britain surviving the aerial onslaught, it was in his view 'invincible'. Although impressed by the courteous and attentive reception received from the British Ministry of Information, del Pozo was even more anxious to leave after the Ministry broadcast on its Overseas Service an account of a speech in which he described the Italian army as hopeless. 'But I was drunk', he explained later.[22]

Towards the end of 1940 some within intelligence circles dared to think that Britain had turned the corner. The Greeks had halted the invading Italians, the Royal Navy Air Arm had dealt a hammer blow to the Italian fleet at Taranto and the RAF was holding its own against the Luftwaffe's daylight raids. But not at night when the bombing of industrial complexes eroded Britain's ability to move on to the offensive and the shipping losses from U-boats threatened it with starvation. At its lowest point, the country was left with barely three weeks supply of fuel oil.

Victory for the RAF in the Battle of Britain did prove to be the defining moment in the war. But not everyone thought so. One of Churchill's fiercest critics, Lloyd George, continued to complain about Churchill's dictatorial methods in conducting the war for which reason he declined an invitation to join the War Cabinet. In one of his increasingly infrequent appearances in the House of Commons Lloyd George blamed the war on the broken promises of the Versailles Treaty at a time when there were democratically-elected governments in Germany to whom a solemn promise had been made that if Germany disarmed so would Britain. Promises given to Germany and the minorities in Hungary, Poland and the Ukraine were not delivered and for no fault of his. 'I protested [to the National Government] over and over again,' he told the Commons, 'that if they did not carry out their pledges it would end in a great European war ... [and] we are now confronted with the most terrible answer that has ever been given to people who have broken their faith.'[23]

Rather than join Churchill's War Cabinet, the Welsh Wizard preferred, in a series of articles for the *Sunday Pictorial*, to advocate a negotiated peace once Britain was in a position to negotiate from strength. Elaborating upon this in a letter to the Duke of Bedford on 7 September 1940 Lloyd George predicted a stalemate if an invasion was beaten off or if Hitler shrank from attempting it:

> We (Hitler as well as ourselves) should then be face to face with a protracted war of devastation and starvation which would bring the whole of Europe into ruin. I am not in a position to judge the chances of invasion. I have only the old world tradition which comes from a long series of failures that it cannot succeed. If it fails our prestige would be higher than ever and we should enter a Conference with our heads high and look Hitler straight in the face as people who have thwarted his vaunted plans of the conquest and destruction of Britain, which is why I am against starting at this moment any movement for peace negotiations.[24]

MI5 considered Lloyd George a defeatist and remembered him for applauding Hitler in the mid-1930s as saviour of a bankrupt Germany. Liddell, head of counter-espionage, noted that the former Liberal Prime Minister talked in a very defeatist way in stating that no useful purpose could be served by continuing the war, that total victory was impossible and that Britain should start thinking of a negotiated peace. Not long afterwards, Liddell observed that Lloyd George had changed his views again and while still not believing Britain could win he no longer thought the moment appropriate for a negotiated peace:

> He thinks therefore we should speed up our war effort to the maximum and that having achieved a few successes we should then come to terms with the Germans. He is surrounded by a group who to some extent hold the same views as himself. The principal people are Horrabin [former left-wing Labour MP and cartoonist], Hore-Belisha

[former Secretary of State for War] and Wardlaw-Milne [Conservative right-wing MP], the whole group consisting of about ten people. They are leading the attack on the Government in the House. No personal attack on Winston is contemplated. Lloyd George's ultimate object is to get into the Cabinet on his own terms. An offer was made to him sometime ago but he would not go in as he felt that his hands would be tied. He would only join the Government if he is to be the big noise on policy.[25]

When one obstacle to LG joining the Cabinet was removed – the death from cancer in November 1940 of his arch-foe Neville Chamberlain – he chose to remain at Criccieth, firing criticism at the Government from his Welsh mountain fastness rather than offer his services. There was no second invitation. Some suspected Lloyd George was saving himself as Hitler's pawn in peace negotiations. In private at least LG continued to sneer at Churchill's conduct of affairs, reputedly gloating over any setback that could be attributed to the latter's dictatorial methods. In his last major speech to the House of Commons LG accused the Government of withholding crucial information about the progress of the war and claimed that despite recent successes the outcome was by no means decided. Britain was raising an army of four million when the invasion of Europe meant facing ten million highly trained and well equipped men:

Are we making the best of our manpower … there is a general sense of dissatisfaction and doubt … The Prime Minister must have a real War Council. He has not got it … There is no doubt about his brilliant qualities but for that very reason … he wants men against whom he can check his ideas, who are independent, who will stand up to him and tell him what they think … No one man however able as he is can pull us through. I invite the Prime Minister to see that he has a small War Council who will help him – help in counsel, help in advice, and help him in action.[26]

After listening impatiently, Churchill swept Lloyd George aside contemptuously on one of his 'rare' appearances before the House:

> It was not the sort of speech which one would have expected from the great war leader of former days, who was accustomed to brush aside despondency and alarm, and push on irresistibly towards the final goal. It was the sort of speech which, I imagine, the illustrious and venerable Marshal Pétain might well have enlivened the closing days of M. Reynard's Cabinet.[27]

Smarting from this rebuke Lloyd George retreated to North Wales from where he consorted with dissidents in organising a failed vote of no confidence in the Government. Churchill, he declared, spent far too much time staring down the barrels of guns and making speeches for posterity to have the drive and imagination necessary for a wartime leader.

The invasion of Britain, and possibly Ireland, had not gone away. If the latter happened then MI5 was ill-prepared to deal with the tens of thousands of Irish refugees and the inevitable influx of German agents. The original plan to put them in barbed wire cages was abandoned because of the public outcry it would cause since many would be loyal British citizens. Internment on such a scale was a nightmare for an agency already facing major reorganisation following the arrival of Sir David Petrie as Director-General. MI5 was also in danger of losing its counter-espionage chief Liddell who, criticised for allowing the agency's records to be lost or destroyed, thought seriously of resigning until at dinner one evening he and his number two Dick White planned their own reorganisation 'over a very good bottle of Richburg'. At about the same time, Liddell's flat was rocked by a stick of forty bombs landing at the back of Lowndes Square not far from the Spanish Embassy, and in another raid the security services interrogation centre Camp 020 at Ham was hit killing one of the internees.[28]

Meanwhile, del Pozo was still rattled by the *Daily Express* exposé of his pro-German sympathies. The Ministry of Information told him to go home, so did the Spanish Embassy but not the Double-Cross System for fear his departure would close down its access to the Spanish Bag for passing fake intelligence. As a national of a neutral country, del Pozo could not be prevented from leaving without causing the diplomatic incident the Foreign Office was so anxious to avoid.[29]

Before del Pozo decamped, another meeting was set up with GW at the apartment at Athenaeum Court on 13 December 1940. Since MI5 still knew relatively little about the Alcazar spy ring, was it possible for GW to pressure del Pozo, the weak link in the chain, to reveal its extent?

'I've come to collect the £5,000 which my chief [Snow] says you have received for us from our friends on the other side,' snapped GW after formalties were exchanged. Del Pozo pleaded that apart from the talcum powder tin stuffed with £3,500 he had not received another penny.

'I was told by my chief to collect it from you today,' insisted GW.

Del Pozo admitted receiving a telegram to the effect £250 was being sent to pay GW but nothing had so far arrived. 'If I receive any money for you I will tell you at once. If I have to leave the country suddenly I will leave the money with Segundo at the Embassy,' added del Pozo.

'When is that likely to be … your departure?' GW asked.

'I don't know. I'm waiting for instructions from Señor Suñer.'

Recognising the name of the Spanish Foreign Minister and the importance to MI5 of linking the Spanish spy ring to Suñer, GW asked, 'Does Señor Suñer know what you are doing on behalf of our friends?'

'No, no, definitely not,' replied the Spaniard, adding nervously, 'My letters are being opened and someone's searched my apartment … He is a short man with a large head and protruding forehead, bald on top, French looking. I know he's been in the room but he wouldn't find anything. Everything is locked away.' MI5 had indeed planted a surveillance officer in an adjoining apartment in Athenaeum Court but not with the intention of arresting del Pozo because that would blow GW by requiring him to give evidence of the Spaniard's espionage activities. Better, advised GW, for the association with del Pozo to continue as a means of trapping other enemy agents sent by Madrid. The Spaniard was small fry. The bigger fish was Alcazar.

The telephone rang and GW waited while del Pozo had a lengthy conversation about his arrangements for leaving Britain. The moment he hung up GW dragged the conversation back to intelligence matters. Did del Pozo know about the explosive road materials being used by Britain?, he asked, planting in the Spaniard's mind an idea calculated to worry a potential invader. What about the German aeroplane that had landed with the pilot dead at the controls but no indication as to the cause of death, implying that Britain had developed a secret weapon? Del Pozo had heard of neither. 'If I had I wouldn't believe it,' he said impatiently. 'Half of what is in the papers is not true.' Before leaving GW was told by del Pozo never to write to him at Athenaeum Court again because his last letter had been opened. After examining the letter GW could see no sign of tampering although, in fact, it had been intercepted, testimony to the GPO's expertise.[30]

The following week GW set off by car for west and north Wales to collect information for delivery to the Abwehr agents 'Federico' and 'Pablo' waiting in Madrid for the diplomatic bag to arrive. His first stop was the Royal Naval Armaments Depot at Trecwn, about three miles outside Fishguard, with its network of underground chambers for storing naval mines. From there he headed up the coast to an army camp under construction at Tonfanau, near Tywyn. Some huts were already occupied by Royal Artillery units, their only defence a couple of Lewis guns. At Llanberis near Caernarfon GW noted the location of an aircraft factory near the site of the disused Glynrhonwy Isaf Slate Quarry, at which 14 per cent of Britain's high explosive bombs were stored. Further along the coast outside Bangor was the Penrhos airfield used by bombers and at Rhosneigr on Anglesey, a large aerodrome, RAF Valley guarding Britain's western approaches.

Outside Chester, a branch railway forked south towards another large airfield. This was Hawarden, packed with fighters, bombers and trainers. On the outskirts of Wrexham, thirty miles due south of Liverpool, there were five aerodromes, the pilots, according to what GW was told by locals, using the parish church as a landmark. Nearby were steelworks, collieries and chemical plants. At Borras, Wrexham were three grass runways for training flights – and headquarters for Western Area UK Warning and

Monitoring Organisation. Returning to north-west Wales GW drove passed an aircraft factory under construction just south of Llandudno Junction, again poorly defended.

His report for the Double-Cross System ended with a paragraph claiming that the whole of Wales was being used for 'military camps and its industries for the production of military material'.[31] How much of this remained in the final document passed to the Germans with the aim of diverting the Luftwaffe away from London and strategic targets in England is impossible to know. The naval depot at Trecwn was never bombed, the arsenal of high explosives at Glynrhonwy Isaf Slate Quarry was buried a year later when the roof collapsed, Penrhos was attacked by the Luftwaffe *before* GW reported its existence, and the Royal Artillery base at Tonfanau was still there in 2011.

Accompanying the military update was GW's latest account of Welsh nationalist activity for Robertson. According to the latest communiqué from the Welsh front line, a violent uprising was imminent among people angry and resentful about the thousands of women and children descending on the Rhondda from England's blitzed slums:

> It is said that a capitalist war has thrown these refugees into homes exploited by the same English Capitalist Government. There is no end to the misery and devastation caused by English Government. On it rests the responsibility for the bare homes of the Rhondda, and ultimately for the wrecked homes of London. It is a scene to delight the Devil – London's homeless ones received by Rhondda's homeless. What a sum of human misery.
>
> Wales has been told by every English Prime Minister from Ramsay MacDonald to Chamberlain, the English Government will not lift a hand to help South Wales. Largesse in the shape of schemes of social service or Depressed Area Acts it distributes with a certain calculated abandon. The real problem it deliberately evades by mass transfers of population, to which only the Assyrian and Babylonian empires offer any parallels.

When the Welsh nationalists argue with South Wales socialists we are told to remember that the class is more fundamental than the nation and that a Welshman's loyalty to his English fellow worker must take precedence over all other loyalties. Unfortunately, however, the traffic along this Rue Internationale is only one way, from Wales to England, never in the other direction.

Now that most of the overseas markets for South Wales coal have been lost there is, under the present system, only one other market in which it can be sold, and that is the home market. An attempt has therefore been made to secure for south Wales coal an increased share of this market, which has hitherto been the preserve mainly of the Midland and Lancashire coalfield. Here was a splendid opportunity to demonstrate working class solidarity, and to rise to the heights of international doctrine, by the sacrifice of part of the prosperity of the English coalfields to the salvaging of the South Wales miner. Alas for the international utopians of South Wales! The English miners have defended their monopoly as selfishly and stubbornly as any of the capitalists they profess to despise.

South Wales is faced with ever rising prices and stationary wages plus an enormous unemployed population. We have no means of gauging the hardships of the European countries under German control. What we do know is that this winter will bring to our fellow countrymen in South Wales, under English control, hardships beyond even the bitter experiences of the last twenty years.

The only hope of the sorely tried people of South Wales is an early peace, bringing the restoration of at least a proportion of the lost European markets. England can, at a pinch, dispense with the Continent; for Wales it is essential. A protracted war means the final ruin of the coalfields of South Wales. If Mr Churchill means to extend the war, then he will, among other things, complete the work he began in 1925. The Welsh nationalist Party, on the contrary, will never cease to reiterate that peace as soon as possible is the supreme interest of Wales.[32]

The approved documents were handed to del Pozo at the Spanish Embassy on 23 December 1940. But the Spaniard appeared more interested in receiving £100 from the talcum powder tin to pay his mysterious contact. A heated discussion followed with GW agreeing to get the money: 'If he [the agent] can tell me why he wants the money [so] I can tell my "master" and get it sooner.'

At first Del Pozo didn't take the bait. 'Sorry,' replied GW, 'but I don't think my "master" will hand over money unless he knows why.' After some hesitation del Pozo revealed that a few evenings previously an agent recently arrived from Madrid had called at his apartment wanting £200 urgently, saying the money was to be obtained from 'Ketteroch', Snow's Abwehr code name. Del Pozo's story was changing. Originally, it was £100 to pay an informant; now it was for a German agent. GW tried to get a name and address by asking, 'How do I get in touch with the agent to hand over the money?' No answer, just an arrangement to meet again at 'Chez Segundo', the Spanish Embassy, on 7 January 1941.

After wishing each other the compliments of the season at their next meeting GW produced what del Pozo wanted most: an envelope containing £300 – £100 for himself, the rest for the mysterious agent. Whether relieved at the sight of the money, or in an unguarded moment but the Spaniard said 'Angel' would collect his share in two days, letting slip the agent's name. 'Angel' was Angel Alcazar de Velasco, head of the Spanish spy ring, posing as Press Attaché at the Embassy and one of the most wanted on MI5's list. Asked how he was certain Angel would call to collect the money del Pozo explained that whenever they needed to talk he walked past Angel's house at a particular time, the signal they were to meet at his Athenaeum Court apartment at the same time two days later. The £200 was payment to Angel for obtaining British plans to invade Ireland in a covert operation to be blamed later on the Germans as a means of forcing the Irish into allowing Britain naval bases on Ireland's west coast. The sea route around Britain's western coast was heavily mined from Land's End to Liverpool, leaving only a narrow corridor for the convoys to enter the North Atlantic at which point they were especially vulnerable to German U-boats waiting to attack before the ships picked up their destroyer escorts.[33]

By now desperate to return to Madrid, del Pozo couldn't sleep and was paranoid about MI5 surveillance. A man in a taxi had followed him to the Spanish Club one evening while the other night he was attacked in Piccadilly and knocked over the head, he said. But there was one last operation he had for GW: help him wipe out the population of Swansea by poisoning its main water supply, the Cray reservoir, near Brecon. The poison for this del Pozo could obtain from a Spanish doctor living in London. That something like this might be planned was no surprise to MI5 which had a section preparing for bacteriological warfare. GW was sent by Rothschild to investigate just how vulnerable Cray reservoir was to such an attack. If it was not adequately protected, then the same could be said for probably every reservoir in Britain, certainly those in Wales's remote mountainous areas.

Arriving at Cray, GW discovered that the purifying plant where del Pozo proposed to introduce the poisonous substance was protected only by some loosely coiled barbed wire and a watchman. The watchman had orders to shoot any unauthorised person approaching the plant, but his rifle was locked away during the day and only issued at night.

'He was dressed in ordinary civilian clothing and indistinguishable from any other person. But he said eight soldiers patrolled the area day and night,' GW reported back to Rothschild. 'The poisoning of the water can be effected quite easily without going anywhere near the reservoir … from the main road which crosses over a number of small bridges built over mountain streams that feed the reservoir. The contamination of any of these streams would be as effective as if the contamination material was placed in the reservoir. In fact it would be easier as there is no danger of detection'.[34]

Suddenly, the Spaniard's plan was irrelevant. Del Pozo fled the country aboard a steamer bound for Portugal, only for it to be torpedoed by a German U-boat off Ireland's west coast. Picked up and taken to the Azores, he finally made it back to Madrid. Not long afterwards the British Consul General in Madrid cabled the Foreign Office: del Pozo had been arrested and sentenced to six months' imprisonment for embarrassing the Falangist Party by expressing support for Hitler. The *Daily Express* had finally got its man only for del Pozo to 'escape' from custody and take refuge in the German Embassy in Madrid.[35]

But rather than GW's cover being blown by del Pozo when interrogated by the Germans in Madrid as might have been expected there were, strangely, no obvious repercussions. The only loss was that MI5 no longer had access to the Spanish diplomatic bag.

For a time GW's attention shifted from nationalism to spying on the activity of Welsh trade unions, some of whom ignored political appeals to set aside their differences with employers until the war ended. Newspapers were prohibited from reporting the details but strikes still occurred, especially over Government premiums paid to factory owners for achieving production targets, which workers saw as a bonus they should share. The right to trade union membership was still Labour's Holy Grail and was vigorously defended by a walkout at steel plants across South Wales when the management at Richard Thomas and Baldwins refused to recognise a union member. GW also reported that his neighbours on Mount Pleasant were leaving Swansea in droves each night instead of sharing air raid patrol duties.

'The position is very hard on the few who, in some localities of the town have an entirely unjust share of the work,' he told Robertson. 'Reasonably able-bodied watchers [ARP] are few in numbers, particularly in the neighbourhood where I reside. I respectfully suggest that the time has arrived when the authorities should compel able-bodied men to remain in their homes […].'

His concern was vindicated on the nights of 19, 20 and 21 February 1941, the Luftwaffe reducing the town centre to a sea of flames, the glow visible in Milford Haven sixty miles away and in Newtown, 120 miles to the north. Incendiary bombs left the grammar and technical schools directly opposite GW's Mount Pleasant home 'blazing like a furnace' and his own house damaged. While factories and military installations escaped, all work at the docks was suspended with shipping unable to enter or leave until an acoustic mine sitting on the deck of a vessel moored in the bay was defused.

'Deaths alone consequent upon this raid,' he reported, 'are said to be between four and five hundred. Many of the inhabitants who were able left the town after the second night of the attack and made their way by any means possible to less vulnerable places outside the town … From what I am able to gather another night attack following the three we had would have completely broken the morale of the majority of the population and driven them desperate. Delayed action bombs have been exploding continually since the raids. It is said there are more than 200 of them … Still no news from our special friend'.[36]

The breaking of the link with del Pozo did not end GW's espionage career. All that happened was that the Abwehr put him on ice again, as it had between the demise of his first contact, Frau de Ridder, and the materialisation of del Pozo. For Robertson, Masterman and the Double-Cross System, the Spanish diplomatic bag was out of reach until the Germans could be persuaded to reactivate GW. In the meantime he monitored the activities of the local nationalists except that they were not doing a great deal. As a member he attended a Swansea branch meeting of Plaid Cymru at 116 Bryn Road on 10 April 1940 along with four other people. The local organiser Wynne Samuel gave a very long talk on Mazzini, the great Italian liberator of the 19th century. 'How the story ended I cannot say as I fell asleep in the middle,' he told Robertson.[37]

For several months GW took a back seat, the eyes and ears of the Double-Cross System in Wales but nothing more. By convincing the Abwehr that it had a team of nationalist fanatics waiting to wage a war of sabotage, he had ensured that German intelligence felt no need to send saboteurs to replace the missing Cubans. Not a single act of sabotage would occur in Wales throughout the war. Moreover, when in 1941 the Abwehr made renewed efforts to establish a more effective organisation in Britain, no agent was sent to Wales where it was preoccupied with delivering explosives to GW's imaginary nationalist cell. The shopping list of intelligence questions supplied to GW by the Abwehr shone a bright light into the dark corners of German military planning at a time when fear of an invasion was greatest. Del Pozo's intense interest in the coastal defences in southern England led to increased fortifications. Surveillance was maintained at Oxwich Bay in case a U-boat did arrive with the promised explosives. Questions the Germans asked about food supplies and public reaction to shortages showed how uncertain they were about the success of their U-boats in severing Britain's North Atlantic supply lines. By skillfully manipulating the replies delivered by GW, the Double-Cross System deceived and confused the enemy far more successfully than it first realised.

In the same way that it groomed its agents to win the confidence of the enemy before they embarked on more challenging assignments, the Double-Cross System itself graduated from manipulating intelligence to planning bogus operations. The two best-known are the case of the 'Man Who Never Was' and the duping of the German High Command into believing the Allies would land in the Pas de Calais rather than Normandy. In the first, 'Operation Mincemeat', the body of a Welsh tramp, Glyndwr Michael, found dead in a warehouse in St Pancras after swallowing rat poison was pumped full of water to give the impression of drowning, and then dumped in the sea off the Spanish coast to wash up on the beach at Tarifa as Major William Martin of the Royal Marines. In his briefcase were documents that persuaded the Germans to move ten divisions to Greece to prepare for an Allied invasion when Sicily was the intended second front. There were other schemes, no less imaginative, in which GW was about to play a part.

EIGHT THE CONFESSION

IN THE AUTUMN OF 1940 SNOW WOULD EXIT the espionage scene in a blaze of intrigue and insinuation, bringing down three other agents in the process. That May the Abwehr asked him to provide another potential agent for training, the new recruit to be delivered to Rantzau at a rendezvous in the North Sea. The German spymaster would arrive by submarine, Snow and his latest recruit by trawler. Seizing the opportunity to eliminate the head of the Abwehr's Hamburg counter-espionage branch, Robertson nominated a reformed petty criminal, Sam McCarthy, code-named 'Biscuit', to accompany Snow on the mission.

From the moment Snow and Biscuit teamed up there was friction. Snow believed Biscuit was a German agent while Biscuit thought Snow one on account of his pro-German sentiments during their train journey north to join the trawler waiting in Grimsby. The entire enterprise was fraught with danger from the outset. The British Army was trapped on the beaches at Dunkirk, yet on 19 May 1940, a week before the mass evacuation the pair sailed from Grimsby aboard a UK Fisheries Board trawler for the extraordinary rendezvous in the middle of the North Sea. What Snow didn't know was that the master had instructions not to go directly to the rendezvous point. Instead a Royal Navy submarine would be waiting there to torpedo the U-boat or apprehend Rantzau if at all possible.

After their first spat on the train Snow and Biscuit watched each other's every move as they headed out into the North Sea. On the evening of 21 May Snow, believing they had reached the supposed meeting place, gave what he claimed was the recognition signal to a plane circling overhead. For Biscuit this was convincing evidence

Snow was a traitor and the rendezvous a trap. The trawler's lights were extinguished and it turned for home. Snow objected and after scuffling with Biscuit was overpowered and held under armed guard until the trawler docked at Grimsby where on being searched by Special Branch officers Snow was found to be in possession of unauthorised documents. His explanation was that they were given to him by W. N. Rolf, his partner in a London business set up by MI5 as a channel for contacting the Societé de Consignation et Affrètement in Antwerp, a known cover address for the Abwehr. As improbable as it might seem, MI5 accepted Snow's story that Rolf was short of money and was using him as an intermediary to sell the documents to Rantzau when they met in the North Sea.

An attempt to retrieve the situation by dispatching a trawler with a naval crew to the correct position for the rendezvous on 23 May was unsuccessful. Fog reduced visibility to such an extent that Snow was able to tell Hamburg in his next radio transmission that they were there but missed the submarine on account of bad weather.[1]

The North Sea escapade shook MI5's confidence in Snow but a month later his differences with Biscuit were patched up, the pair agreeing it was a genuine misunderstanding over each other's modus operandi. But there was one loose end: Rantzau's new recruit had still to be delivered for Abwehr training, this time to Lisbon in neutral Portugal. Since the end of cross-channel espionage traffic Lisbon had become the new focus for clandestine activity.

On Snow's recommendation Biscuit was sidelined and Walter Dicketts chosen for the part of 'sidekick', as Snow called all his accomplices. The Welshman had first met Dicketts playing darts in the Marlborough public house at Kingston-upon-Thames some months earlier. Of average height, hair well-greased, wearing a light brown tweed sports jacket and grey flannels, his shoulders thrown well back, Dicketts was a loud and pretentious confidence trickster with a string of convictions. Because of a prison sentence for fraud he was unable to regain his First World War commission in Air Intelligence. But he did speak German and could represent himself to the Abwehr as a man with a grudge. Dicketts, code-named 'Celery', was first recruited by the Double-Cross System as an informant and paid thirty shillings a week to hang around bars and hotels in the

London area eavesdropping on conversations and reporting suspicious persons. That he considered the pay 'paltry' and beneath his assumed station in life was another grievance to add to his anti-British credentials when interrogated by Rantzau.[2]

Shortly before they were due to leave for Lisbon Snow received a radio SOS from Rantzau. An agent with a top secret file about the infrared detectors the RAF was fitting to its bombers for locating enemy night fighters needed a 'friend in England'. 'Can you bring the file to Lisbon?' radioed Rantzau. 'How can he contact you without [revealing] your identity and can Charlie micro it?'

Snow set up a dead letterbox for the infrared agent in Craven Hill, Paddington, the package to be delivered between 7–13 February at 9.30 a.m. Liddell, Robertson, Masterman, and Cowgill (MI6) wrestled with the problem of what action to take when the infrared man arrived there. If the package contained vital information that could not be allowed to leave the country then Liddell favoured 'bumping him off'. But if they did eliminate him MI5 might never discover if the German agent had a hidden radio transmitter. Snow was told to ask Rantzau to arrange for the package to be delivered earlier, in the next twenty-four hours, on the assumption that if the last-minute change of plan proved impossible then MI5 could safely assume the agent did not have access to a transmitter. Hamburg's reply was that delivery was delayed until the day before Snow left for Lisbon, in which case he was to memorise the salient points in the document before sending it to Charlie for microdotting later. Rantzau still believed Snow and Charlie were his people.

A camera with a telescopic lens was set up in a house directly opposite the dead letterbox. Officers were to trail the German agent back to his base or until dusk when the arrest would be made rather than risk losing the man in the blackout. By 10 a.m. that morning there was no sign of the infrared man. The only interest in the house was from a suspicious-looking individual who glanced in its direction as he walked passed. The next morning at about the same time the same person appeared to take a long hard look at the postbox before being followed to Whiteleys department store in Bayswater where he was employed as a floorwalker. The watch was later called off although John Gwyer, a security analyst at MI5, did suspect the floorwalker was either the infrared man or his emissary.[3]

Snow flew to Lisbon from Bristol Airport. Celery left earlier for Portugal aboard the SS *Cressado*. The night before his flight Snow stayed at the Cumberland Hotel in Marble Arch, to be driven first thing the next morning to Bristol Airport by Jock Horsfall, an MI5 chauffeur ferrying agents around the country. That evening, Horsfall was in the corridor outside the Welshman's room when he overheard a telephone conversation between Snow and a woman during which some kind of code was used. By the time this was reported Snow was already en route to Lisbon but as a precaution Robertson ordered his telephone tapped just in case other family members were implicated.

Celery's arrival in Lisbon was delayed by atrocious weather in the Bay of Biscay, the SS *Cressado* at one stage reported as having been sunk by a German U-boat. The delay gave Snow two weeks alone with Rantzau to whom he allegedly confessed that for the previous three months he was a controlled British agent. Whether he did and whether he warned Celery about this has never been clear although Masterman and Robertson, and the Double-Cross section subsequently devoted hundreds of man-hours trying to figure it out and the consequences for the network of British agents. Masterman concluded that the 'riddle of the Sphinx and the doctrine of the Trinity are simple and straightforward affairs compared with this'.[4]

The various hypotheses to explain what did actually occur rely wholly on the accounts of those involved. Did Snow confess to Rantzau that he was controlled by the British? Did the German spymaster then persuade him to become a triple agent? Was Snow always in the pay of the Abwehr? Was Snow so jealous of a new rival that he deliberately sent Celery on a mission into Germany from which he was not expected to return? Not only was Celery briefed to infiltrate the Abwehr by convincing Rantzau of his pro-German, anti-British sympathies but also instructed to report on Snow's relationship with the German spymaster and on German espionage operations in Portugal. After entering Germany for espionage training MI5 hoped Celery would return with valuable intelligence about Abwehr operations.

What makes this affair more intriguing is an eleven-page document entitled 'Major Ritter's [Rantzau] final report on the [Snow] case' in which Rantzau makes no mention of Snow's alleged confession. Even more puzzling is that the English translation of the original written by Rantzau in Berlin on 31 July 1941, describing what occurred between Snow, Celery and himself in Lisbon the previous February, is included in Snow's MI5 dossier. Without any mention of how it was procured, this top secret German document is attached to a report prepared for MI5 by security analysts John Gwyer and John Marriott dated 17 November 1941, *only* four months after Rantzau wrote it for his Abwehr bosses in Berlin. At the end of the war it is reasonable to assume the Rantzau report might have been among documents captured by the Allies. But was it leaked to MI5 as early as 1941 – and if so, by whom? As unlikely as it seems, after returning from Hamburg Celery suggested to Snow he suspected some kind of relationship existed between Rantzau and Robertson:

I cannot understand this business over there, a chap like [redacted] sitting in an office and here I am on this bloody job risking my life. I don't know what it was but I think he was a little bit in with Robby [Robertson]. It may have been something I said but for a long time he never shook hands with me. I don't know what I did. I probably stepped on his corns somewhere. Another thing I cannot understand you know, Robby said to you in front of me at the last meeting, 'Tell the doctor I want to meet him'. He may think the war is going to be over. Don't you remember he also said, 'Where you are going there is no censor and you can say what you like'. Look at the position he has put me in. If I go back to England and say that, where is Robby … I have seen so many things. I know exactly what is going to happen and I want to be assured that there is going to be no trouble when we get back to England … I don't like that little fellow [MI5 agent] in the house [where Lily and Celery's wife were living]. I think they will probably start some mucky business with the girls. If there is mucky business God help them when I get to Bristol …[5]

Snow's story for MI5 was that on arriving in Lisbon on 14 February 1941 he was collected from the foyer of the Metropole Hotel by the resident German agent Dobler (alias Duarte) and led to a black Opel saloon car in which Rantzau was waiting. During the drive across the city, Snow asked Rantzau cheerfully, 'How's the wife?'

Nodding, the Abwehr spymaster replied, 'How's Lily and the baby?'

'Very well,' answered Snow.

'We are going to have a little talk. It's all very interesting,' said the German as the Opel pulled up outside a block of flats. Taking the lift to the third floor, Duarte unlocked the door, the three entered and sat down.

'I've something very interesting to tell you, and I want a truthful reply,' said Rantzau immediately.

'Okay, shoot,' replied Snow.

'I've information that you are in contact with British Intelligence,' said Rantzau grimly.

Without a moment's hesitation, Snow replied, 'That's perfectly true. I've been trying for over two and a half months to get over to see you about it, and I've sent you SOS signals as arranged but your operators could not figure it out.' From Rantzau's expression he guessed that the game was up and, knowing how the Abwehr could 'beat up' on a subject during interrogation, decided to admit everything.[6]

'Tell me roughly what happened,' invited Rantzau.

'Well, they walked in [on me] about two and a half months ago. Somebody had squealed.'

'Who do you think double-crossed you, GW or Charlie?'

'I don't know … I can't tell you. They went right through the house. They never found any papers; only the codes and the transmitter, that's all.'

'What about Lily? Do they know she helps? Was she cross-examined?'

'As far as I know, yes she was. She knew nothing … only that I had a radio transmitter in the house. I never mentioned anything about Lily.'

'If I didn't know you as well as I do and worked with you for so long,' said Rantzau, 'I would never trust you as far as I can see you, but when you tell me things like that I know you are speaking the truth.' But Snow knew too much about the Abwehr and its operations for Rantzau to let the Welshman return to Britain. If necessary, he would hold him hostage in Lisbon, he said.

'That suits me,' replied Snow. 'The only thing I can do is contact the British Embassy.'

'What do you think [of the situation]?' Rantzau asked.

'I didn't want to be in front of a firing squad. The only thing was to tell them [the British] I would work for them.' Nodding his head, Rantzau paused and then added mysteriously, 'I've got a solution worked out for the whole thing.'[7] His plan was for Snow to return to Britain as a triple agent using certain code words inserted in radio traffic to indicate whether the intelligence transmitted was accurate or bogus.

Rantzau asked for the names and descriptions of the MI5 officers who raided the house in Kingston-upon-Thames. The men, according to Snow, were 'medium English people, thin faces and I think a policeman among them … All I know is that they were called Doctor and Professor, and there was one Herr.'

'What about the radio messages you have sent us [before the raid]?' Rantzau asked.

'You can take it from me that everything that has been sent over has been genuine.'

'You're sure?'

'You can check up on them,' replied Snow. Rantzau admitted the intelligence was 'very useful'.[8]

'Tell me about Celery. I am very interested in Celery and I shall stay here until he arrives,' said Rantzau.

'He is definitely 100 per cent for you … double crossing them. I've known him for about twelve months … from Richmond. He seemed to have pro-Nazi views and after that difficulty getting into the air force I thought he was suitable.' The conversation then turned to more personal matters, Snow showing Rantzau photographs of the baby.

The following morning they met in a flat belonging to a German girl. Rantzau asked about Caroli, code-named 'Summer' by the British. His radio transmissions had stopped. What had gone wrong?

'He was scared. Someone was making inquiries about him and he beat it,' said Snow.

'That's okay,' said Rantzau. 'He's got seaman's papers and we will see him again. What about Celery?' It was then Snow confided that Celery was not as pro-German as he pretended.[9]

A car collected Snow from the hotel that evening and he was driven to Estoril on the coast and a large private house with a veranda extending along the front, the house set in its own grounds at the top of a hill overlooking the sea.

Dobler sat drinking coffee and blowing smoke rings. Four other men were waiting. Rantzau took Snow aside and whispered, 'There's one thing I forgot to ask you this morning. What about your men in South Wales?'

'There's nothing to worry about,' replied Snow. 'They're okay. We can go on with the sabotage in South Wales. These are my men, not GW's.' In a large sitting room Rantzau proceeded to give a talk about sabotage illustrated with exploding pens, time clocks and detonators. A large pocket watch was fixed to the back of a torch battery and a detonator attached but it failed to explode. At the end of the demonstration Snow was given various explosive devices to take back to Britain, including torch batteries, shaving soap, a talcum powder tin containing timers, two exploding fountain pens in special holders, and more small blocks of wood concealing detonators. When these were subsequently surrendered to Rothschild's counter-sabotage section of MI5 for scientific examination it was discovered that while the torches were manufactured in Germany the batteries containing the timers and detonators were made in Britain.

What MI5 totally failed to understand was why, after allegedly confessing to being a British agent, Snow was then given £10,000 (£287,000 at 2005 prices) by Rantzau to fund his espionage activities in Britain, including GW's Welsh nationalist cell. Instead of being terminated, as might have been expected, Snow's pockets were filled with money and a new set of radio codes for contacting Hamburg.[10]

When told of this, Liddell noted in his diary, 'There has been some rather disquieting news about Snow. It seems the Germans were not satisfied with his traffic and went for him … in spite of this he has been given £10,000 and a new contract. Very curious but no chance of getting at the facts until he returns … There is also the rather curious fact that he [says] he was ill and wants his wife [Lily] and child to join him in Lisbon. The whole thing is rather unfortunate but it was bound to come to an end sooner or later. We have to get other strings to our bow'.[11]

At their last meeting alone before Celery's arrival Snow was instructed by Rantzau to send Celery to the Channel Islands to collect another radio transmitter, otherwise someone from South Wales would have to go. After his setbacks Rantzau had orders to establish a new network of agents in Britain. 'You understand the instructions: when Celery arrives you are both coming to Germany at once. Dobler will arrange everything,' said Rantzau as Snow climbed into the car for the drive back to the hotel, adding cheerily, 'Give my respects to Lilly. I've clean forgotten to buy her a present but I've left instructions for Duarte [Dobler] to buy her one.' Unfortunately for MI5 Rantzau also neglected to issue Snow with a fresh supply of specially treated writing paper and secret ink capsules, which the Germans changed regularly to confuse the British censor.

The stress was evidently getting to Snow who was drinking at least a bottle of brandy a day, some mornings so hung over he couldn't crawl out of bed. Celery eventually reached Lisbon on 23 February and went directly to the hotel. 'I've had a terrible journey,' he muttered. 'I must have a drink.' Over drinks Celery admitted being told by Robertson before leaving England to report what Snow did, where he went, to whom he spoke.[12]

'It looks like a double-cross to me,' remarked Snow. 'Don't you think Robby [Robertson] is a bit scared by something?'

'Remember what happened in the club before we left,' replied Celery. 'Robbie said "there will be no censor there, and you can say what you like as far as I am concerned … and tell the Doctor [Rantzau] I would like to meet him".'

'What do you think of the situation?' Snow asked. 'I have instructions [from the Germans] to give you money and whatever else you want.'

'Well, that's more like business,' replied Celery cheerfully. 'You know how I went around and did all the dirty work [in England] getting the passports, visas, everything … If I had not met you what would I have done?'

'You will find the people here quite different from that,' said Snow pulling out a handful of notes to show Celery.[13]

Rantzau had postponed his return to Hamburg to meet Celery. That he was worried by the rumoured sinking of the *Cressado* is evident from a conversation an SIS (MI6) agent reported from Lisbon in which a German agent named Kuno Welzien was heard to boast that the *Cressado* was delivering an agent regarded 'as a valuable means of planting false information on the British'. Even if Celery's mission was to infiltrate the Abwehr as Snow claimed Rantzau believed the loyalty of the petty crook could still be bought.[14]

When the three men met in Snow's room at the Metropole Hotel Snow was already drunk and, crucially, unable to recall exactly what he told Celery about confessing to Rantzau about being a British double agent. Despite hundreds of pages of testimony taken by MI5 from the main protagonists precisely what was said in that hotel room remains unclear. Snow did remember sitting on the bed alongside the Abwehr agent Duarte (alias Dobler) listening while Rantzau questioned Celery who, if he had known of the 'confession', would almost certainly have refused to enter Germany for espionage training as he did a few days later. There could have been another reason for Snow's heavy drinking that particular day. According to Celery, he was afraid he would be arrested and 'shot' the moment he returned to Britain and that Lily and the baby were being held hostage to guarantee his return!

But none of this appeared to ruffle Snow's natural ebullience when with a flourish he introduced Celery to Rantzau, 'This is my man … returned from the grave [a reference to the rumoured sinking of the *Cressado*].'

'Yes,' said Rantzau, 'we have been trying to find him for a long time. We have had submarines looking for him. We thought he was in Madeira but he is here. I am very glad he is here. I have put off so many appointments [in Germany] because I knew he was an important man.'

'He's 100 per cent for you,' said Snow.

'Is that true?' Rantzau asked.

'100 per cent … I'm with you 100 per cent,' replied Celery, before complaining about his MI5 pay and conditions, and adding, 'If I pull this off [in Germany] I am going to get a staff position when I get back … a lieutenant in the RAF, and be of enormous use to you. I am ready to go.'

'This man is working for British intelligence and he's 100 per cent for you,' Snow assured Rantzau. 'He has given me his word … maybe you can use him.'

'Well. We know a little about this man,' replied Rantzau.[15]

According to Snow, Celery then said his assignment included learning everything he could about the anticipated German invasion of Britain. For this his reward would be a commission in the RAF, at which point Snow interrupted saying, 'I live in a very dangerous spot. I'm in south west London and I don't want to be mixed up in this invasion.'

'The mass attack of the invasion will come through Gravesend,' said Rantzau. 'I think you ought to go to Wales. That's all I can advise you at the moment.'

After the Germans left, Snow and Celery continued drinking, first with the crew of the *Cressado*, and then neat gins in the English Bar until the early hours of the morning, when they returned to the hotel where over yet more drinks in the lounge Celery asked, 'You are 100 per cent for the Doctor, aren't you?'

'Yes. Why?'

'I am, too. I would never take this trip [to Germany] unless I knew you were 100 percent for him because I would not trust the people on the other side.'[16]

The next day Celery told Ranzau that Snow was likely to be executed when he got back to England. Rantzau looked across and asked, 'What do you think of that?'

'That's all eyewash, they're probably fooling!' replied Snow.

'You could always work in Germany,' suggested Rantzau.

'No, I've got Lily and the baby to go back to … I must go back.'

Celery wasn't much interested in moving to Germany either. 'I've got to go back as well, you know,' he told Snow later over a drink. 'When I get back [after the German visit] I am going to have so much dope that you are going to get a decoration and we shall be able to get Lily and the baby out of England without any difficulty,' he added, in a reference to the internment order hanging over her.

On several occasions afterwards Celery asked for reassurances from Snow that Rantzau could be trusted to return him to Lisbon after training in Germany. 'You know,' Celery threatened, 'you have put your life in my hands? I can go to the Embassy now and get them to wire England with information about you.'

'You can do it if you want to but I am positive the Doctor is playing straight [with us] and we are both 100 per cent for him. You have no doubts in your mind about making the trip?'

'None whatever,' replied Celery. 'I am looking forward to it.'[17]

Celery collected a German passport in the name of Walter Dunkler from their Lisbon Embassy located in a castle overlooking the city, then bought a new hat, coat, shirts and a suitcase. Their last evening together was spent at the Arcadia Hotel nightclub with a pair of German girls. Celery slipped away at midnight with one of them while Snow remained to watch the cabaret with the other. Before leaving, Celery turned to Snow and said, 'If it was not for you I would never do this … you won't double-cross me?'

'No,' replied Snow, 'I've given you and other people my word that I will see you go into Germany and come out.'

'You won't double-cross me in any shape or form? And you won't say anything in England about this?' he added, indicating his female companion.

'No,' Snow repeated, 'I will see that you come out again. No, I shall say nothing.'

'What about the money?'

'You will get plenty of money for the trip … and you'll be looked after, given money when you are there.' Back at the hotel Snow asked the hall porter to prepare a packed lunch for Celery – sandwiches and whisky.

The next morning, shaking Celery's hand in the hotel foyer, Snow said, 'You are a very brave man.' After embracing his German girlfriend Celery headed for the railway station where a diplomatic car was waiting for the drive to Madrid, and from there by plane to Hamburg.[18] The interrogation by the Abwehr was tough but there never was any espionage training, only a quantity of propaganda material and some tendentious information about the absence of air raid damage in Hamburg despite almost nightly RAF raids.

By the third week Snow was drinking with friends in the Arcadia nightclub having given his 'sidekick' up for dead when in walked Celery. Casting around for a quiet corner to talk he explained how he was picked up at the Spanish–Portuguese frontier by the German agent Duarte (Dobler) and his Spanish girlfriend. Excitedly he whispered, 'I must see you at once … shall we get a table?' The moment they were settled out of earshot, Celery blurted, 'I have had the most remarkable experience of any person.'

'Did everything go alright then?' Snow asked.

'I've never seen such an organisation … I have never seen such a country … I have never seen such people as in Germany!'

'What do you mean?'

'I've got enough stuff here to blow the whole works.'

'In what way?'

'In papers and documents … I was allowed to go everywhere … given a free hand. I went down the docks in Hamburg, to Blohm and Voss. I have got all the dope on shipbuilding, submarine production, aircraft production, the number of aircraft in commission in Germany, and approximately the number of men they have … I had a meeting with Dr Goebbels's secretary … they were tickled to death with the information I gave them regarding improvement in their propaganda. When I arrived in Hamburg the Doctor wasn't there but he arrived a few days afterwards.'

'What is the food situation in Germany?' Snow interrupted.

'There is any amount of food there. There is nearly twice as much butter there as you get in England.'

'There ought to be,' said Snow. 'They pinched it from other countries. Were you there for any raids?'

'Yes, there was one [lasting] six hours.'

'Where were you?'

'I was in a shelter with some staff officers.'

'Is there much damage in Hamburg?'

'The only place I saw damage were a couple of buildings in St Pauli.'

'You were in an air raid shelter for six hours, and no damage!' retorted Snow in disbelief.

'No, none … nor in Berlin … in Hamburg bombs dropped in the country on the opposite side of the river to Blohm and Voss.'

'How many machines went over?'

'About 60.'

'What is the matter with our people?' remarked Snow, exasperated at the RAF's failure to hit its targets.[19]

This was just what German intelligence wanted the British to believe. No attempt was made to intimidate Celery; not once was he threatened with violence. Rantzau's instruction to the interrogators was to discover ways to use a man who had 'all the appearance of a crook, who would do anything for money'. Celery spoke often about being in low water financially and being compelled to accept work that was beneath his qualifications. The Germans cultivated Celery's love of money, Rantzau buying him with a down payment of £200, some US dollars, and the promise of much larger amounts in England paid by Snow. The German spymaster calculated that so long as Snow had a financial hold Celery could be prevented from running to MI5. He might squeal when the £10,000 was exhausted but by then it would be difficult to provide a convincing explanation for having said nothing sooner. By keeping Snow operational and above suspicion Rantzau believed his agents in South Wales were secure. If Snow eventually collapsed, there remained a great deal to gain from the false information planted on Celery whose immediate value to the Germans was as part of an elaborate plan to protect Snow, one of the three men Rantzau most trusted, the others being the Welsh nationalist fanatic GW, and Charlie, the Manchester photographer, both of whom were British Double-Cross agents.[20]

When Snow returned to England on 27 March 1941 and admitted to 'confessing', Robertson guessed that the Abwehr was already picking at the strands of the Double-Cross System's Gordian knot. In too many cases those strands ran back to Snow, the very first brick in the edifice. GW followed in October 1939, but it was not until a year later that Robertson picked up a third member for the team, a Dane Wulf Schmidt (alias Harry Williamson), code name 'Tate'. When Schmidt parachuted into Britain in 1940 MI5 was waiting having been alerted to his arrival by Snow. The immediate consequence of Snow's confession, if true, was that the Abwehr was certain to realise that another of its supposed agents, Tate, might also controlled by the British since the Germans paid him through Snow. Tate was a prolific agent feeding the Abwehr masses of false intelligence and later playing a vital part in the combined intelligence operation to persuade Hitler that D-Day would be launched across the Straits of Dover to the Pas de Calais, rather than to Normandy. Robertson could ill-afford to lose Tate, so named because he resembled the music hall comedian Harry Tate. From Snow, Tate's umbilical cord led to 'Balloon' who, in turn, used one of the most famous of all double agents, 'Tricycle', otherwise Dusko Popov, for transmitting fake intelligence to Hamburg. Rantzau believed Tricycle was his master spy in the United States when, in fact, he was another double agent controlled by Robertson. Popov was born in 1912 in Titel, Austria-Hungary to a wealthy Serbian family, before moving to Dubrovnik when young. He spoke fluent German and had many highly placed German friends, but secretly despised the Nazis. Recruited by the Abwehr early in the war, Popov immediately offered himself as a double agent to Britain. Well-rewarded for his services Popov enjoyed a playboy lifestyle in between carrying out perilous wartime missions. In London he always stayed in the same suite at the Savoy Hotel, earning his code name Tricycle for his penchant for three-in-a-bed sexual encounters. In 1941 Popov was sent to the United States by the Abwehr with ample funds and detailed instructions to discover all he could about the defences at Pearl Harbor. Reputedly it was Tricycle who warned FBI chief J. Edgar Hoover of an imminent attack on Pearl Harbor, only for Hoover to ignore the tip-off. Tricycle, Tate, Balloon, and GW were all at risk because of Snow's 'confession' at a time when pressure on agents to provide intelligence about military installations along the south coast suggested the invasion was imminent. In particular, Rantzau wanted specific information about apparent obstructions in fields in the Aldington, Stowting, Lyminge, Hawkinge and Folkestone areas. After German reconnaissance aircraft spotted lines of pylons, the Luftwaffe needed to know whether the wires were electrically charged, what gauge, the height of the pylons and material from which they were made. These were, in fact, part of the RAF's early warning radar installation.[21]

Unravelling the truth about what exactly happened in Lisbon would prove beyond the capacity of MI5's most skilled interrogators. On one matter British and German intelligence was agreed:

Snow was virtually impossible to question, his story rarely consistent, his constantly shifting ground leaving interrogators with the distinct impression that the Welshman had a foot in parallel universes. Although Snow was given every opportunity to recant his 'confession' he never did.

Snow might reasonably be described as a spy from a long line of terraced houses located somewhere in the South Wales valleys. It is hard to imagine one of the polished, public school educated agents of post-war fiction uttering the immortal line to his spymaster as an opening gambit, 'How's the wife?' Snow resembled a car salesman or insurance agent sheltering from the rain in a shop doorway but never the secret agent of popular fiction shuttling between foreign embassies. Resentful of the English, Snow's bunk up over the wall and escape to Canada did little to dislodge the chip on his shoulder. The condescending attitude of his English associates in MI5, some of whom regarded him as barely literate, might have fed into his anti-English prejudices but not nationalism which was only ever a ruse, a paper-thin excuse for double-crossing, double-dealing by a relic of inter-war espionage stranded by the uncertain tide of a real war. Nor was Snow strong on patriotism. Only when all options were exhausted did he rush to the colours – and then from behind prison walls. His motivation was the lure of easy money. Listening to careless talk, while wandering around the country at someone else's expense noting the locations of factories, airfields and other military installations, was intellectually undemanding and hugely rewarding. Dodging shadows, using secret passwords and starring in imaginary plots were bread and water for a man happiest when assuming a false persona. By the time war started Snow's life was fashioned by deception and fuelled by women and alcohol.

Arrested on returning to England he stood before Robertson, Masterman and Marriott, all intent on discovering the truth behind the alleged 'confession'. Later, Dick White, deputy head of B Branch – and the only man ever to run both MI5 and MI6 – was given a crack at Snow. Liddell, who oversaw the interrogation, became more convinced than ever that the Welshman could not distinguish between fact and fiction and was only in it for the money. But MI5 had to get to the bottom of the Lisbon affair to protect its other agents.

The questioning, beginning with a preliminary interview on 28 March 1941, was complicated by Snow's admission to having confessed to Rantzau to being a British double agent. That he had nothing to hide was evident the moment he stepped off the plane at Bristol and surrendered the £10,000 given him by Rantzau to the waiting MI5 agents, together with assorted sabotage devices and explosives to the delight of Lord Rothschild's counter-sabotage section. In addition, before leaving Lisbon he briefed the resident MI6 agent at the British Embassy – in this case the Air Attaché – about his meetings with Rantzau.

Snow's interrogators knew from dealing previously with the little man to remain focused if they were to have any hope of discovering (1) what action Rantzau decided to take when told Snow had been 'walked in on' by MI5 (2) whether Snow told Celery about his 'confession' before the latter entered Germany and (3) what story the pair cooked up for Major Robertson's benefit as regards their activities in Lisbon.

The steno-typist's verbatim record covering hundreds of pages provides a unique psychological profile of two British spies who with unsophisticated cunning confounded their intellectually superior controllers at MI5. Naturally suspicious, Snow deftly fended off the most probing questions, sometimes inarticulately but always with a veneer of honesty and co-operation. The Welshman succeeded in reducing three days of interrogation to a level of incomprehension and equivocation that left the men from the Double-Cross System no nearer the truth. By the end Marriott concluded that he was 'more than ever convinced that Snow is a case not for the Security Service, but for a brain specialist'. An interrogation that set out to navigate a maze of conflicting claims and counter-claims was reduced to becoming a merry-go-round.[22]

Marriott began the questioning on April Fool's Day 1941 by asking, 'I want to know what story the Doctor thought you were going to tell us [after your confession].'

Snow: I am not supposed to tell you anything.

Marriott: But we knew that you were out there. What does the Doctor think you are going to tell us now?

Snow: That everything is going satisfactorily. That I had met the Doctor, introduced Celery to the Doctor, that he was okay, and had gone into Germany. I know nothing about the story that Celery was to tell you as a result of going into Germany. He [Rantzau] told me we should come back here and he would make arrangements for Lily and myself to get out of the country.

Marriott: But didn't he [Celery] discuss with you what he was going to say to us?

Snow: No, he never discussed that at all, no so far as I remember.

Marriott: But if he was double crossing … ? He would have told you what he would say to us.

Snow: He said, 'I will boost you right up to the skies and help you any way I can, and you will get a decoration.'

Marriott: You say that Celery is double crossing us.

Snow: Your man in Lisbon thinks the same way.

Marriott: Do you think Celery is of the opinion that you were double crossing us?

Snow: I do not know. No … I will tell you why because afterwards he tried to find out about the German girl and tried to get some dope out of her, and stood her drinks and gave one of the other German girls 200 escudos, and she gave him her address in Paris. He said to me later, 'Who are you working for?' I said, 'What did she say?' He said she had given him the address in Paris and told certain other things.

According to Snow, he and Celery met four German dancers – Ruth, Lottie, Sadie and Dopie – in the Arcadia nightclub. The eldest, he said, was Ruth, aged about 33, 'thin face, slightly Jewish nose, of medium build, not married as far as I knew, with good teeth' and spoke six languages. Celery warned him not to be seen with the girls because they were returning to Germany on Berlin's instructions.

During Celery's absence Snow visited the Arcadia club every evening and attempted to recruit the older one Ruth as a British agent in Paris where she had a flat.

'Wasn't it very silly of you, mistrusting Celery as you did, to go recruiting agents in Portugal?' Marriott asked.

Snow: How did he know?

Marriott: Because you told him.

Snow: I didn't tell him a word.

Marriott: Or because she was a German agent and told him.

Snow: The night Celery found this out [the attempt to recruit Ruth] I was feeling pretty rotten. At ten o'clock he rushed back to the hotel and asked if I was going to the Arcadia. I said yes. He came down afterwards … he had been talking to Ruth for hours. Lottie was crying on his shoulder all the time … she was more homely than the others. She's the one he gave the 200 escudos to.

Marriott: Did you ever see him with any other woman there?

Snow: There was a woman in the hotel … from France … he said he met her on the train [except] … I thought he came by aeroplane to Lisbon. He used to go to her flat. I don't know what happened there … he is so definitely pro-German he will go to any lengths … absolutely money-mad. All he did when he came back was [ask for] money, money, money … the Doctor had told him to call on me for as much money as he required.

Marriott: If we can't trust Celery the whole thing is finished.

Snow: I will not leave this country again with Celery.

Marriott: Do you want to go on?

Snow: Definitely, I have done a lot. And a lot has been done through me.

Marriott: What can be done now?

Snow: There is this transmitter in the Channel Islands. The Doctor raised Cain about [what happened to] the parachutist. I told him that I had sent two men from Wales there to snoop around the pubs and that they heard he came down from an aeroplane and fired his revolver. The Doctor said it was getting too wasteful and he must provide another method to get men to this country. Celery says it's easy.

Marriott: He's a pilot. It isn't everyone who knows the way to the Channel Islands by boat. If you don't trust him you can't use him. He might stay away.

Snow: He won't stay away without his wife. He doesn't know about the new transmitter. I didn't tell him. If he is not playing straight we can get him to get the radio. If he is not playing straight he will help to get the man [the agent] here. It must have been talked about in Hamburg. The Doctor is very keen on this method. He lost too many men the other way. I don't know about him [Celery] going back in a month's time. I don't know what dope he has got. I should be very much inclined to doubt whether he has anything big to tell Churchill, that the war will be over in a fortnight.[23]

During a lunch adjournment, Marriott quietly quizzed Snow about Germany. The Welshman had previously expressed profound admiration for German efficiency and believed nothing could stand against it. Snow now believed England would probably win the war, Marriott adding, 'His ignorance of and indifference to even the most important of current affairs are almost fantastic. His position now, however, appears to me to be that he is beginning to suspect that his German idol has feet of clay and although his reasons are not good ones, they seem for the moment to carry some weight with him … and together with his jealousy for Celery provides us with a soft spot he is not particularly anxious to cover up.'[24]

The following day when Celery was questioned, he told of a conversation with Rantzau in Hamburg. The German knew Snow drank heavily and lived on his nerves, but seemed 'really fond of the little man' whom he trusted because he had never 'let me down' in the four years they worked together.

Celery: He must have been giving you some very good information.

Rantzau: No, Snow has not given me very much but I think he is going to be very useful to us in other ways.

Celery: What other ways?

Rantzau: Don't ask too many questions but Snow is a very clever chemist. In fact, in some ways he is brilliant. I am very fond of Snow but he is a Goddam lazy son of a bitch and he won't get going unless someone gives him a good kick in the pants. Snow spends a hell of a lot of money but we don't mind … we have plenty of it here.

In a final attempt to get at the truth, Snow and Celery were brought face-to-face. Dick White conducted the interrogation but the easy charm and manners of a man described as the perfect English gentlemen, the David Niven of MI5, proved no match for the two compulsive liars. Again and again during a whole day of interrogation White took them over the same ground: did Snow confess to Rantzau he was a British controlled agent, and did he warn Celery of this before he was taken to Germany for training by the Abwehr?

White: I am sure you are both aware of the seriousness of the position. Therefore I want to hear first of all from you Snow [about] … the nature of your warning to Celery in Lisbon.

Snow: Yes, Celery knew exactly that the Doctor knew I was in touch with British Intelligence before he left for Germany. That is right, isn't it?

Celery: I had gathered as much but I didn't know.

Snow: You didn't know?

Celery: You never told me anything about it. You never mentioned it to me.

Snow: You mean to tell me you didn't know?

Celery: I'm telling you. After making my report [on returning from Germany] you told me you had blown the whole project to the Doctor, and had warned me accordingly. You never made any such statement. When did you break it to me?

Snow: I believe I warned you when I saw you in the room.

Celery: You believe you did. I don't want to know what your beliefs are, I want to know exactly.

Snow: Do you remember me telling you in front of the Doctor? I remember this definitely, telling you in front of the Doctor that the Doctor knew everything about me in connection with the British Secret Service. Don't you remember you sitting there, the Doctor sitting there, me sitting on the bed with Dobler, and I said to you, 'The Doctor knows everything, you understand?' I definitely did.

Celery: I say you didn't, and I am also informed that you warned me personally that you had blown the entire party to the Doctor, and that your advice to me … was to assure me that you were the only person who could look after me [and to] put my whole trust in you, that you would see me back again as you had given your word of honour. You wavered on the last day and were obviously very nervous and you said to me on the pavement when I was getting into the taxi to go to Estoril Station, 'You are a very brave man Celery. Don't go if you don't want to.'

The exchanges between the two deteriorated further until separating fact from fiction became virtually impossible such were the infantile depths of their wrangling.

Snow: Don't you remember me phoning down at your request to the bar for two gin fizzes because you said you felt so rotten?

Celery: We went down to the bar and sat in the bar ourselves.

Snow: Half a minute. You said to me in the office let's go and have a drink. I said, 'Don't have a drink down here, come up to my room'. We went up to the room; I phoned down to the bar.

Celery: No.

Snow: I phoned down to the bar and got them to send it up.

Celery: No. You had some sherry in your room. You said, 'I only have beer here'. I said, 'I don't want beer'.

With the banter between the pair descending into farce, White sought to refocus the interrogation on why Rantzau gave Snow £10,000 after he confessed to being a British agent. But he was no more successful, both men continuing to squabble over the smallest matters.

White [to Snow]: When did you tell Celery you had received £10,000?

Snow: The first day I met him.

Celery: No.

Snow: I showed you the money.

Celery: He told me he had £5,000 then. The other £5,000 comes at a different date.

Snow: I didn't tell him how much I had. I said £50,000.

White: How do you explain it? Because you say also that you told him that the Doctor knew everything. You are under the control of the British and yet he has given you £5,000. Did you tell him that?

Snow: I said, 'Look here; look at these people. Look at the way they give money away. They don't quibble about money.'

Celery: 'Look what they think of me,' that's what you said.

Snow: I said, 'Now look at the way they treat people. This is what they do. They don't even think about expenses at all.'

White said it was curious that at the moment the Germans knew Snow was under British control they give him such a large sum of money as a reward.

Snow: I see your point. The point is this though … I don't exactly know what I said but I showed him [Celery] the money anyhow and what I said about it I just don't remember now. Whether I made any explanation or not, I can't remember.

White [to Celery]: Do you remember?

Celery: He made no explanation at all. He simply said, 'Look what they think of me and how they feed me.' And he had it under a bundle of dirty washing locked up first of all in the wardrobe, which I thought was very unwise.

Snow: No, I didn't.

Celery: Oh, yes you did. Later you put it in a suitcase. First you had it pushed under a dirty shirt. You said it was the best place to keep it.

Snow: No, I had it in my case first and I had it in the wardrobe afterwards … I remember that definitely.

Celery: You lifted the shirt up. I can see you doing it now.

Snow: In my case.

Celery: In your wardrobe. I said you ought to put it in the safe and you said the safe was too small.

Exasperated by the continuous bickering, White cut in suggesting that maybe they were both drunk since the points of disagreement were largely minor ones. 'Definitely not,' replied Snow.

Turning to Celery, White asked what he thought was the relationship between Snow and Rantzau.

Celery: That he [Snow] was double crossing us and acting for Germany while pretending to act for us … that was the reason for my going to Portugal, to check it, to clear it up as to which side in fact Snow was actually working for.

White: Did you ever tell Snow that you were one hundred per cent for the Doctor?

Celery: Yes, certainly.

White: When and why was that?

Celery: Well, that was my role, all those remarks were my role that I was to get as close in contact with the Doctor until I was certain of which way Snow was working, and I was to follow him wherever he went.

White: What discussion followed?

Celery: I never had any discussion with Snow about it at all. He always refused to give me any information. Always made me feel I was an amateur whereas he'd been in it for years, and if I knew everything that was going on it would upset me. The less I knew the better and then I would not fall into traps.

Celery was next questioned about his interrogation in Germany and those in British intelligence in whom the Germans had the greatest interest. 'They knew about Major Robertson? They knew that he was in touch with Snow?' White asked.

Celery: I gathered as much. They asked me if I had met anybody in the Department. They knew that I had worked for it in the last war. They had my whole record.

White: How did they speak of the Department?

Celery: I replied that I might have met him [Major Robertson]. I gave a totally wrong description. I thought I was probably laying myself open to traps. But if they should say, but this isn't the man at all, I would say, I haven't met him then. It must have been somebody else. They asked me who I had met that Snow knew.

White: Can you remember exactly what the Doctor said?

Celery: I think he said, 'Do you know any of the people who Snow is in contact with in England? First of all, the people who are working with him. I stuck again to the agreed story. That was that I had heard of a man called Biscuit and had seen GW for ten minutes. That again was our agreed story.

White [to Snow]: How did the Doctor know the name of Major Robertson?

Snow: I don't know. He asked me if I knew a Roberts or a Robbins connected with the War Office. I said yes, I know plenty. As a matter of fact the night before I came over, I said, I had dinner with one of the big shots connected with the War Office … Richardson. So I know plenty of them there. He asked me for descriptions of these people and I gave them to him – wrong.

Before adjourning for lunch, White gave Celery a brief account of comments attributed to him by Snow in an earlier statement to Masterman and Robertson.

White [to Celery]: On your return from Germany you told Snow, 'The Doctor's best friend and the only one he has to look to is Goering,' to which Snow replied, 'I didn't know he was such a big nut … that's nice for me. The only man I'm responsible to is the Doctor. Anyhow I've got £5,000 out of them and an extra £5,000 for my loyalty. Actually it's more than that because I had very heavy expenses in Lisbon, approximately £10,000. Celery is a most expensive man.

I had to go out and buy gold watches and bracelets for him, his wife and for my wife.'

The mention of gold watches had hit a nerve. When the verbal ping-pong resumed after lunch Celery was champing at the bit to correct the idea that he was 'expensive'.

Celery: I would like to ask another question about the last statement about me being a very expensive man. You've got a detailed statement of the monies that Snow gave me whilst I was there and a fairly detailed statement which I can improve on of what he spent elsewhere. I'd like Snow to tell you what amounts of money he gave me. You can check that up with the money I brought back and the money I spent over there.

Snow: I gave you quite a lot.

Celery: You bought me an overcoat and a hat, two sets of underclothes, and two shirts, that right?

Snow: A suitcase … 1,000 escudos, 500 escudos, a case, and 100 dollars.

Celery: That was on the Doctor's instructions.

White dragged the interview back to the still unanswered question at the centre of the 'confession' story: why had Rantzau given Snow £10,000 *after* he confessed to being controlled by the British? By the afternoon session Snow had thought of an answer!

Snow: Rantzau said, 'This is the finest situation we can be in. This is dandy.'

White: Why?

Snow: He said, 'You can come and see me any time now. You can get stuff through, they won't bother you.'

White: Then in addition to the money they gave you these explosives, fine pieces of mechanism which you would have thought the Doctor would not like us to know about. How do you explain that?

Snow: 'Well,' he said, 'you will be able to get all that stuff in now without any difficulty.'

White: But if you get it in and immediately hand it over to the British, what good is that?

Snow: Ah, I'm not supposed to do that. I'm supposed to use that with my men in South Wales who I'm not supposed to tell you anything about.

Snow frequently sprinkled statements with mysterious references to his 'men in South Wales' as distinct from those supposedly controlled by GW. White asked whether Rantzau was aware MI5 knew all about Snow's 'men in South Wales'.

Snow: He asked me once about the sabotage men in South Wales, and I said they were perfectly safe.

White: But didn't he ask whether the British Secret Service was keeping a close enough watch on you to know when you were communicating with these men in South Wales?

Snow: I don't remember.

White: Are you saying he believed you could correspond with your men in South Wales without British intelligence knowing? I haven't had the advantage of meeting the Doctor but is he a stupid man?

Snow: He's a very shrewd man. He's very dull on some points.

White: He must think we are extremely stupid, mustn't he?

Snow: Yes, definitely.

White: I'm supposing that the Doctor looks at it like this: he says you are under British control but that may well be an advantage, your sub-agents are intact, the British don't know about them, you can walk through the port control without any hindrance and you can take in therefore as much as you like, a great deal more than you have ever taken in before and this is a definite key point, an advantage from the German point of view because unknown to the British Secret Service you can distribute these explosives to your men in South Wales. I think all along the mistake you two men have made is to have these suspicions of each other and to be too ready to cast these suspicions on each other.[26]

Despite the long hours of questioning nothing was certain, except that evidently Rantzau still thought Snow a German agent otherwise he would never have given him £10,000 and the sabotage materials. Aided and abetted by Celery, Snow had confounded and exhausted their interrogators with an almost incomprehensible account of what really happened in Lisbon. Baffled and beaten, Masterman, nevertheless, still rated the little man as the 'W. G. Grace of espionage' for his service to Britain even though Snow might by then have become a triple agent. Whatever the situation, he was of no further use to the Double-Cross System.

Before deciding the next step, Robertson sought advice from a Harley Street specialist. Snow had complained about a pain in his side, a GP diagnosing a weak heart, or so he said. But MI5 was more interested in Snow's mental state than his general health explained Masterman when he called at the address in Harley Street to arrange the consultation and press upon the specialist the need for utmost discretion.[27]

'I asked Dr [name redacted] to observe complete discretion in the matter,' Masterman told Robertson. 'I then explained that the patient who would visit him at 12.30 p.m. was a man who was doing certain confidential work, and that it was essential for us to do all that we could to find out how far he was likely to be reliable. I said that we realised that no doctor would speak about the health of one of his patients without the patient's leave. It had, however, been suggested by Snow that he would like Major Robertson to go with him to the consultation, and that I thought he would probably volunteer the suggestion that Major Robertson should be told all about his state of health.

'If, on the other hand, Snow did not want his state of health reported to other people, Dr [redacted] would confine himself to telling us what he thought of Snow as a man and whether he regarded him as the sort of person whose word could be at all trusted.'

The specialist was also asked to advise on whether Snow should be admitted to a nursing home. For the purposes of the consultation Robertson posed as Snow's friend but the results were classified and under no circumstances to be sent to the GP.[28]

Snow arrived at the consulting rooms accompanied by Robertson and 'Mrs Snow' [Lily]. After listening to a catalogue of various ailments, mostly imaginary, the specialist found the only problem was venereal disease for which Snow was being treated at St Thomas Hospital. Otherwise his general health was good but he should stop drinking a bottle of brandy a day.

Afterwards Robertson asked the specialist privately what he thought. Snow was unquestionably a malingerer, said the consultant, and if he really was drinking as much as he claimed then he must have the constitution of an ox because there was really nothing wrong with him apart from high blood pressure. In the opinion of the specialist Snow was mentally sound but 'very sly', a consummate liar prepared to deceive anyone so long as it suited his purpose.[29]

The end came quickly. Snow was called again to a meeting in Imperial House with Robertson and Masterman on 10 April 1941.

'Will you sit here,' said Robertson pointing to a chair.

'I generally sit here,' replied Snow.

'I will come alongside you, if you like ... Well, it is about 9.30 or quarter to ten ... I had to memorise this ... of stating your case in front of our witnesses.'

'Yes,' said Snow.

'And both together in the same room at the same time,' Robertson continued. 'And we have come to the conclusion that the only line we can take with regard to your particular case is that as far as you are concerned in connection with us, you are no longer of any use to us. We are therefore proposing that you should send a message over tomorrow saying you are exceedingly ill, and that your nerve has gone, and that you are not prepared to go on with the game. Is that all right?'

'Um,' Snow.

'And also ask for instructions from the other side as to what you are to do with the various equipment that you have.'

'Yes.'

'On your rendering of the case naturally the Doctor must expect that British Intelligence Service knows exactly what message is being sent over by you.'

'Quite, quite – I follow.'

'Therefore this will cause him furiously to think, and it throws the ball into his hands. Do you follow?'

'Exactly. Quite.'

'Now that is the situation,' Robertson stressed.

The decision to terminate Snow had been taken earlier at a meeting of White, Robertson, Masterman and Marriott, chaired by Liddell, at which all agreed that by giving Snow £10,000 Rantzau had shown the Abwehr's intention to keep the party alive, either to maintain its own prestige or to use Snow as paymaster for other German agents sent to Britain. Like his British counterparts Rantzau probably believed there was still much to be gained from studying information the Double-Cross System allowed Snow to transmit since this would enable the Abwehr to eliminate from its calculations intelligence the British security service regarded as unimportant. That Rantzau wanted to keep Snow 'alive' was the most convincing argument for closing the case, Liddell said. Snow's reactions might throw some light on the extent of his involvement with the Abwehr. Failure by Rantzau to reply with instructions about Snow's radio transmitter could be taken as confirmation the German had also decided to close the case as well as additional proof that Celery was never warned in Lisbon about the 'confession'. At the very least MI5 was justified in enforcing the 18B internment notice served on Snow at the start of the war. The only decision still to be taken was whether to lock him up or remove him from the country. White was confident Rantzau believed both Snow and Celery were controlled by British intelligence but was keeping them in play as couriers for money and sabotage materials. White also thought it likely that Rantzau accepted Snow's word that his agents in South Wales were not compromised and could still be used for sabotage.

After listening to the judgement Snow pleaded, 'Can't I do anything to help the country at all?'

'What do you suggest you should do?' Robertson snapped back.

'I will do anything.'

'I mean, what description,' said Robertson, inviting an explanation.

'Well, I am not a fool. I have had a good education, and have had excellent experience, and if my education and experience is wasted ...'

Robertson: You have had ample opportunity all these months of doing jobs, haven't you ... I mean quite frankly, you have been tremendously idle.

Snow: Oh, there is no doubt about that. I haven't bothered with anything.

Robertson, impatiently: No, you haven't done anything. You have just lived on the fat of the land with an enormous salary – a salary which would make a Cabinet Minister's salary look stupid at the present rate of taxation.

Snow: Quite.

Robertson: Well then, roughly speaking, you will accept that position, will you?

Snow: If you say so, I have nothing more to say. I should certainly like to do something for the country, all the same … not that I want to be paid for anything.

Asked by Robertson exactly what he had in mind Snow said he was now in a far better position to plant fake intelligence on the Germans since Rantzau was expecting him to operate as a triple agent, and make arrangements to bring in Abwehr agents through the Channel Islands.

'And then,' suggested Robertson, 'he outlines a case to you for setting up another transmitter for collecting sabotage material for running agents in this country …'

'A wonderful scheme,' said Snow applauding himself for dreaming it up.

'Such a wonderful scheme,' said Robertson disdainfully, 'that it compares favourably with all the other wonderful schemes that he has put up to you, none of which has ever come off. We have had exceedingly little benefit from any of the schemes that the Doctor has put up to you … I suggest he puts these up as sort of smokescreens. He gives you a fairly large sum of money, which he must be a fool if he thinks you can get it into the country. He must be rather stupid thinking that you can get explosives through.'

Robertson: It is absolutely inconceivable that if he accepts your story that you were walked in on by us two and a half months ago, that we would allow you absolutely carte blanche to do anything that you liked without checking up on you … absolutely inconceivable … Isn't he rather upset at having lost all the contacts which you are supposed to have, in the shape of Charlie, GW, Biscuit …?

Snow: He didn't mention that at all.

'Do you mean these aren't his friends at all … GW, Charlie?' Masterman interjected.

Snow: He wasn't a bit interested in them at all … he regards me as his man … I don't think they mean anything to him at all, not in the slightest. If he lost them all, it would mean nothing to him. He is very cold-blooded when it comes down to business.

Robertson then said after examining Snow's various statements they were of the unanimous opinion he did not tell Celery the game was up before he went into Germany.

Snow: Well, I did tell him before he went to Germany.

Robertson: Well, that is our opinion, and that being the case, you definitely sent a man on a most dangerous mission … You sent him knowingly, I maintain, to put the worst construction on it, to his death probably.

Snow: That's a lie … I did not. I did nothing of the kind…Dobler knows … and Dobler wasn't tight.

'Who was tight then? You were?' Masterman asked.

Snow: Yes.

The conversation went around in circles for most of the morning until Robertson ended the interview by reminding Snow the plan was still for him to transmit a message to the Doctor the next day explaining that his health and nerves had collapsed, that he was throwing in his hand, and asking what should he do with the transmitter.

'… In the meantime if you want to communicate anything to us when you have thought over this interview … well, you know my address,' said Robertson finally.

'Lily?' Snow asked.

'Yes. She's waiting in the car for you.'[30]

MI5 had not ignored the possibility Snow had become a triple agent paid by Rantzau under another name into a bank in the United States, or Canada. Personal letters to Lily intercepted by Special Branch suggested they were planning a new life together in Canada.

Despite everything Snow probably still considered himself a patriot. During wartime a double agent is usually defined as a man who though supposed to be an agent for Power A is working under the direction and influence of Power B. But a large part of Snow's espionage activities occurred pre-war when agents saw nothing disloyal in working for two governments simultaneously, and being paid by both. Masterman believed Snow was 75 per cent on the British side, the rest of the time employed by Rantzau. No one would ever know who got the most value.

In his last transmission Snow told Rantzau he was seriously ill from which the German concluded that Celery was a British agent who, having rejected the financial inducements offered him in Germany, informed on Snow. His continued radio silence meant Snow was either in prison or had retired on the £10,000. 'I was obliged to assume,' wrote Rantzau later, 'that Snow's position as one of our agents was now known to the British. Evidently, since his transmitter had closed down, the British were not proposing to employ him as a controlled agent. Why they had not taken this opportunity could only be guessed – perhaps because they had not succeeded in extracting enough information from him to make it possible.' [31]

Like the British, Rantzau had also to consider the repercussions for his spy network. If Snow squealed, GW and Charlie could expect to be picked up. But Snow, in Rantzau's view, was 'abnormally difficult to interrogate'. The British decision to close Snow down instead of using him as a channel for transmitting phoney intelligence convinced Rantzau he had told them very little and that GW and Charlie remained undetected. Judging by GW's traffic through the Diplomatic Bag at the Spanish Embassy in London he was not acting under British control.[32]

Snow would spend the remainder of the war, firstly in Stafford Jail, and afterwards in Dartmoor. Interned under Regulation 18B as a serious threat to security, he was the only British national detained in Dartmoor where the most dangerous aliens were held.

Whatever doubts there were about Snow's loyalty some within MI5 still believed he had more to offer the security service, either about the personalities involved in German intelligence or by making a remarkable 'recovery' from his 'breakdown' to resume radio transmissions. At no time did he appeal against his internment nor withdraw his 'confession'. When it was suggested Snow was interrogated again with a view possibly to reactivating him Masterman told the Twenty Committee:

> If we cross-examine him again we are unlikely to get more of the truth and may easily get a great deal of twisted invention and baffling lies. If the object of cross-examining him again is to get to the bottom of some of the unexplained mysteries, I think that the enterprise is unlikely to be successful. He

> will give us more or better information (if he has any) only
> if he judges that he will thereby obtain better conditions or
> avoid worse punishment.[33]

Masterman agreed Snow might be resurrected at some point in the future, his health restored and able to resume duties as a German agent. The Germans had no idea whether Snow's illness was real or faked. If it was a breakdown Rantzau would not be surprised if he made a full recovery in about nine months, which would be about the right time to reopen communications. 'He could say,' Masterman suggested, 'that he had had difficulties in finding a secure hideout whence he could safely transmit; that in health he was still enfeebled and would therefore start only with weather and odd scraps of news, since he could not get about the country to collect information, and that his old organisation was of course dispersed.'

Masterman's proposal was for Snow to transmit innocuous information until Rantzau's confidence was sufficiently restored to resume sending fake intelligence. He would not, of course, be permitted to transmit messages himself and as before MI5 would provide an expert radio operator to imitate Snow's 'fist'. But Masterman's proposal was rejected by the committee.[34]

That Snow was regarded by the Abwehr as the linchpin in its British intelligence network, when no such spy ring existed, was in part due to a man who, for all his faults, was one of the great masters of deception in the Second World War, a man described by Masterman as providing information of 'incomparable value' to British intelligence.[35]

On the debit side the Welshman confirmed that Britain was developing radar although the Germans probably already knew. Much of the information Snow supplied to the Abwehr was before the outbreak of war and related to the RAF. Captured Abwehr files in the National Archives in Washington DC list the various topics on which he provided 'intelligence', some so imprecise they were most likely culled from local newspapers:

> Identified RAF headquarters in France in the vicinity of
> Strasburg.

Described balloon barrages set up to protect RAF and Royal Navy communications centres near Portsmouth.

Reported on personal surveillance of Croydon Airport.

Gave exact description of the camouflage of the administration building in Croydon.

Briefed Ritter (alias Rantzau) about survey work at Llanstephan in Wales for new airfields.

Supplied general information about conditions in Wales.

Described the addition of new batteries of seachlights to improve coastal defences at West Hartlepool.

Personal observations on a train journey transporting 600 RAF officers to St Athan; eavesdropped on conversations.

Sketched the location of an oil refinery for the Royal Navy at Skewen, its tanks being filled with crude oil arriving via Swansea docks.

Informed Ritter (alias Rantzau) that most of the synthetic fuel used by the RAF came from Powell Duffryn Steel and Iron Company at Merthyr on the road to Treharris.

Reported that ten RAF planes were shot down at Southampton, Portsmouth and Ilford by accidental fire from own anti-aircraft guns.[36]

Snow spied for cash and expenses. On each occasion he met Rantzau in Brussels, Antwerp or Hamburg he was paid £200, this increasing to £800 on his last visit to Lisbon. The notes, all forgeries, were always handed over by Rantzau although he did consider a parachute drop somewhere in the Bristol Channel area until Snow vetoed the idea for fear the Home Guard might pick up his wages.

At their first meeting at the end of 1936 Rantzau had asked Snow why he was prepared to work against the interests of his own country. His only reply was that as a 'true Welshman' he had no sympathy for the English. Snow was an enigma and paradox at one and the same time.

After he was imprisoned, Lily and her baby, together with Snow's 21-year-old son Robert, and Mrs Kaye Dicketts (Celery's wife) were all issued with detention orders to be enforced in the event of an invasion. Accompanying the orders were explicit instructions issued to John Marriott from Sir David Petrie, Director-General of MI5 appearing to authorise the family's execution if Germany invaded:

As soon as you have learnt that an invasion has begun you will carry out the following orders:

1.   You will proceed to Weybridge and take charge of Mrs Snow [Lily] and baby, and of Mrs Celery.

2.   You will yourself (Marriott) take Mrs Snow and baby to North Wales, and you will see to it that Reed, in the other car, takes Mrs Celery and Snow's son to the same destination.

3.   You will satisfy yourself that Reed has destroyed by burning, all documents, and that he has dismantled and packed into his own car all Snow's W/T apparatus.

4.   On arrival in North Wales you will report to the R.S.L.O. Captain Finney: Tel Colwyn Bay 4787 – Office, Colwyn Bay 2862 – Home; Address: Melfort, Kinmel Road, Colwyn Bay.

5.   As it is of vital importance that Mrs Snow should not fall into the hands of the enemy, you must be prepared to take any step necessary to prevent this from occurring.

6.   You will, so far as is possible, remain in company with Reed's car, and should the capture by the enemy of Snow's son appear probable you will assist him in taking any step necessary to prevent this from occurring.

In order to assist you to carry out these instructions, you will see to it that you are provided with the following:

1.   Not less than £10 in cash.

2.   Petrol coupons for 20 gallons.

3.   A revolver.

4.   Two pairs of handcuffs (for Mrs Snow or Snow's son, or both).

5.   A pass for your car.

You should familiarise yourself with the route to North Wales, and should, at this office, learn all the routes your car pass will entitle you to travel over. After you have reported to Captain Finney in North Wales, you will assist Mr Mills in taking charge of the persons controlled by this section and will co-operate with the RSLO in arranging for their disposition.

These orders are to be burnt when you have learnt them by heart.

N.B. Orders under D.R.18B have been made and are now in this office.

Signed D.P.
3/4/41[37]

Since there never was an invasion Snow's family survived. Hitler postponed 'Operation Sea Lion' indefinitely to concentrate on 'Operation Barbarossa', the invasion of the Soviet Union. Snow's son Robert was, however, detained from March 1941 until the war's end on the Isle of Man with hundreds of others considered a threat to national security. Robert, who was very attached to his father despite his faults, had the crazy notion that if he 'confessed' to being an enemy agent Snow's sentence would be reduced or at the very least father and son could serve their time together in Dartmoor or on the Isle of Man. All that Robert ever did was help his father erect an aerial in the loft for a radio transmitter.

After his parents parted, Robert, then aged 21, chose to live not with his mother who he said was forever 'pestering him for money' but with his father and girlfriend Lily. When Snow senior was interned, Robert offered himself to MI5 as an agent and 'confessed' to having been a Nazi spy. In a letter to Robertson he claimed to have information enabling him to obtain access to enemy territory:

I have information regarding the means which enable me to gain entrance and exit into occupied and enemy countries. Therefore, I offer my services to the State. If you will arrange for me to see you as soon as possible, we will be able to fully discuss the details of my proposal.[38]

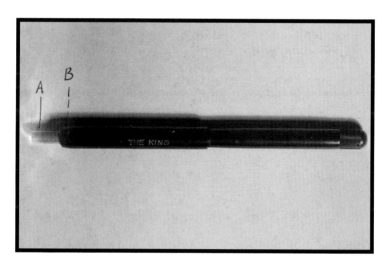

1. Inside the exploding fountain pen (TNA)

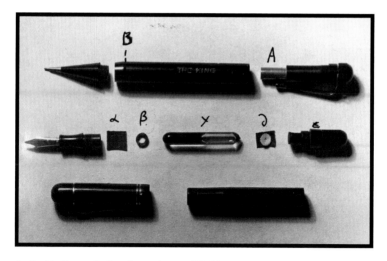

2. Fountain pen and holder assembled for use (TNA)

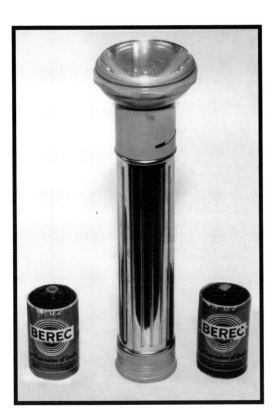

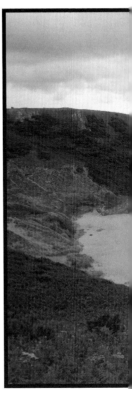

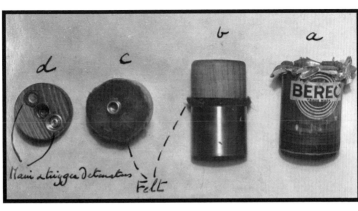

d   c   b   a

Main trigger detonators

Felt

3. (top left) Torch and batteries Snow and Williams brought back to London after meeting with Abwehr agents in Antwerp (TNA)

4. (bottom left) Torch batteries with time clock and detonators concealed inside (TNA)

5. (above) Penmaen, where a German U-boat tried to land explosives

6. *Talcum powder tin, shaving soap and sprinkler (TNA)*

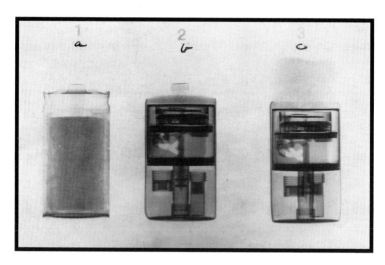

7. *X-ray photograph of talcum powder tin containing time clock and detonators, and exploding shaving soap (TNA)*

8. (above) The fishing boat Josephine *at Fishguard after being boarded by the Royal Navy (TNA)*

9. *(right) The master of the* Josephine*, Cornelius Evertson (TNA)*

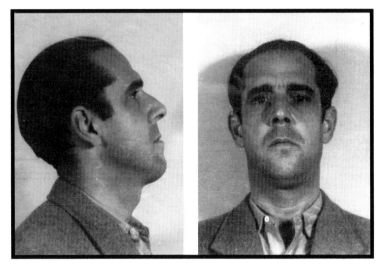

10. One of the three Cuban saboteurs, Silvio Ruiz Robles

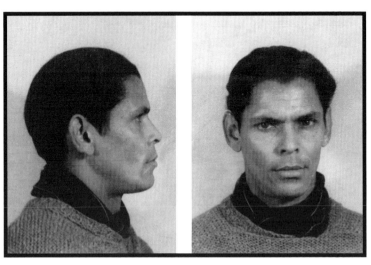

11. One of the three Cuban saboteurs, Pedro Hechevarria

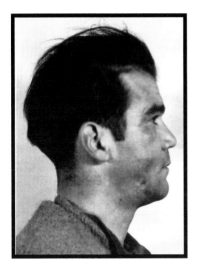

12. One of the three Cuban saboteurs, Nicholas Pasoz-Diaz

13. Cray Reservoir near Brecon, which German agents planned to poison

14. *After the Swansea Blitz: the old Grammar School opposite Williams's home in Mount Pleasant* (South Wales Evening Post)

Robertson and Masterman saw Robert at the War Office. His story was that while lunching alone at the Mars Italian Restaurant in Frith Street, Soho, a man sitting opposite asked, 'You are [Snow] junior?' The person seemed to know all about him, and eventually asked him to join 'them'. Robert believed this was an invitation to become an enemy agent, enabling him to enter occupied territories as a British spy.

After listening to the young man's implausible story the two Double-Cross controllers said he was not qualified to become an agent; that he would never be trusted; that the safety of other persons would never be risked in his hands, and that he grossly overestimated his own capabilities. In response, Robert admitted he only wanted to secure the release of his father and to this end would take any risk. Told again and again that there was no way he could be of assistance, the young man became piqued, and rashly claimed in an effort to exaggerate his own importance that he previously worked for the Germans. Before the war, he had mapped the aerodromes in south London, including Biggin Hill, and sent the plans to a Hamburg address his father used for communicating with German intelligence. Sending the plans to Germany was an act of bravado, and his father was very angry. Asked about his father's sympathies, Robert said they seemed to be pro-German at the outbreak of war but he was now entirely pro-British.[39]

This bungled attempt to emulate Snow senior's aptitude for deception had catastrophic consequences for the son. Although Masterman and Robertson did not believe a word they were obliged to refer the conversation to Special Branch. Whether stubborn or stupid Robert refused to retract anything and was interned for the remainder of the war on the Isle of Man. The Home Office refused to allow him to serve his sentence with his father in Dartmoor.[40]

The immediate consequence of Snow's imprisonment was the termination by the Double-Cross System of agents Celery, Biscuit and Charlie. Celery was kept in play for a few more months, visiting Lisbon again in June 1941 where he attempted to persuade an agent named Sessler to switch sides, which the German agreed to do on condition of free passage to the United States. Nothing came of this and Celery's MI5 file was closed in July 1941 and arrangements made for him to work in Rio de Janeiro for MI6. Everything seemed in place including payment of an indemnity to an employer in Rio when MI6 objected that MI5 were encroaching on its overseas territory. What happened to him next is a mystery. Apart from Masterman's terse explanation that Celery 'entered the business world and disappeared from our ken', there is a hint of something more sinister in his reference to the case being closed because of Celery's 'misfortune'. Fortunately for the Double-Cross System the demise of Snow coincided with the rise of GW and the opening of a new channel for duping the Germans.[41]

Author's note: Volumes 21 and 22 of Snow's MI5 file (TNA, KV 2/450) contain shorthand notes of his story and interrogation. Snow's story can be found at 1081a, his interrogation at 1091a, 1092a, and 1093a. In conjunction with above, first read 1090a and 1097a.

NINE INSIDE ALCAZAR'S SPANISH SPY RING

GUY LIDDELL, HEAD OF COUNTER-ESPIONAGE at MI5, was plainly excited. 'We have scored a great success with Alcazar de Velasco,' he wrote in his diary. 'He has handed GW £50 in the presence of Calvo.'

Only a month previously Liddell had instructed his Regional Security Liaison Officers to increase surveillance on Spanish diplomats suspected of involvement in espionage. If necessary, they were to be provoked, even if this meant the Spanish Ambassador lodging an official complaint with the British Government. 'Our consuls are continually being harassed abroad and I see no reason why in the case of Japs and Spaniards we should not rather obviously follow their consular officials about,' said Liddell. 'This might well act as a deterrent and, in the light of our knowledge of what these people are doing [this] cannot very easily be a cause for serious complaint'.[1]

That the tentacles of the Spanish espionage ring reached beyond London was corroborated when GW reported that the Cardiff consul, a fervent pro-German sympathiser code-named 'Parsley', was spying on shipping movements in and out of Bristol Channel ports. MI5 also knew about 'Queenie', the owner of a café in Bute Street, Cardiff, from which seamen and others wanting to enter the United States illegally could obtain false identity papers.[2]

The cash transaction between the German agent Alcazar and GW in the presence of Luis Calvo, a Falangist journalist attached to the Spanish Embassy and employed by the news agency owned by General Franco's brother-in-law Ramón Suñer, proved Calvo's link to the spy ring operating from the embassy. Brooman-White, who ran MI5's Celtic Movements section, wanted to arrest Calvo and a number of other Spaniards immediately. Robertson opposed this because it meant sacrificing GW. Masterman also lodged a special appeal with Liddell on behalf of their Welsh agent. In the end Liddell agreed not to act prematurely but wait to see where the Alcazar trail led. Not so long ago Alcazar had evaded the clutches of British security by skipping the country but was now back and in business, courtesy of a visa issued by a Foreign Office still reluctant to declare him *persona non grata* for fear of reprisals against British diplomats in Madrid.[3]

After lying low for four months on Robertson's instructions, GW was sent by the Double-Cross controller to knock on the side door of the embassy in Belgrave Square to inquire ingenuously about del Pozo's return. Robertson guessed Rantzau was still holding GW available for future operations despite the unexplained circumstances surrounding Snow's elimination. Segundo, the Embassy porter, opened the back door to the embassy, and after welcoming GW like an old friend gave him Calvo's address, Flat 24, 19–21 Chesham Street SW1. The Welshman it seemed was still on the Abwehr's pay roll.

GW wrote to Calvo introducing himself as an inquiry agent acting on behalf of a mutual friend, del Pozo, with regard to a sensitive matter. His confidential report was now available for delivery. GW included a stamped addressed envelope for Calvo's reply which he received a few days later, the Spaniard offering to deliver the report to del Pozo if they could arrange to meet in London.[4]

Robertson and Brooman-White saw GW at the Bachelors' Club to plan the next move. GW was to exercise the utmost caution, be diffident and apprehensive, and appear unwilling to hand over his report until satisfied Calvo was the right man to discuss confidential matters. Then drip feed him with bits of information about the meeting with Rantzau in Antwerp, the sabotage training, and the arrangement with del Pozo for passing information through the diplomatic bag. Once GW had Calvo's confidence he was to offer to sell the Spaniard a top secret document, 'Plan IV'.[5]

From the club, Robertson and GW went to Imperial House. Once a 1930s hang-out for Soviet spies it was now a front for various sections of MI5. All the offices were anonymous, sparsely furnished, behind War Department issue curtains, windows criss-crossed with brown adhesive paper to catch the flying splinters if the Luftwaffe called. Cold and unfriendly, it was not surprising MI5's top controllers preferred the comfort of the club. Unlocking a desk drawer Robertson pulled out a folder marked 'Plan IV', asking GW to make a note of the main headings but not the details. The story for Calvo was that the documents were stolen by 'Sullivan', a Government messenger who wanted £25 for the folder. To tempt Calvo into buying GW was to show him the list of contents but nothing further at that stage.[6]

MI5 had been looking for an opportunity to reopen a channel to the Abwehr for passing fake intelligence. The Air Ministry was concerned to draw the Luftwaffe away from towns and factories towards airfields. Since the enemy had to drop its bombs somewhere it was better if these were directed at airfields which were better defended by ack-ack batteries. But the 'Sullivan' folder purported to show that airfields were poorly defended. One document entitled 'Damage Report' gave details of the large number of British aircraft destroyed when the Luftwaffe attacked airfields. Another minute noted complaints about inadequate training for ground defence personnel.[7]

On arriving at Paddington Station for his meeting with Calvo GW crossed the platform to a telephone box and dialled the Spaniard's flat, Sloane 4040. A woman introducing herself as Natasha answered. Calvo was not at home and he should ring back in an hour, said Natasha. Like his compatriot, Calvo had soon fixed himself up with a mistress, in this case a Russian, Natasha Anton, whose favours Calvo shared with an American FBI agent named Fellner, then operating undercover in London. By the time GW rang back the GPO was already tapping the line:

GW: Is that Sloane 4040?

Calvo: Yes.

GW: Is Mr Luis Calvo there, please?

Calvo: Speaking.

GW: Mr Calvo you remember I wrote you some time ago from Swansea. My name is Williams.

Calvo: Oh, yes.

GW: I wonder whether I could make an appointment with you, either this evening or whenever is convenient to you.

Calvo: Well, this evening I shall be here until about a quarter to eight.

GW: Well, I'll come along at a quarter to eight to see you.

Calvo: All right. Thank you. Good-bye.[8]

GW had his first meeting with Calvo at 7.15 p.m. on 23 June 1941. Chesham Street was a fashionable white-fronted Victorian terrace, pillared porticos guarding each entrance like a miniature acropolis for those owning one. Calvo rented his, paid for by the embassy a five-minute walk away. Very convenient, GW must have thought, leaving the tube at Knightsbrige and heading across Sloane Square into Chesham Street.

The flat was on the first floor at the head of a circular staircase. As they shook hands, Calvo nodded reassuringly at the man at his door, recognising GW from a photograph he had been shown by the Abwehr in Madrid. A small passageway led into a large, elegantly furnished, carpeted sitting room with a window overlooking Lowndes Mews at the rear of the building. Beside the window was a table and telephone. There were three other doors, one ajar leading to the bathroom, the others all firmly closed.

Calvo was much the same height and build as del Pozo but with a healthier complexion. He was also more cautious, pausing and taking a mental step back before answering a question, unlike del Pozo who jumped in with both feet.

'The inquiries you made for Sn. del Pozo? What were they about?' he asked tentatively. 'Does he owe you money? If so the Embassy will deal with it.'

'I'm afraid they were of a confidential nature and it would be improper for me to state their nature to anyone except to someone who would be able to convey them direct to Sn. del Pozo,' explained GW, adding with a wink, 'Of course, you may know that I am a Welsh nationalist.'

'I think I understand,' replied Calvo. 'Del Pozo was a fool. Got himself into trouble because of what was published in the newspaper. He was sent over here by a Spanish political party to obtain first-hand knowledge of the extent of the German bombing. But as a result of the press articles complaints were made about him by the British authorities … and he was sent back to Spain … he left by boat from Liverpool, was torpedoed on the way and obtained another ship from the Azores to Spain, where on arrival he was put in prison. His father is a very influential man so he has probably been released by now,' explained Calvo, adding after a pause, 'Where did you meet del Pozo?'

'Mostly at the Athenaeum Court, where he lived, sometimes the Cumberland Hotel, and at the Spanish Embassy. Segundo let me in.'

'That wasn't sensible … dangerous to meet in the same place so many times. Segundo is also a fool. He's only the porter.'

Looking at his watch, Calvo said, 'I have an appointment. Can we meet again? When do you return to Wales?'

GW said that he was in London on business for a few more days. The Spaniard thought for a while before replying, 'Will you meet me somewhere tomorrow evening?'

'Yes.'

'Where?'

'Anywhere you like. You know London better than I do perhaps.'

'Well,' said Calvo, 'I will meet you at the Sloane Street entrance to Knightsbridge Underground Station tomorrow evening at six o'clock and we will go for a run in the car. I am very interested in what you have said.'

Walking across to the window, Calvo pointed to a grey Vauxhall FXF 843 with white 'CD' number plates parked below in Lowndes Mews. 'That's my car,' he said before letting GW out of the apartment.[9]

The following evening the rush hour was in full flood, the civil servants streaming in and out of the Sloane Street entrance to the underground, mostly older men now that the younger generation was conscripted into the armed forces. The moment Calvo's grey Vauxhall drew up, GW climbed in and they drove off to a quiet corner on the edge of Hyde Park. It was early summer, the evening long and warm, but the car windows were tightly closed as Calvo explained that he could pass on any reports GW had for Madrid.

Choosing his words carefully, GW replied, 'Are you aware the information I was asked by del Pozo to obtain was not intended for the Spanish authorities?'

Calvo hesitated, at first professing ignorance of the arrangement before admitting, 'Yes, I do know. It came to my knowledge at a time when I had to complain of del Pozo's conduct in this country and was told not to bother because he was doing very good work here and what had been published in the English Press was more or less a blind for his other and more important activities.'

'Why then put him in prison when he returned to Spain?' GW asked.

'To satisfy the British authorities who complained … prison was merely a matter of form … the Spanish and German authorities are working together, hand in glove … every Spaniard is sincerely grateful for what the Germans have done for Spain … had it not been for the Germans the Reds would have controlled the country … taken over the government and Gibraltar at the same time … so England has something to be thankful for … England should not have declared war on Germany.'

Calvo then asked how del Pozo happened to be working with someone he had not known previously and who lived at the other end of the country. That was confidential, replied GW, to be revealed only to someone trustworthy.

After a slight pause, Calvo replied, 'I would like you to have more confidence in me. [Tell] me something about your inquiries. I am sure we can work well together and you will not be sorry.'

The relationship was at a critical point. The Spaniard was clearly eager to please and GW judged this was the moment to reveal his Welsh nationalist credentials as leader of a group of collaborators. English financiers, he explained, were living off profits made in Wales while closing factories and leaving the Welsh to starve.

Calvo was impressed by GW's rant against the English. 'The Welsh are like the Spanish in the north of Spain,' he said sympathetically.

Confident that Calvo was on side, GW proceeded to describe his recruitment by the Abwehr in Belgium to sabotage the British war effort. Then from an inside pocket he withdrew the sheet of paper listing the contents of 'Plan IV', the so-called 'Sullivan' document.

'I have this,' said GW. 'It came from a friend in one of the government departments. He wants £25 for the original.' Calvo was astonished that GW had obtained such an important document and promised to send it to Madrid immediately.

'It will have to be translated and coded but I can promise you I will make it my business to get it to the proper place as quickly as possible,' said the Spaniard excitedly. At which point GW screwed up the sheet of paper as if to destroy it. Realising his intention Calvo snatched it from his hand, flicking on a cigarette lighter to burn it until GW warned that was certain to attract the attention of the police.

'I'll burn it back at the hotel. I never carry incriminating material a moment longer than I need to,' said GW retrieving the paper.

Leaving Hyde Park they drove directly to the Spanish Club and over drinks GW was introduced to a Harley Street doctor and a woman who knew the Gower. Afterwards he took a taxi back to the Imperial Hotel in Russell Square.[10]

When GW delivered 'Plan IV' to Calvo's apartment a month later the mistress, Natasha, opened the door. In the background the Spaniard was engaged in a lengthy telephone conversation. Replacing the receiver he said Madrid had authorised him to take delivery of any intelligence gathered on behalf of del Pozo, and he could guarantee it would reach GW's 'German friends' without delay. Behind a closed door another man was waiting and listening.

'I now have the documents we spoke about at our last meeting,' said GW, handing over the dossier. 'They are very secret and confidential and must be delivered to my friends.'

After glancing through the papers, Calvo replied, 'They seem of great importance … but I don't understand them … I'll see they are safely delivered to your friends … by next week without fail.'

Suddenly, the door of an adjoining room opened and a swarthy individual entered, and took a close look at GW before speaking quietly to Calvo in Spanish. There were no introductions and he was gone within minutes. The stranger, said Calvo, had recently arrived from Spain, spoke no English, and would stay with him for two months. Before leaving, GW handed Calvo copies of the nationalist newspaper *The Welsh Nation* and some party leaflets to send in the diplomatic bag along with the 'Sullivan' dossier.[11]

The mystery man was Don Angel Alcazar de Velasco, Alcazar or Angel to MI5, and Guillermo in the Kriegsorganisationen (KO), an Abwehr espionage section in neutral Spain before the outbreak of war by Admiral Wilhelm Canaris, head of German Military Intelligence. It was one of six major KOs, the others in Portugal, Switzerland, Sweden, Turkey and China. At the centre of Abwehr collaboration in neutral countries, the Madrid KO was permitted to operate freely by General Franco and maintain surveillance posts either side of Gibraltar to report on shipping movements through the Straits. Canaris, through his involvement in the Civil War, had an intimate relationship with the Spanish Secret Service, the Sirene, which for all practical purposes was an arm of the Abwehr. Robertson's Double-Cross section knew from GW's description that Alcazar was back, and saw another opportunity to feed the Germans bogus intelligence. On his last espionage mission to Britain Alcazar had not posed too great a threat, most of his output indifferent and of no real value to the Germans to whom he boasted of managing an espionage ring of a dozen agents. Robertson doubted this but guessed correctly that Alcazar would claim the credit for obtaining 'Plan IV'. The description of the damage caused to British aircraft on the ground so delighted the Luftwaffe that Goering showed it to the Führer who authorised the payment of a bonus to Alcazar. Now the intelligence-hungry Abwehr wanted more of the same.[12]

The next day after meeting in the lobby of the Imperial Hotel in Russell Square Calvo drove GW to the Embassy Chancellery to explain the arrangements for using the diplomatic bag. Once again out came a list of targets for GW to report upon: shipping movements, cargoes, food shortages, and the location of military installations and munitions factories. At this point Alcazar entered the room and without waiting to be introduced shook GW's hand vigorously before opening a small leather case and handing him ten £5 notes, all forgeries. Alzazar then disappeared, leaving Calvo to explain, 'You're alright. He has recognised you by your photograph.'

GW asked for another £500 to keep his saboteurs happy while he awaited the delivery of explosives. The Germans had tried, said Calvo, but the U-boat couldn't get close enough to shore because of the shallow water in Oxwich Bay. He would ask their 'friends on the other side' to try again. In the meantime, what did GW think of Hitler's deputy Rudolf Hess landing his aircraft in Scotland.

'No idea,' replied GW to the sudden change of tack.

'Definitely in connection with the invasion,' said the Spaniard, smiling knowingly. 'He came to make arrangements with their agents and friends, with the Scottish nationalists and you!' GW frowned. No one knew for certain why Hess had come, although there was speculation he was an emissary from Hitler to negotiate a peace deal with those opposed to Churchill and the war.

'He had all the names and addresses with him in the plane,' Calvo continued, 'including yours. When he failed to complete his mission Hess burned the plane and the list.'[13]

There was only one item on the agenda for the next meeting of the Twenty Committee: the future use of GW. Having successfully penetrated the Spanish espionage ring for a second time should the Welshman be used to hang Calvo and Alcazar, gather intelligence for Rothschild's anti-sabotage team, or pass more Sullivan-type documents? Opening the meeting Masterman said that GW was so important only the Twenty Committee should be allowed to direct his movements.

'It must also be remembered that we cannot dictate to the Germans exactly how he should work,' added Masterman. 'They may show much greater interest in his sabotage potential than in his documents, or vice versa, and we must, if the deception is to be maintained, adapt ourselves to some extent to their requirements.'

An immediate problem for Masterman as chairman of the Twenty Committee was inter-departmental rivalry. Not all Committee members were keen to share their secrets and methods of operation. MI6 (the Secret Intelligence Service, formerly SIS) was the worst offender. Britain's great advantage in the secrets war was that the code-breakers at the government's Code and Cipher School at Bletchley Park had with the assistance of Snow tapped into the Abwehr's intelligence traffic. But MI6 was reluctant to distribute these decrypts to the rest of the intelligence community for fear of compromising their own agents in the field as well as alerting the Abwehr that its encrypted messages were being read, in which case codes would be changed. The lack of co-operation also extended to BJs, the Japanese intelligence equivalents. But Masterman believed the Twenty Committee should have routine access to these ISOS messages, which among other things revealed the levels of trust the

Abwehr had in agents it thought it controlled but were in reality run by Robertson's Double-Cross System. Sir David Petrie, Director-General of MI5, backed Masterman who afterwards received translations of the most recent decrypts for distribution to committee members before each Thursday's meeting, at the end of which copies were collected and destroyed.[14]

The intercepts showed that although GW had two periods of inactivity since being recruited by Rantzau in Belgium in 1939 the Abwehr's agents in Madrid, Frederico and Pablo, continued to describe him as 'a good friend of the Germans.'

Brooman-White still wanted to blow GW to hang Calvo. Masterman would have none of this, insisting he would have to be ordered to do so by a much higher authority. 'I think we are still a long way from committing ourselves to such a course,' he said. 'Even if this was to happen we have to be absolutely satisfied that GW's evidence is conclusive and Calvo perishes as desired before we make up our minds to sacrifice GW. I think that at present the outcome of such a move is very dubious.'

Rothschild voted to continue running GW until the Germans delivered samples of their latest explosives and timers to Oxwich Bay in Wales or some other location. The prospect of an invasion might have receded after Hitler attacked Russia in June 1941 but German saboteurs would be just as big a threat when the allies landed in France, the planning for which had already started. Robertson was for using GW to pass 'Sullivan-type' documents to the Germans through the Spanish Bag, his most successful channel for conducting strategic deception.[15]

The committee was deadlocked. 'Whatever is eventually decided,' said Masterman, 'we instruct GW to report on 7 August [to Calvo] in the manner already approved in principle by us: that he should bring a certain amount of information, and suggest that he is temperamentally and by education better suited to sabotage than to espionage, and enquire how far his "Sullivan" documents have been appreciated. We shall then see from the answers given to him, in which direction the Iberian-Teutonic cat seems disposed to jump; the delicate question as how to force the sabotage card after that is a matter for us to decide.'

'Care must be taken in drafting the "sabotage prospectus" so as not to give personal or geographical details,' said Masterman. 'Handing this over may have unfortunate repercussions. In other words we accept Rothschild's prospectus [with regards to sabotage] and not Brooman-White's [to blow GW]. In the meantime new "Sullivan" documents can be prepared in case we need them.'[16]

But would the intelligence handed over on 7 August convince Calvo and Alcazar? GW's document compiled from his further travels around Wales had been stripped of its credibility by interested parties during the vetting process. Even then, no one could be absolutely sure it did not contain information, no matter how small, that fitted neatly into a larger picture the Abwehr was piecing together for itself.

Alcazar greeted GW with a Nazi salute when he arrived at the Chancellery. As Calvo read through the latest intelligence Alcazar shook hands with GW, then bid him adios and left the room. 'Very interesting,' said Calvo, 'but you say nothing about factories and their output.'

'I am only prepared to work in Wales on the business [sabotage] I had agreed,' was all GW could think of in response, adding, 'If I obtain the particulars you require about factories it is possible my country will be bombed and my countrymen injured or killed.'

'Can your friends still be depended upon?' Calvo asked.

'Definitely.'[17]

Evidently not satisfied with GW's latest intelligence, Calvo arranged another meeting for that evening at his Chesham Street flat when he hoped the Welshman would have something more interesting to offer.

Robertson was lunching at the Bachelors' Club when GW arrived to report on his meeting with Calvo, clearly 'depressed by the scantiness of the information he was passing over'. The problem was that the majority of what GW put forward for approval was simply not approved. After listening to his complaints, Robertson produced two agreed documents, one written by Rothschild dealing with the sabotage angle, and the other by Brooman-White about GW's Welsh saboteurs. In this, emphasis was given to GW's role as a fanatical Welsh nationalist, his slogan 'Wales for the Welsh', and his aim, the removal from Wales of English munitions factories and aerodromes. He was to explain that by confining themselves to sabotage, his group hoped to control the amount of damage and minimise the risk to Welsh lives while persuading the English to take their munitions factories elsewhere.

From the club, GW went straight to Imperial House to prepare the new intelligence document. By the time he had finished typing it ran to several thousand words but was still unconvincing. Did the Germans really want to know that shops in Wales were displaying notices saying they had run out of cigarettes, sweets and chocolates, and that public houses were closing for part of the day because they had no beer?[18]

Calvo was disappointed, dismissive, not giving the report a second glance before pulling out a notebook and reading from a long list of questions from their 'friends on the other side':

When was England going to occupy Eire?

What did English people think of the possibility of an invasion and what measures were being taken?

Was the convoy system working?

Shipping movements and the merchandise being carried.

Rationing, and what effect the German blockade was having on hungry workers.

The location of munitions factories.

The signs were ominous. Without some material improvement in the weight of the intelligence there was a real risk the Spaniard would withdraw completely from the operation. GW was in a tight corner with nothing to fall back upon except a vague promise of another 'Sullivan' document. Momentarily placated, Calvo asked to be driven to a cabinetmaker's workshop on the King's Road where GW's petrol tank was filled from a cache of black market petrol. No money was paid or coupons asked for. Calvo signed a chit and they returned to Chesham Street, not to his flat but to one on the ground floor where Alcazar was waiting. After a lengthy conversation, in which GW's name was often mentioned, Calvo translated:

'He says everything is now alright. The money will come along in about a fortnight in dollars or English notes … he tells me Hess came to Scotland with instructions concerning the invasion. Something went wrong … otherwise someone from Scotland would have come to see you with definite instructions as to the part you were to take.'

Alcazar spoke again to Calvo. 'He says that after the victorious conclusion of the war by Germany, which will also control Spain, you will be invited to Spain where you will be introduced to senors Franco and Suñer; and you will have a good time.'

Alcazar was plainly excited by the prospect of another document from 'Sullivan'. '[He says] if you can get any plans for fortifications and other things of importance we shall be very pleased to have them,' translated Calvo once more.[19]

For the next rendezvous the Double-Cross System concocted a top secret document entitled 'GHQ Corps and Divisional Signs'. Before producing it GW was to offer Calvo some scraps of paper 'Sullivan' had supposedly picked out of a wastepaper basket in the offices of the Home Defence Executive as proof of his friend's access to sensitive material. It was plain from the Abwehr's shopping list that the Germans were especially interested in the insignia of various British regiments to aid front-line commanders estimate the likely strength and capabilities of opposing forces. The insignia worn by the Royal Tank Regiment and the markings on Churchill tanks were of particular interest. Was, for example, the tiger's head on a red shield also worn on the uniform? Were those troops billeted at certain locations English or Canadian, infantry or supply, and what were their regimental numbers? German High Command needed to know how the remnants of the British Army were reorganised after its decimation at Dunkirk. Uniform identification was of interest to the British Army, too, in the event that invading German parachutists wore British uniforms. To prevent a panic the War Department had a bizarre scheme for painting the right boot of every British soldier blue!

'Sullivan' wanted £100 for the 'Signs' document, which must be returned to the ministry by 10 a.m. the following morning before it was missed, GW told Calvo. After consulting Alcazar he would meet GW again that evening in the mews at the rear of the embassy. GW was making his way there when the Spaniard drove up, beckoning him to get in the car before driving off to a quiet corner in Hyde Park. As soon as they were parked, GW pulled out the 'Signs' document: 'My friend wants it back by ten o'clock tomorrow'.

'Alcazar says you have to give us the original. We can't make a copy.'

'Surely you can photograph it?'

'I don't have the means and I can't type a copy. I'm a poor typist. You will have to tell your friend to let me keep the original or make a copy. Nor can I promise to pay him. I am just patriotic and doing this for Alcazar because he cannot speak English.'

GW shrugged as though not interested in Calvo's motives, adding, 'I would much prefer they gave me some material for sabotage as they originally agreed. Wales is a veritable arsenal. One need only go a few miles to find numerous military works in the course of construction where good work could be done if I had the material.'

'How could we send the material to you?' Calvo asked.

'Difficult question,' replied GW. 'It's up to them to find ways and means. One possible way is to send it aboard a ship from Spain to Swansea with a member of the crew who would make himself known to my friend [WW], an Immigration Officer whose duties take him aboard all the ships and is known to our friends on the other side.'

'A good suggestion. When Alcazar returns to Spain in about a month he'll mention it to them.'

Quick-thinking, and rarely caught off guard, GW was delivering a virtuoso performance for a retired police inspector with no previous experience of espionage or the stage! Like Snow, he was a natural with an innate capacity for escaping tight corners while extracting useful information from difficult subjects. And Calvo, his nerves ragged, forever looking over his shoulder, was proving increasingly difficult to handle. GW was not to write to him, or be seen near the embassy. Instead of taking a train to London for their clandestine meetings it was much safer if he drove. But GW did make one mistake: he mentioned Snow, Calvo recognising the name immediately and asking what had happened to him, a question GW fended off by quickly moving the conversation on.

Before parting outside the Dorchester Hotel GW promised to make a further attempt to obtain the original 'Signs' document. 'Can you trust this man?' the Spaniard asked nervously.

'He's an Irish nationalist. I know him very well and can trust him,' and as proof handed Calvo the scraps of paper from 'Sullivan's' wastepaper basket in the offices of Home Security. Without even a glance the Spaniard bent down and pushed the papers under the car mat, muttering, 'I am not interested in this business and I don't want to be found with any papers from a Government department in my car … I don't know what happens when Alcazar leaves.'[20]

Alcazar, who was preparing to leave Britain for Madrid, was waiting at the embassy with Calvo when GW delivered the document. Alcazar stuck it in his pocket immediately, his face beaming, as pleased as 'a dog with two tails', recalled GW. Then with a glance at his watch, and adios, Alcazar was gone.[21] Messages intercepted later by the Radio Security Service between the Japanese Embassy in Madrid and Tokyo contained extracts from this and the earlier 'Sullivan' document. Like Snow, Alcazar was a mercenary selling the same intelligence to both Berlin and Tokyo, only the price changing. Although most of his agents in Britain were controlled by the Double-Cross System, he had others in neutral Brazil, according to Alcazar who after the war claimed to have smuggled Hitler's deputy Martin Bormann to South America.[22]

TEN THE MALTA CONVOY
AND SINKING OF *ARK ROYAL*

THE DOUBLE-CROSS SYSTEM COOKED UP an even bigger
piece of deception for the Nazis – a ghost convoy bound for Malta. In
the meantime Calvo set about making arrangements for the Abwehr
to dispatch the long-awaited consignment of sabotage materials by
ship from Spain to Swansea. Waiting to take delivery was 'WW', the
Immigration Officer originally intended to play the part of fanatical
nationalist. Spain asked for photographs so that the courier could
identify 'WW' when the ship arrived in Swansea.

'Shall I bring the photographs or post them?' GW asked in a call
to Sloan 4040. Hesitating for a moment Calvo replied, 'By registered
post to me at the embassy'.[1]

On Robertson's instructions GW contacted the Spaniard again a
week later to explain that the situation had changed. The Immigration
Officer had been transferred to a desk job which meant he no longer
visited every ship arriving in Swansea. He needed to know what vessel was being used for the arms shipment if he was to meet it.

Instead of replying, Calvo booked a seat on the first available
flight to Lisbon. The reason for his sudden departure, he explained
to an Embassy official, was because 'what had happened was a very
grave matter'. From tapping the Sloan 4040 telephone MI5 discovered that Calvo's panic attack was triggered not by the proposed arms
shipment but by a suspected Red plot to assassinate Alcazar who had
promptly fled the country when told about it. In another bugged
call the terror-stricken Calvo pleaded with his Spanish news agency
employers to reassign him to Lisbon, anywhere but London. He even
lobbied the Argentine Ambassador about the possibility of getting
work in Buenos Aires.[2]

Dick White, deputy controller of the counter-espionage branch, wanted Calvo arrested before he had a chance to board the flight on 24 October as a 'salutary lesson to the Spanish colony' even if it meant blowing GW. The Spanish Diplomatic Bag had become a double-edged sword as far as White was concerned. Each time it travelled between London and Spain it was carried by an Embassy diplomat who then spent a month in Madrid before returning. During that time it could be assumed the Germans used the bag to send instructions to their agents in Britain. 'Action against Calvo,' White said, 'would at least show the people concerned that such work is not without risk and that we are capable of hitting back. It may thus to some extent put a damper on proceedings. At the moment, they regard us as amiable imbeciles … the question is are there any further dividends to be collected from GW now that it seems fairly evident that Calvo is not going to continue to play in Alcazar's absence.'

Masterman was totally opposed. 'The only certainty,' he told White, 'is that the Spaniards will in future exercise greater precautions in passing on information from this country and that is precisely what we do not want. Surely, it is preferred that Calvo should return [to Britain] with the belief that we are easy to hoodwink, and that his successor need not worry too much about his method of communication.'[3]

Masterman and Robertson were convinced GW had further uses if he could avoid being implicated in Calvo's arrest which was sure to lead Rantzau to dig into the Welshman's past contacts, in particular Snow. If that happened, Robertson and Masterman expected their agents to fall like dominoes. Nothing, they argued, was to be gained by destroying GW, an agent patiently and successfully invented to win the confidence of the enemy. Calvo would simply be replaced in the spy ring by others about whom they knew nothing at all. Since GW was recruited by Snow (alias Johnny) the Abwehr would surely terminate Rainbow with whom Snow had direct contact, leading to Tate being compromised, this in turn threatening Tricycle, MI5's top double agent in the United States. The Twenty Committee postponed a decision by arranging for the Foreign Office to delay Calvo's departure until January 1942.

In the meantime, GW was used for one of the most important strategic deceptions of the Second World War. The Malta Convoy operation had its origins in two loosely connected events in July 1941. An intelligence leak at an unnamed British port resulted in German U-boats ambushing a convoy bound for the beleaguered island garrison on Malta, sinking one destroyer and damaging a cruiser and supply ship. MI5 discovered from an Italian naval intercept that the ambush near Gibraltar was due to a lamentable breakdown in security during the loading of the ships. Packing cases were clearly labelled 'Malta', and the provisions loaded aboard were addressed to the 'NAFFI, Malta'. Furthermore, when the convoy was assembling there were vessels in the port destined for Eire and other neutral countries over which British intelligence had little control.[4]

That the convoy was caught by U-boats was not due entirely to the intelligence leak. Admiral Karl Doenitz, commander of Germany's U-boat fleet, had been ordered by Hitler to transfer a large number of submarines from the North Atlantic into the Mediterranean to protect Field Marshal Rommel's supply route from Italy. The German offensive in North Africa was stalled by a serious shortage of supplies after 70 per cent of the total Italian tonnage serving Rommel's North African operations was sunk by the British Navy. The first six U-boat reinforcements passed through the Straits of Gibraltar at the end of September 1941 followed by another four at the beginning of November, and together did temporarily reduce the effectiveness of Malta for attacking Italian merchant shipping. Believing that the Mediterranean, rather than the Atlantic, had become the main theatre of operations, Hitler insisted that Admiral Doenitz continue to maintain a strong U-boat presence in the area. Whereas this for a time curtailed enemy submarine operations against the North Atlantic convoys, it increased the danger for allied shipping in the vicinity of Gibraltar.

Admiral Doenitz regarded the Mediterranean as a 'mousetrap'. Passing through the Straits submerged was easy enough on the strong current flowing from the Atlantic but getting out was a nightmare and only possible at night. 'The most important task of the German Navy and therefore of the German U-boat arm … which overshadowed in importance everything else,' wrote Doenitz in his memoirs, 'was the conduct of operations against shipping on Britain's vital lines of communication across the Atlantic. It was along them that flowed the sources of British strength, provided in the most part by American power; and it was, logically enough, the safeguarding of these lifelines that Britain regarded as the foremost of her strategic aims at sea'.[5]

It was clearly to Britain's advantage that the German High Command continued to believe it was using the Straits and Mediterranean as a supply route when in fact greater use was being made of the much longer but more secure route around the Cape of Good Hope. With this in mind the Double-Cross System concocted a story for GW to plant on Calvo for delivery to the Abwehr through the Spanish Bag.

GW telephoned the Spaniard on the morning of 21 October to say he had something important and must see him immediately. Calvo, though not sounding especially interested, finally relented, 'All right, come along [to the apartment]'. No sooner did GW enter the sitting room than Calvo waved him away with 'Good morning. I have nothing for you.'

'I have something important for you,' replied GW. His story was that he had heard from 'WW' that a large convoy was assembling in Belfast before departing for Malta in the next few days:

> My friend was very excited. He explained that on Saturday a party of 60 RAF personnel with their kit bags arrived at Swansea Docks en route for Belfast where they were to transship to one of a convoy sailing from there on Thursday 23 October. One of the RAF's men's kitbags was marked 'Malta'. Apparently the attention of the Senior Control Officer was drawn to the kitbag … and he reported it immediately to Headquarters, because late on Sunday afternoon a senior military officer arrived from London to investigate the matter. There was a terrible row as the RAF personnel had been told that the voyage was very secret and nothing was to be marked which would indicate that the destination was Malta. All the port staff who were in contact with the RAF men had been interviewed by the Senior Military Officer and told that under no circumstance was anyone to disclose

that the RAF men were on their way to Malta. Should anyone make such a disclosure he would be dealt with under
the Defence Regulations, and severely punished. The RAF
man whose bag had been marked with the word 'Malta' was
placed under arrest and taken to London the same night by
the Security Police.

I have ascertained that this draft of RAF men is only a
small part of the number of men who are being taken from
various parts in England and Wales to Belfast for transport
to Malta on 23 October.

It must have been intended that the strictest secrecy
was to be maintained about the destination of these men
otherwise there would have been no need for the sudden
appearance of such a high military officer to investigate the
circumstances connected with the disclosure made by the
word Malta on the man's kit bag.

A large number of new motor lorries loaded with
motor cycles have been parked near the docks for shipment
to the Middle East on 23 October. The ships are to form a
convoy which leaves from Belfast and are going through the
Mediterranean.[6]

The resemblance between this and the circumstances surrounding
the July attack by U-boats on the convoy at Gibraltar is too remarkable to be a coincidence. The strategy behind the dispatch of GW's
'ghost' convoy was to reduce U-boat attacks in the North Atlantic
by persuading the German High Command to continue with its
increased submarine presence in the Mediterranean.

GW insisted his intelligence should be sent to his 'friends' without delay. Time was short. 'The convoy leaves on the 23 October,'
replied the Spaniard. 'I don't think this will get over in time as it takes
a week to get there.' GW pressed him to act faster.

'The convoy is due to leave Belfast on the 23rd but it is always
possible sailing may be delayed by a day or two,' GW suggested. 'In
any case it will take at least a week to reach the Mediterranean; that
gives our friends at least a few days to make arrangements to intercept if they get this information a week from today.'

'All right, I will try and get it off at once,' promised Calvo. 'And the money for this [information]?'

'Don't you worry about the money,' said GW. 'If we can let them have the goods they will let us have the money. I am a Welsh nationalist and would like to see this material from Wales at the bottom of the Mediterranean.' Calvo smiled. The following day GW told Masterman and Robertson at the Bachelors' Club that the Malta Convoy report was on its way to Berlin.

Three weeks later on 13 November 1941, HMS *Ark Royal* was torpedoed and sunk by Lieutenant Guggenberger commanding U-boat *81* as the aircraft carrier headed for Gibraltar from Malta. The crew survived but GW was able to boast when he next met Calvo, 'The information I gave you on the last occasion has turned out very useful to our friends. They must have missed the convoy, but they got the *Ark Royal* and crippled the *Malaya* ... I should think that they ought to be very satisfied with that bit of work and should send something substantial for our trouble.'[7]

Nothing cemented GW's reputation as the Abwehr's master spy more than the Malta Convoy operation. 'Oh, yes,' said Calvo, 'they are interested in what you do but there is difficulty in getting the money over here. I shall see about it when I get back to Spain.'

But had the Double-Cross System blundered by inadvertently alerting the U-boat wolf pack that the *Ark Royal* was closing on Gibraltar? Rather than a coincidence was the Malta Convoy a tragic error? When Masterman's Twenty Committee authorised GW to alert the Germans to a convoy passing through the Straits why wasn't it warned that the *Ark Royal* and its escort would be approaching Gibraltar at about the same time?

Masterman regarded the partnership between GW and Calvo as 'brilliantly successful', the Welshmen passing documents of great importance to the war effort. GW had the best channel for transmitting information too bulky or detailed to be sent by radio and by surviving periods of apparent neglect had confirmed his reliability to the Germans. 'I cannot help feeling,' said Masterman, 'that if a reliable one such as GW were blown at this stage, they (the Germans) may feel disposed to distrust all their agents, and even perhaps close down on several of them rather than take a risk by keeping them going'. If Snow had confessed to Rantzau in Lisbon why then was his protégé not compromised? Not even the knowledge that GW was a retired police inspector had 'stuck in their gills' as might have been expected, admitted Robertson. Had the Abwehr's eagerness to recruit Welsh nationalist extremists as collaborators at Hitler's behest blinded Rantzau to the trap the Twenty Committee set?[8]

'Minotaur' was GW's next assignment. Code-named after the mythological Greek creature dwelling at the centre of a labyrinth, the plan was for the minutes of a War Cabinet meeting to be offered to Calvo by 'Sullivan'. By then the imaginary 'Sullivan' was portrayed as a mercenary unconcerned with what the Spaniards did with the documents, as long as he was paid. On this occasion he was asking for £125. The War Cabinet minutes were to be copied and handed back for 'Sullivan' to return to the file the next morning before they were missed. From a telephone box outside the Bachelors' Club GW set up a meeting with Calvo at his Chesham Street apartment for later that day. No sooner had he arrived and he was explaining excitedly how his contact 'Sullivan' was now in a position to obtain secret documents about matters dealt with by the War Cabinet. For these he wanted immediate payment.

'I haven't got any money, not until I get back from Spain,' replied Calvo. He was leaving soon for Madrid but would return fifteen days later. 'I'll see our friends and I'll get all the money you need,' he promised.

'I don't think my friend will agree to wait but I'll try.'

'Are you able to change dollars?' Calvo asked.

'No problem, my prospective son-in-law works in a bank. He can make the exchange without suspicion.'

'Be careful,' warned Calvo. 'Don't telephone me from Swansea or Cardiff and when you are in London never mention names on the telephone. Just say something about a motorcar or tyres … I'll understand and say when I can see you … Notes, large English notes – can you change them without arousing suspicion?' GW nodded.

'All right, I will see you get money.' With this, GW agreed to ask 'Sullivan' to hand over the War Cabinet minutes on the promise of payment later.[9]

At about eight o'clock that evening GW was walking along Lowndes Mews towards the rear entrance to the Spanish Embassy when a torch flashed in the darkness ahead. Before it was doused he caught a momentary glimpse of an RAF officer and a woman fumbling with a key to the side door of the Embassy. There was no sign of the couple when the porter, Segundo, let GW in and, without a word, led him into a room furnished with three desks, typewriters, piles of books and newspapers, a steel safe in the corner and a large photograph of General Franco hanging on the wall. Calvo was waiting, apologising again for not having money to pay 'Sullivan'.[10]

'Well, I've got the document,' said GW waving an envelope containing the Cabinet minutes. 'But my friend has to replace it before nine o'clock tomorrow morning. He's prepared to wait for payment on condition he gets it as soon as possible.'

Opening the envelope, Calvo read quickly, before commenting, 'Not so very interesting.'

'Suggest you read it again,' advised GW. 'I think it's very interesting and I am sure our friends will agree.'

Calvo shrugged. 'I've got a dinner appointment, so we'd better go to my place and type a copy immediately.' During the drive Calvo promised to have the money when he returned from Madrid.

'I've had promises like this twice before,' GW told the Spaniard. 'Unless you have the money then I can't work for you any more. People want to be paid for information.'

'It's difficult for us,' explained Calvo. 'All Spaniards in this country are under suspicion. That's why Alcazar hasn't returned. He was afraid. That's why you must be careful not to implicate me in any way.'

'Don't worry,' GW said reassuringly. 'I know my business. I don't take risks with my own personal freedom.'

'The other side,' said Calvo, 'have been in touch about sending me dollars. Alcazar says they are quite willing to pay … it's just that I prefer to wait until I'm in Spain and I can deal directly with them.'

With the 'Top Secret' document copied, the pair drove to the Ritz Hotel where the Spaniard was dining with friends. For their next meeting on 10 December, Calvo asked GW to provide a detailed report of the situation in Wales with particular regard to factories and airfields for him to take to Madrid. Could he also persuade 'Sullivan' to obtain more 'Top Secret' documents?

'I'll try,' GW promised. 'But he's taking a great risk and won't do it unless he's paid. So far, he hasn't been.'

'I promise I'll have money when I get back. I want to get something out of this for myself, as well.'

In the absence of Alcazar, Calvo was now playing a greater role but acutely aware that Britain hanged spies, his nerves were shot to pieces, repeatedly reminding the Welshman not to take risks. 'Are you not afraid of being followed in Swansea?' he asked.

'I'm an Inquiry Agent. My job is to gather evidence. That means I'm often away from Swansea in connection with these proceedings. Don't worry.'[11]

The following day GW met Robertson and Masterman not at the club but in Imperial House to discuss the next move. Calvo was now well and truly on the hook. Were they to spring the trap on the Spanish espionage ring or continue to exploit Calvo's access to German Intelligence? Unless Calvo had the cash to pay the fictitious 'Sullivan' it was agreed GW was not to offer any further documents apart from the regular 'Welsh Activity' report which Calvo wanted by 10 December. The content needed to be more convincing than previously, GW reminded his controllers.

'Better if we write it for you this time,' said Masterman. 'I'll arrange it. You'll get it in plenty of time … and we'll check out that sighting,' in reference to the RAF officer seen entering through the back door of the Spanish Embassy.

From 24 to 27 November, Special Branch officers kept the door and those using it under round-the-clock surveillance. On one side of the entrance was the name Berdasco, a Spaniard apparently occupying a flat above an adjoining garage. The other side had two bell pushes, one for the Chancery, the other for 'Fowler' or 'Weston'. There was also living accommodation above the Chancery. For the three days the premises were watched no one in uniform entered or left the premises, only a young woman 'of the servant class' wearing an RAF badge and evidently on her way to the local shops. A car registered to the Military Attaché Colonel Alfonso Barra stopped at the entrance on a number of occasions, as did the one driven by Calvo. The only sighting of RAF personnel was at the address immediately opposite where an RAF officer was seen to leave and return. After three days surveillance was withdrawn, Special Branch concluding that GW had the wrong address.[12]

The approved version of the latest 'Welsh Activity' report GW delivered to Calvo to take to Madrid is not available, only the draft with the objections of interested parties scribbled in the margins. On the assumption that these more sensitive paragraphs were omitted, the agreed document was still a substantial block of intelligence about the location of airfields, factories and munitions dumps in Wales. While waiting for approval, GW submitted his expense account for espionage work: £70 for visiting London between June 1941 and November 1941, car upkeep (£50), and £50 to pay friends for information, and £125 for settling a 'debt' with a friend.

GW's latest communiqué told the Germans that a new airfield for Coastal Command had been built on Fairwood Common, near Swansea; that there were airfields at Pembrey and Stormy Down for training pilots; that St Athan near Barry was 'very large and used by fighter and bomber aircraft'; that Coastal Command was operating from a base between Dale and Roch in Pembrokeshire; and that Milton Airfield, Pembroke Dock, was a base for bomber aircraft.

Not only did these exist but so did GW's list of factories, including a recently built synthetic oil plant at Glynneath; an installation for filling shells and mines with explosives at Castle Hill in Milford Haven; the location again of the Trecwn underground storage facility for mines three miles south of Fishguard employing 4,000 people; two magnesium works at Port Tennant (Swansea); and another producing aluminium propellers for aircraft at Waunarlwydd (Swansea). Factories in various stages of construction were mentioned, as was the location of underground oil storage tanks at Milford Haven.

Deleted was the site of the army barracks at Brecon, and the Sunderland Flying Boat base at Pembroke Dock for U-boat spotting in the North Atlantic. References to packing cases containing aircraft, and locomotives and rolling stock awaiting shipment to the Far East from the Bristol Channel ports were also omitted. GW was sufficiently pleased with this latest offering to address a note to the Abwehr asking for a pay rise:

> I would again call your attention to the difficulty of obtaining interesting information without a means of inducing the giving of such information. I have a motorcar but the quantity of petrol that may legally be obtained is not sufficient to enable long and frequent journeys to be made into the country, but here again it is possible to obtain any quantity of petrol if one is prepared to pay what is asked for it. You must realise that there is not much that I can do unless you are prepared to supply the necessary money to carry on. In regard to materials it is very necessary that you should supply me with what I require to work with. Opportunities often present themselves when something useful could be done if I had the means.

For once Calvo was impressed, GW seizing the opportunity to present him, too, with an expenses account for £325. The Welshman saw no reason why he shouldn't claim from both sides. The 'Welsh Activity' report seemed packed with revelations, begging the question to what extent the Luftwaffe followed up the information.

The Double-Cross System did insert an additional paragraph about Marshal Semyon Timoshenko, Stalin's People's Commissar of Defence, and commander of the defence of Stalingrad. 'This is very interesting about Timoshenko,' exclaimed Calvo excitedly, spotting the name. GW's impromptu reply sounds as though he was momentarily caught off guard.

'Yes, it's one of the chief topics (of conversation) in Wales,' he said, adding, 'Timothy Jenkins is a very common Welsh name.'

'You have done very well,' said Calvo.

'Are you are returning to this country?' GW asked. 'If you are not then I suggest you make some arrangement for me to receive some money as I am spent out.'

'The question of making other arrangements to send you money does not arise, as I am definitely coming back,' replied Calvo. 'I wouldn't go if I thought there was a likelihood I couldn't return to this country. I shall bring you money.'[13]

Their final meeting was early in the New Year. After exchanging formal greetings, Calvo said he would leave on 19 January for fifteen to twenty days. GW's last report, some nationalist party pamphlets, and his expenses account had all reached their destination, he assured the Welshman.[14]

During Calvo's absence, GW spied on the failure of lazy Welsh factory workers to support the war effort. But the mood was more optimistic, he added, now that the United States had declared war following the Japanese attack on Pearl Harbor in December 1941.

The backs-to-the-wall attitude that galvanised the British in the first years of the conflict had been replaced by indifference, according to GW. Production in many of the munitions factories had declined on account of mismanagement, and at Gloucester an aircraft factory worker told him there were 'large numbers who do practically no work, their time sheets during the week often marked with many hours of "waiting time" due to a shortage of raw materials on the assembly line although the stores are filled with (these) essential materials'.[15] Aware that in some cases poor management was impacting on productivity, Ernest Bevin, the Minister of Labour, instructed companies to report whenever more than ten men were idle, suspended or discharged.

'The Japanese intervention is one of the main topics of conversation locally,' reported GW. 'Many caustic comments are being made against the authorities on account of the unpreparedness against such an attack shown by both America and Britain. The people, however, are fully convinced of the ultimate success of Britain and her Allies, but they are bitter at the fact that we are continually being caught "napping" by our enemies'. A month later the speed of the Japanese onslaught through the Malay Peninsula took the British by surprise ending in the fall of Singapore, Britain's greatest defeat in the Second World War.

Besides his part in the campaign of misinformation GW provided an intriguing commentary on events and attitudes in Wales during the Second World War. There was praise for the Russians fighting on the eastern front, continued support for Churchill as a war leader, a general acceptance of rationing but impatience over delays in opening a second front in France. After the fall of Singapore most were confident the Japanese would eventually 'get a dose of their own medicine'.[16]

On 28 January 1942, GW complained of 'slackness' among workers in the munitions factories after taking a note of remarks made by young women employed in the Royal Ordnance Factory at Bridgend:

'At Bridgend, the workers seem to think of nothing else but payday. "Roll on Friday" is the most popular saying amongst the workers.'

'Outside the factory we are spoken of as "Churchill's Ideal Army", but "Churchill's Idle Army" would be more appropriate.'

'The supervisor visits us once only during each shift.'

'When we are approaching the extent of our quota we are then told to go slow.'

'Most of the girls are sick of not having sufficient to do to occupy their time; some take a week off occasionally to break the monotony. Nothing is ever said about it.'[17]

GW was becoming obsessed with the apparent decline in the war effort and accused workers at some Welsh factories of not pulling their weight:

I regret to say there are indications of some factories and docks not being all out in the war effort. The following are a few of the facts I have been able to gather recently from items of conversation, which I overheard or in the course of conversation with others:

The Mannesmann Tube Works at Llandore (now owned by the Newport and South Wales Tube Company) have a shell-making department, but no shells have been made during the past two months, although the employees, numbering over a hundred men and women are at the works every day doing nothing, and receive their full wages every Friday …

> At Palmer's Dry Dock, Swansea, many of the employ-
> ees are frequently told to work overtime although the men
> know, and have pointed out to the officials, that there is
> nothing for them to do. This involves the payment of rates
> of wages at time and a half on weekdays and double time on
> Sundays for doing nothing …
>
> I am also informed that it is common practice when
> employees at factories engaged on the manufacture of war
> materials are disabled and unable to work, they are told not
> to go on 'compensation', but if they possibly can they are to
> go to the factory and receive their full wages.
>
> I have made it my business to try and find out why
> such a state of affairs should exist in factories engaged in
> the manufacture of vital materials of war at such a time as
> this. The reason, I am informed, is that the labour is subsi-
> dized by the government and as long as the men are on the
> premises their wages, plus a certain percentage, are received
> by the management irrespective of whether the work for
> which wages are paid is being carried out or not.
>
> I have been able to gather that the workmen are not
> in agreement with this ramp, but are more or less obliged
> to participate.[18]

As a double agent, however, his days were numbered. The Security
Executive (ADBI) decided to arrest Calvo when he returned to
Britain, and as chief witness against him GW would cease to be of
further use to the Double-Cross System.

Masterman and Robertson knew that GW's usefulness would
cease the moment Calvo was arrested, assuming he returned to
Britain. Masterman, in particular, regarded the possible loss of GW
as a 'major disaster'. The Welshman would be an even greater asset
once Britain moved on to the offensive and that could be soon,
now that Churchill, President Roosevelt and Marshal Stalin had
agreed on the urgency of opening a second front in Europe in 1942.
Preliminary planning foresaw a vital role for Double-Cross agents in
feeding misinformation to the Germans about the possible location
for an Allied landing. With direct access to the Abwehr through the

Spanish Bag GW was certain to be involved in this. 'It has always been the opinion of the Service members of the Twenty Committee', wrote Masterman in vigorous defence of GW, 'that the best opportunities of passing effective operational misinformation would come when Great Britain undertook offensive action, and for this reason it is highly desirable to take as few risks this winter as possible in order to keep good agents alive until this stage of the war is reached.'

If an arrest was made, he said, the consequences would be far-reaching, leading to retaliatory arrests of MI6 agents in Madrid and a major conflict with Spain. Arresting Calvo and breaking the Spanish spy ring might push Franco into the arms of the Axis powers.

'If it is the policy of the HM's Government to provoke such a conflict at this time, in order, for example, to clear the air and bring the Spaniards to better behaviour by a confident display of power, then there is a strong prima facie case for the arrest', wrote Masterman, adding, 'If on the other hand, it is the policy of the Government to pursue the plan of maintaining good relations with the Spanish Government on the present lines, then there is a strong case against [the arrest].'[19]

One consequence of the round-up would be to confine the transmission of information concerning the war effort to accredited Spanish diplomats, which while more accurate would be more limited than GW. In effect, the flow of information would become a trickle, the Double-Cross System losing a channel for manipulating German military intelligence at a critical time. As it happened the invasion was postponed for three years because Britain was not ready.

MI5's indecision was not mirrored in Madrid where the Abwehr agent Pablo concealed new instructions for GW in the diplomatic bag before it was returned to London. GW was to collect a wireless transmitter from the Spanish Embassy left there by Alcazar some months earlier and if help was needed in operating Calvo would find an instructor or import one from Spain.

'So what do you want me to do?' Calvo asked before leaving Madrid.

'You will not have to do anything', replied Pablo. 'GW will do everything.' By now Alcazar had convinced the Abwehr the British were preparing to invade Ireland. GW was set the task of confirming this. Besides written instructions, the diplomatic bag contained an operating manual for the radio transmitter, codes and signals. Reports were to be written in invisible ink, the capsules for making this also enjoying diplomatic immunity. There were the names and addresses for dead letterboxes in Madrid – and the money the Abwehr had long promised but not delivered was finally on its way.

The date and time for GW's first radio transmission to Hamburg was set as 15 March 1942. The diplomat charged with delivering the bag full of espionage paraphernalia to London on 10 February was an Embassy official named Brugada. Calvo was to follow on a later flight. But just before leaving Madrid Brugada received a scribbled note from Alcazar: 'Do not do anything about the wireless; do not give it to GW or to anybody'. Something had spooked the Spaniard. Had he heard that Calvo would be arrested the moment he set foot in England, in which case the Abwehr would not want its 'top agent' caught in possession of a radio transmitter? When the bag arrived at the Embassy, and after inspecting the contents, the Ambassador ordered them burned, and the radio transmitter destroyed.[20]

If Masterman had known any of this his case for continuing with the Welsh agent would surely have prevailed. Petrie, Director-General of MI5, left the final decision on arresting Calvo and sacrificing GW to Guy Liddell, controller of the counter-espionage branch. Liddell had the Spaniard picked up as he stepped off the plane at Bristol Airport on 13 February 1942. From there he was taken to Camp 020, the secret interrogation centre for enemy agents, leaving the Double-Cross System to work out the consequences. The very first thing was to warn Captain William Stephenson, the wealthy Canadian businessman who ran British intelligence in North and South America from the Rockefeller Center in New York, that his top agent Tricycle could no longer be confidently regarded as enjoying the full trust of the Germans. 'We are doing what we can to save as many of our agents as possible,' cabled Masterman.

While Masterman fretted over the fate of the Double-Cross System, Calvo was interrogated at Latchmere, an ugly three-storey manor on Ham Common in which Camp 020 was housed. A former mental institution, it was set back from a narrow country lane and hidden from the curious by a stone wall. Camp 020 was run by a Rhodesian Lieutenant-Colonel Robin Stephens, known as 'Tin-Eye' because of his heavy-duty monocle. Latchmere was for civilian detainees, not prisoners of war, and therefore not covered by the Geneva Convention. Although prohibited by Stephens, physical pressure was occasionally used by interrogators. Before switching sides, Tate was badly beaten after parachuting into Britain as a German agent. Stephens had refined psychological intimidation into an art form, using every trick, lie and bullying tactic to extract information, some subjects reduced to so pitiful a state by threats and intimidation they could only be carried back to their cells. The camp commandant cared not for morality, only results.

'Violence is taboo,' wrote Stephens, 'for not only does it produce answers to please, it lowers the standard of information.' Stephens put the unprecedented success of Camp 020 down to the rule of non-violence. 'In the first place it [striking a man] is an act of cowardice. In the second place, it is not intelligent. A prisoner will lie to avoid further punishment and everything he says thereafter will be based on a false premise,' he said.[21]

Known as 'Tin-Eye's No-Man's-Land' Camp 020 broke captured German agents before releasing them to work as British double agents. By all accounts Stephens was a daunting character with his monocle wedged firmly in his right eye, thick black hair pasted back severely off his high forehead, a hiatus between his green army sweater and top of his trousers, ranting about the 'loathly Germans' and 'scrofulous Bosches', in fact, a caricature of an SS interrogator.[22]

On arrival at Latchmere Calvo was subjected first to 'shock' interrogation designed to catch the fearfully apprehensive prisoner sufficiently off guard to confess. That was followed by systematic interrogation at all times of the day and night until Stephens, once satisfied everything of value had been extracted, handed the prisoner over to MI5 or for execution. Six enemy agents suffered the latter fate, Stephens's greatest regret that many more didn't follow them to the gallows. Calvo, according to Stephens, broke after a 'war of attrition' lasting from his arrest on 13 February until 3 March 1942. From then onwards the Spaniard talked freely, most of his confession confirmed by other sources.[23]

The brief for the interrogators at Ham was to build a case against Calvo if they could without implicating GW, so allowing the Welshman still to be used. Masterman took the view that since GW had twice previously been resurrected by the Abwehr, why not a third time. Stephens's concern was that GW had been used as an agent provocateur, which might 'raise doubts in the minds of those hypersensitive in the Foreign Office and the Home Office'. But the need for GW's evidence to obtain a conviction disappeared by the time Stephens finished with Calvo.[24]

'My present view,' Stephens reported, 'is that Calvo has found himself in a desperate position and is endeavouring to ingratiate himself. As to whether he intends finally to offer himself as an agent double or whether he considers himself cunning enough to regain his freedom is at present undetermined but an examination of the twelve written statements he has made since 3 March 1942 indicates that a formidable indictment can be made against Calvo without reference to GW at all.'

With the confession in the bag, Stephens telephoned the good news to Masterman, at the same time mentioning that GW, according to Calvo, was expected to contact the porter Segundo whose instructions were to refer him to Brugada, the Abwehr's new man at the Embassy. Stephens's personal recommendation for Calvo was that he be 'hanged by the neck until he be dead'.[25]

It was only when a prisoner broke and was talking freely that Stephens allowed outsiders to sit in on the interrogations. Now that point was reached, Robertson sent along one of his best officers, Tommy (Tomas) Harris, to participate in further questioning. Harris was a Spanish-speaker born in Hampstead, who would be remembered most as the MI5 handler of Juan Pujol (alias Garbo), a Nazi-hating Spaniard from Barcelona. Rejected as an agent by the British at the outbreak of war, Garbo tried the back door: in 1942 signing up with the Germans who sent him to London where he immediately switched sides. Together, Garbo and Harris invented thirty fictitious agents, one of these a Welsh nationalist leader of a group of Fascists in Swansea called the 'Brothers of the Aryan World Order'.[26] But Garbo's greatest coup was his part in persuading the German High Command that the main attack on D-Day (Operation Overlord) would come in the Pas de Calais (as Hitler had always believed) and not Normandy, a ruse sustained by sending 500 fake radio messages to Berlin via Madrid from all parts of the Double-Cross System's imaginary world.[27]

After receiving the all clear from Stephens, Robertson was preparing to reactivate GW when there were two security breaches at Camp 020. Despite strict instructions to the contrary, one of Calvo's interrogators let slip that MI5 knew of his relationship with GW. Soon after this the Spaniard smuggled a note to a diplomat named Viturro during a visit, thought to expose GW as a double agent. However, another of Robertson's agents working inside the Spanish Embassy, 'Sweet William' (alias William Jackson), discovered that the note made no mention of GW, but was to the effect that Calvo believed he was being detained on suspicion of currency irregularities.[28]

Robertson met GW at the Bachelors' Club on the morning of 3 April to discuss how best to reopen the link with German intelligence. At all costs, nothing should be done to encourage the Germans to start digging into the past because that was certain to lead to the unmasking of others. There were two alternatives for GW to consider overnight: either he inquired for Calvo at the Embassy, or he volunteered to be detained in Camp 020 as a way of convincing Calvo, and ultimately the Abwehr, that he, too, had been seized as a German agent. In the case of the second option GW might be held in Camp 020 for several months playing the part of Calvo's espionage accomplice while encouraging him to confess everything to save both their necks. After considering this for a moment, GW said if it was the latter then his family would move to Milford Haven. 'In any case,' he added, apparently unperturbed by the prospect of incarceration alongside some of Britain's most dangerous enemies, 'we've been contemplating leaving Swansea for a while.'[29]

On the train back to Swansea GW thought through the Camp 020 proposition. 'Should you deem it necessary,' he wrote to Robertson the next day, 'that I confront LC I could either (a) profess not to have seen him before and deny all knowledge of him or (b) try and persuade him to make a clean breast of everything with a view to preventing any further action by the authorities other than our detention for the duration of the war, and thus ensure our personal safety and freedom after the war.'[30]

As it happened, the failure of Calvo to incriminate GW presented the Double-Cross System with an excellent opportunity to move further on to the offensive, away from operations previously designed to

contain the enemy threat to Britain's security and armaments industry. Calvo had not squealed; GW's cover was not blown. That implied
GW was so well-embedded in the German espionage apparatus that
he might be able to reopen the link not through the Spanish Embassy
but direct to the Abwehr through his old stamp-collecting contact
Mme. de Ridder.[31] But first Robertson chose the more obvious route
to the back door of the Embassy. If GW was assumed by the Spanish
to know nothing about Calvo's arrest he might be expected to call to
inquire if he had returned from Madrid.

GW rang the bell on the side entrance to the Embassy in Belgrave
Square. Segundo opened the door and after exchanging formal greetings GW inquired about the whereabouts of Calvo. 'I don't know,'
replied the porter. 'He go back to Spain. No come back.' GW explained
that Calvo had said he was planning to return in fifteen days. That was
a month ago. 'I don't know,' repeated the porter in broken English. 'He
no come back. Sometime Secretary go back to Spain for one month
and stop perhaps two months, sometime longer.' At this point GW
thought it better not to press the matter further, and left.[32]

A severe bout of influenza gave GW four weeks to contemplate
the next move. Doubting whether the link with German military
intelligence could be reopened, he offered to resign:

> May I take this opportunity to respectfully suggest that you
> will kindly consider, consequent upon the trend of recent
> events, whether the need for my services has now ceased.
> Personally I feel that the probability of any further contact
> is very remote. However, I shall be glad to receive your
> instructions and will be pleased to comply with any direc-
> tions you may have for me.[33]

Robertson was not as pessimistic and asked GW to hold himself in
readiness in case the situation changed. For this he would receive a
small retainer. 'It doesn't seem possible,' replied Robertson, 'for us to
dispense with your services entirely, which, as you know, we shall be
most reluctant to do.'

ELEVEN THE MAN FROM BRAZIL

GW NEVER KNEW HOW CLOSE HE CAME to meeting the German agent Josef Starziczny in Swansea. The Abwehr planned to parachute Starziczny into the Bristol Channel area with instructions to head for the home in Swansea of the man it thought of as its top British agent, GW. Terrified at the thought of jumping out of an aircraft, Starziczny tried to avoid the mission by claiming it was too risky because he was widely known in England. In the end, a stomach ulcer came to the rescue and he remained in hospital for three weeks. The agent who replaced him dropped into the Bristol Channel and was presumed drowned.

In February 1941 the name on the passport of the man arriving aboard a steamer at Santos in Brazil was Nils Christian Christiansen, in his suitcase a radio transmitter with a range of 15,000 kilometres, more than enough power to reach Hamburg and Berlin. He was, in fact, Starziczny, sent by the Abwehr to spy on British shipping moving through the south Atlantic.[1]

Starziczny's espionage career had started in Mexico City as an employee of Telefunken at the outbreak of war repairing a clandestine radio transmitter installed in the gardens of the German diplomatic mission. A combination of technical problems and the close attention of US agents from across the border meant the transmitter never did work properly. Starziczny was then sent to the United States to set up a network of low-power radio transmitters for German agents to transmit intelligence to South America for relaying to Hamburg. The agents also had dead letterbox addresses in Sao Paulo and Rio de Janeiro for sending coded information hidden in private correspondence. It was from this traffic that the FBI first discovered the

Dot, the micro-photographic reduction of secret documents to the size of a full stop concealed on the inside of an envelope flap.[2]

Starziczny spoke little Portuguese but soon had a companion who did – Ondina Batista de Oliveira Peixoto, the 37-year-old girlfriend of an elderly baron living at the Waterfall Hotel on Copacabana Beach. Ignoring instructions not to consort with local women, Starziczny set up home with Ondina in Apartment 82, Francisco Sa, 5, near the beach, later moving into what became the headquarters for Germany's Brazilian espionage operations , a two-storey house in Rua Campos de Carvalho, 318, Leblon, Rio de Janeiro. Starziczny's mission was to 'collect all possible information about the merchant ships of countries at war with Germany, especially the British, tonnage, type of cargo being loaded, destination, and armaments'. Very soon thousands of tons were being dispatched to the bottom of the Atlantic by U-boats guided to their targets by Starziczny and the agents he employed at Santos to obtain details of shipping movements in and out of Brazil's main Atlantic port.[3]

While Brazil remained neutral, the Rio police ignored the activities of the not inconsiderable German community among which Starziczny and Ondina were prominent, enjoying a lavish lifestyle funded by cheating the Abwehr. All that changed, however, when a U-boat sank two Brazilian merchant ships with considerable loss of life, and the Brazilian government sent Elpidio Reali, head of an elite crime squad based in Sao Paulo, to crack down on the Rio Germans. Reali trailed Starziczny to the front door of his house in the suburbs and early on the morning of 15 March 1942, armed with a search warrant, knocked on the door. Once inside the detective discovered a treasure trove of espionage paraphernalia: a small laboratory, cameras, telephoto lenses, and a radio receiver. When he tried opening a locked suitcase Starziczny shouted, 'Don't, you'll blow the house up!' Another box was stuffed with tissue paper on which were the records of ship movements in and out of Santos, their tonnages, whether carrying food, troops, munitions, in some cases routes and destinations.[4] The name of one ship jumped off the page. It was the *Queen Mary*, the great liner now a troop carrier having departed Santos three days previously with 4,000 American troops aboard bound for Adelaide in Australia via the Cape. Without a moment to lose, Reali picked up the nearest telephone to alert the British Ambassador who radioed the master of the *Queen Mary* to change course immediately as it was almost certain a German U-boat was stalking the ship. When the *Queen Mary* failed to reach her next port of call, Buenos Aires, on schedule, she was reported missing, the Germans broadcasting she had been sunk although by then the troop carrier had given the U-boats the slip and was safely out of range.[5]

Returning to Starziczny's house Detective Reali found the mistress was now awake and wandering about in a dressing gown claiming to be his housekeeper and not knowing anything about the German's activities. 'That suitcase,' Reali asked. 'You said it will blow the house up.' Deciding resistance was futile, Starziczny shook his head and replied, 'No, you can open it.' Inside, Reali found the high-powered long-range transmitter – and a book from which two micro-photographic copies of typescript fell out as the detective leafed through the pages. At the sight of these, the panic-stricken Starziczny reached for a revolver concealed on a shelf – the one he was supposed to use on himself rather than be taken alive. Reali had found the Kriegsmarine's secret transmission codes.[6]

'That will take me before a firing squad,' moaned Starziczny. 'The Gestapo will never forgive me.' Brazil, said Reali, did not have the death penalty and if he co-operated the Gestapo would never get him. Starziczny's confession was soon flashed to Allied intelligence services around the world.[7] In Berlin, the capture of the Kriegsmarine codes triggered a major emergency and for three days and nights the same message was transmitted to German agents over and over again: 'Warning! Warning! Lucas [Starziczny's code name] stuck … Code in hands of enemy … Change the code … Keep in touch.'

Not only was the breaking of the Brazilian spy ring a major coup for the sharp-eyed detective of a neutral country but Starziczny's confession was of particular interest to MI5 after the Foreign Office received a cable from its embassy in Brazil:

> German agent named Josef Starziczny … arrested in Brazil … made a statement on German espionage in UK … stated that the head of the German espionage service in UK is a man named Gwilym Williams who lives in Swansea in

a house number 42 in a street called Mount something.
Starziczny later identified this address from a map of
Swansea ... stated GW or his emissary met Colonel Ritter
[Rantzau] in Lisbon in August 1940.[8]

Not unnaturally the mention of GW in the Nazi agent's confession
set alarm bells ringing along the corridors of MI5 back in London. If
Masterman found Snow's Lisbon confession in February 1941 more
baffling than the 'riddle of the Sphinx and the doctrine of the Trinity'
then the various hypotheses springing from the Starziczny confession was a Gordian Knot of Cyclopian proportions. If it was true,
as Starziczny claimed, that GW was the principal German agent in
Britain, then the Welshman was almost certain to be executed as
a traitor while all those with whom he had associated during his
three years working for the Double-Cross System would be suspect.
Could GW, the retired Swansea police inspector, possibly have been
a German plant?

The vital point in Starziczny's confession was his claim to have
known GW personally and visited his house in Swansea. If this was
substantiated then there was a real possibility of 'obtaining genuine
incriminating evidence against GW', according to Robertson.[9]

Starziczny's arrest was publicised widely not only in South
America but also in the London *Daily Telegraph*, which on 6 May
1942 reported that the Brazilian police had uncovered a German spy
ring with agents in Britain, Canada and Portugal.[10] For MI5 to ignore
the Brazilian report would be tantamount to informing the Germans
that it already knew GW was an Abwehr agent. Until the security
service discovered the truth it should, according to Robertson, act as
if the revelation about GW was genuine:

From what Christiansen [Starziczny] has said we should
have no difficulty in identifying this man [GW]. On the
other hand, having identified him we should equally have
no evidence upon which it would be possible to arrest him.
Since GW has now discontinued his activities as an agent
no amount of surveillance or examination of his correspondence would reveal anything incriminating. The vital

point on which we should seize would be Christiansen's [Starziczny] statement that he had known GW personally and visited his house in England [*sic*]. If this statement could be substantiated there would be the possibility of obtaining genuine incriminating evidence against GW.[11]

In fact, GW was not the only Double-Cross agent whose loyalty was being questioned. The German had also mentioned Tate in his confession. GW and Tate, he said, were the Abwehr's principal agents in Britain. If that was the case, then the Abwehr would have expected GW and Tate to be arrested by MI5 following Starziczny's confession.

The only way to be certain about GW and Tate was for MI5 to send its own man to Brazil to question Starziczny, said Robertson:

If we are at once to acquire all the information we need from Christiansen [Starziczny] and conceal from the Brazilians by the type of question we ask how much we already know, it seems essential that an officer from this department should go to Brazil and assist in the inquiry personally … It is true that GW has now ceased work and the question of his arrest might therefore be considered academic, but this is not wholly true since we are particularly anxious to avoid any reinquiry by the Germans into GW's, and therefore Snow's earlier history.[12]

Starziczny was not the first Abwehr agent to identify GW as their main man in Britain. Had not Pablo and Frederico, the two Madrid-based German agents, spoken of GW as being a 'good friend' of Germany? Had not Snow claimed to Robertson that GW confessed to admiring the Third Reich and what the Nazis had done for Germany? Had not Alcazar greeted GW with the Nazi salute? And why was GW not compromised by the Snow 'confession', or by Calvo's arrest? Or was GW simply the victim of his own success in playing the role of a Welsh nationalist fanatic?

In the meantime GW still had his uses. Since the political tensions in Wales were of continuing interest to MI5's Celtic Movements section, it became GW's business to inquire into the post-war aspirations of the Labour Party. After speaking to an official in Swansea it was evident the party was expecting to form a post-war government, its priority the redistribution of wealth, GW was told. What he really wanted to know but was afraid to ask for fear of drawing attention to himself was whether Labour would seize power if constitutional means failed.[13]

The cost of the Second World War led to demands for increased taxation of the wealthy so that the burden was more fairly distributed. Clause Four advocating common ownership of the means of 'production, distribution and exchange' had been part of the Labour Party constitution since 1918 and remained throughout the war years a potent force amongst the party faithful in Wales and elsewhere. Churchill saw British socialism as little different to the ruthless regime of Nazi Germany requiring a Gestapo-esque body to enforce it. Remarks to this effect during Churchill's first election broadcast of the 1945 campaign are generally thought to have contributed to the Conservative Party's overwhelming defeat.[14]

In addition to reporting on the political undercurrents, GW continued eavesdropping on conversations, one in particular between two naval officers attracting his particular interest:

> The principal subject of the conversation was the successes of the Japanese. One of the officers said to the other, 'You can mark my words, before the war comes to an end it will be necessary for the British, Germans, Italians and all the white people to stop fighting each other and get together and fight the yellow races. I include the Chinese as well as the Japs as there is not much love for white people by the Chinese. If they were well enough equipped they would give us something to think about, as there are so many of them.'[15]

Home-grown extremists and union leaders sometimes suspected of distributing seditious material amongst the armed forces were under MI5 surveillance during the war. 'But morale,' GW told Robertson, 'is keeping up very well. Everyone seems quite happy now that the RAF is giving some of the German towns and occupied territory something to go on with. It is the opinion of many that we are likely to have a hard winter in so far as food is concerned, and everyone who is able is hard at it planting as many vegetables as possible for use later in the year.'[16]

The skill in producing a convincing piece of strategic deception came from including events capable of withstanding close scrutiny by the Abwehr. GW continued to concoct documents sufficiently credible for Garbo to feed to the Germans now that the Spanish Diplomatic Bag was no longer available.

GW's latest report focussed on activity at Swansea Docks, and in particular three cargo ships: the SS *Tolten*, SS *Canadian Star* and SS *Ocean Valour*. The *Tolten* (10,000 tons), after being in port for several months for repairs, was being loaded, according to GW, with 7,000 tons of coal, some general cargo, and four aeroplanes in packing cases in the hold, another six on deck. All bore British markings.

'Sixteen passengers were due to sail on the ship … for Australia,' wrote GW. 'I gathered this was one of the "lease and lend" ships completed in January and taken over by our Government in February of this year. She came to this country from America via Australia and was damaged en route.'

The second ship, Blue Star Line's SS *Canadian Star* was also being repaired in Swansea. The third, the SS *Ocean Valour*, had recently sailed after taking on 500 tons of bunker coal – insufficient, dock workers had told GW, for it to reach its destination, Southampton.

The *Tolten* and *Canadian Star* waiting at Swansea for cargo to be loaded and repairs completed were sitting ducks for the Luftwaffe. The *Ocean Valour* limping towards Southampton low on coal, the master casting around for a nearer port to unload his precious cargo of food, was an easy target for a prowling U-boat.

Nothing could be more convincing. The *Canadian Star* had been damaged by a U-boat the previous year en route from Liverpool to New Zealand. The *Ocean Valour* was built at Southampton and launched only a few months earlier, so it was feasible she would be returning to her home port to unload her cargo. The *Tolten* traded regularly between Australia and Britain.

The truth, however, was very different. The *Tolten* was a Chilean freighter sitting at the bottom of Barnegat Bay, New Jersey, after being hit by a torpedo the previous year, only one of its crew surviving to tell the story. The *Canadian Star*, a refrigerated ship with thousands of tons of food for war-weary Britain, was then steaming across the Pacific after being damaged and delayed on the outward voyage from Liverpool by a gun battle with a German U-boat caught on the surface off southwest Ireland. Repairs were carried out not in Swansea but on the other side of the Atlantic at Curaçao in the Caribbean. The *Canadian Star* would be sunk by a U-boat but not until the following year when the convoy of which it was part was attacked off Cape Farewell, Greenland. As for the *Ocean Valour*, she survived the war to be finally scrapped in Naples in 1967.[17]

How GW pieced together this account is in itself puzzling. The story of the *Canadian Star* he could have picked up from the *London Gazette*, which published an account of the commendation awarded to Captain Charles James Whatley Jones, the ship's master after the brush with the U-boat. Perhaps the sinking of the *Tolten* was mentioned in a list of lost merchant shipping. The *Ocean Valour* may well have loaded bunker coal in Swansea but more than enough for the last lap of its voyage to Southampton. The purpose of the exercise was to waste the time and energy of U-boat skippers hunting ships that existed but either at the bottom of the ocean or on the opposite side of the world. There was always the attendant risk, however, that the Luftwaffe might bomb Swansea again!

Robertson called GW to London to discuss what future use, if any, might be made of his services. As usual it was at the Bachelors' Club, just the two men together. At what was to be their last meeting Robertson asked whether GW had any ideas for reopening his contact with the Spanish Embassy. The Welshman shook his head, replying, 'I've thought about it a great deal but can't think of any schemes'. Neither could Robertson who, in the circumstances, reluctantly decided there was no alternative but to close GW down. 'But,' he added, 'if you do get an approach at any time from any of your old confederates, or directly from the Germans, you will keep us informed? You have our telephone number.' GW nodded and asked, 'The car – will you require me to use it in future?' After a moment's hesitation, Robertson replied, 'Probably will. We'll pay you for it on the old basis.' But there was no longer any need for the MI5 telephone installed at GW's house. Arrangements would be made to have it removed.[18]

Walking away from the Bachelors' Club for the last time GW must have dwelled on the events culminating in the end of a career as one of Britain's top double agents. If it really was all over then it had ended in a prosaic whimper not a bang, almost as though the past three years had vanished like footprints in the sand. His recruitment in Antwerp by the Abwehr and explosives training; the mysterious Mme. de Ridder and her network of stamp collectors; his on-off relationship with the impetuous Falangist Party journalist del Pozo; the Calvo and Alcazar connection; the countless pieces of misinformation he fed through the Spanish Diplomatic Bag; all this while delivering a virtuoso performance as an angry, English-hating Welsh nationalist collaborator who had swallowed Rantzau's promise of an independent Wales.

GW's reply to Robertson accepting the inevitable termination of his espionage work read like a thank-you letter from some long-serving employee pensioned off after a lifetime's service:

> I must agree that the services I am now able to render do not justify my retention in your employment, but I am most pleased to know that our association has been satisfactory to you. I only wish that I had been able to give greater satisfaction, but I don't think that the inability to have gratified such a wish is entirely due to any fault of mine. However, if at any future time I should renew acquaintance with my former business associates, or anyone in the same line of business, I can assure you that you will be informed immediately of the transaction …
>
> I think that I shall dispose of the car at the first favourable opportunity as I shall be unable to justify its use on the road after this month.
>
> May I take this opportunity to express to you my sincere appreciation of the great courtesy you have shown to me at all times during the period of our association, and to wish you every success in the future.

> Will you please convey my kind regards to all your associates with whom I have had the pleasure of their acquaintance in the course of my transactions with you.[19]

It is hard to imagine the fictional James Bond writing a goodbye letter, preferring instead to exit the scene with his trusted Walther PPK blazing away in one hand, the other around the waist of a sinuous blonde or dry Martini. That said, GW knew all about dead letterboxes, secret inks, and exploding fountain pens, and had no small part to play in a Double-Cross System that claimed it controlled every enemy agent the Abwehr sent to Britain during the Second World War.

Robertson had one last shot at resurrecting his Welsh superspy after the MI6 officer sent to Brazil to investigate the Starziczny confession absolved GW from all suspicion. Under British interrogation Starziczny admitted he had never met the Welshman, that everything he knew about GW, including the location of his home in Mount Pleasant, Swansea came from Colonel Werner Trautman, head of the Abwehr's radio communications at Hamburg *Ast*. It was Werner who said GW, as the head of German espionage in England, supplied their agents with ration and identification cards, and that he, or his emissary, had met Colonel Ritter in Lisbon in August 1940.[20]

The Hamburg station handled intelligence traffic between Britain, Ireland, north and South America. Trautman had taught Snow Morse in the summer of 1939 when he visited the station with his blonde girlfriend Lily. Working closely with Rantzau, Trautman knew the identity of German agents in the field and, but for speed of the German advance, would have instructed GW in operating a radio transmitter had he been able to keep his appointment in Hamburg.

Once cleared by MI5, GW was asked by Robertson to re-establish contact with Mme. de Ridder, the stamp-collecting enthusiast, by sending her a letter and photograph through a contact in Lisbon. GW was to draft a suitable letter while Robertson would arrange for the package to be delivered to Lisbon by an intermediary. 'I am afraid this is a little ambiguous but I feel you will understand,' Robertson added.

GW's letter to Mme. de Ridder was craftily designed to deliver a message to the Abwehr agents on the Iberian Peninsula that he was still at large and available for operations. The code used was their common interest in stamp collecting and the 'rare specimens' mentioned an invitation to the Abwehr to reactivate him:

It seems ages since I last heard from you. I often wonder how you are getting on, and whether our friend Louis Mercader is still interested in the collection of stamps. I do not suppose he is very busy with his stamp collecting these days. After the very pleasant evenings you and I had together in 1939 I too have been enthusiastic concerning stamps. I did start collecting but owing to the war had to give it up. I have been looking forward to receiving specimens from you and Mercader. Perhaps it's too difficult for you to send them or perhaps you have been fully occupied in other directions. However, I would be most pleased to hear from you and to receive some of the rare specimens you promised during the happy evenings we spent together.

Times have changed haven't they? There is not much opportunity for travelling now, but I do sometimes pay an occasional business visit to London. During a number of these visits I had the pleasure of meeting a number of Spanish gentlemen, by the name of Piernavieja del Pozo, Alcazar and Calvo who were on business in this country, and in the course of conversation I gathered that they, too, had made your acquaintance whilst on business at Lisbon and Madrid. When I last saw these gentlemen they told me they intended returning to Spain for a period in connection with their business. Unfortunately they do not appear to have returned to London as I have made enquiries at their places of residence and business and was informed that they had not returned. They, too, were keenly interested in the collection of stamps and promised that when they returned they would bring me some rare specimens. Had they done so, I would have increased my interest. I would have been most pleased to have had them as I have many friends in Wales who are also very much interested in rare specimens, and often ask me how I am getting on with my collection.

Do you remember the photograph I had taken one day when I last paid you a visit? In case you have forgotten me I am enclosing one now as a souvenir so as you will know I have not forgotten you. I shall be pleased to hear from you and to know that you are quite well.[21]

On receiving the proposed letter Robertson asked MI5's regional liaison officer in Cardiff to find a suitable seaman to act as courier between Swansea and the German Embassy in Lisbon. 'He is to take the letter with him to Lisbon and hand it over personally to an official in the German Embassy,' explained Robertson.

Not everyone on the Twenty Committee agreed to resurrect GW. The new secretary John Marriott, in particular, thought to attempt to reopen the Spanish channel was wrong. 'The Spaniards have a long record of broken promises and failure to produce money, sabotage material or coherent instructions,' he told Robertson. 'From our point of view the Spanish line gets involved in all sorts of complications and it seems to me if a character like Alcazar, who is apparently prepared to use almost anything in the shape of an agent whether he exists or not, does not himself approach GW, then there must be some strong reason for it.' In his view, it was a mistake to revive GW at all.

'We are no nearer a solution of the Snow case than we were eighteen months ago,' he added. 'Having managed to wind up Snow without blowing any of our agents, we should make a mistake in trying to revive a portion of it, since this will cause the Germans once more to direct their attention to a position which was just as unsatisfactory for them as it was for us.'[22]

Snow might be locked up in Dartmoor but MI5 was still unsure what side he supported. The only redeeming factor was that the Abwehr was no less confused. Marriott believed that in attempting to reactivate GW the Double-Cross System would trigger renewed German suspicions about the link between Snow, GW, del Pozo and Calvo.

Whether the de Ridder letter was ever sent is not known. Since Robertson had the final word, not Marriott, the courier might still have delivered it but the Germans either failed to take the bait or by then knew that GW was a controlled British agent. Whatever the case, GW was finally closed down on 5 August 1942 although retained to 'write a few letters'.

'I think you can safely take it that the work for which I may require you,' wrote Robertson, 'will only necessitate you giving up possibly a half hour or so every now and again in writing a few letters for me.' There was nothing, he added, to prevent GW taking another job.[23]

TWELVE THE AFTERMATH

SNOW SAW HIS INCARCERATION IN DARTMOOR as another assignment. The only British subject among the most dangerous aliens, he became an MI5 stool-pigeon eavesdropping on conversations and pumping fellow inmates for information. Robertson visited whenever the little man thought he had something interesting to offer although Snow's tip-offs were mostly the product of his overactive imagination. But he did alert MI5 to the source of leakages of information from the internment camp on the Isle of Man.[1]

Under Regulation 18B there were two categories of prisoner detained for engaging in acts 'prejudicial to public safety and the defence of the realm'. The first were those with the potential to become enemy agents and held for the duration of the war. The second class comprised persons at risk of being subverted and interned as a precaution. The latter were held on the Isle of Man, their correspondence routinely checked and visitors strictly screened, internment peaking at 1,600 in August 1940, dropping to 400 a year later.[2]

Snow was first held in Stafford, a prison since the twelfth century, the most recent building dating from the eighteenth century and last used for Irish republicans after the 1916 Rising. Refurbished in 1940 to accommodate the influx of Defence Regulation detainees it remained a grim establishment with a harsh regime. The governor's instructions were that Snow was not to be trusted even though he had once worked for MI5. All his correspondence was forwarded to Masterman for vetting as was any complaint he had about his welfare.[3] Visitors were only allowed after security clearance and the prison staff were instructed to report suspicious conversations he might have with other inmates. One such inmate, Johan Dirk Boon, a Dutch Fascist, told the governor Snow was planning to escape to Ireland.

Snow had boasted to Boon about his activities as a German agent: how he had taken photographs of tanks and aircraft, told the Germans of a Canadian army camp later bombed by the Luftwaffe, that he carried a German passport, had been in Berlin two days before the outbreak of war, and had a secret bank account in New York through which he was paid by the Abwehr. If the Germans invaded then the guards at Stafford had instructions to shoot all inmates, according to Snow.[4]

Believing he was in the company of the most important spy in England, Boon agreed to participate in the escape plan. When they got to Dublin, Snow promised to arrange for a German U-boat to take him home to Holland. First they bribed a warder to get them a small saw. Whatever this was intended for it didn't work, and the warder was asked to loan them a key from which Snow took an impression on a bar of soap which he gave to Boon to make a cardboard positive, at which point Boon lost his nerve and informed the Governor. The Dutchman told MI5 Snow's only interest in life seemed to be making money; that there was nothing idealistic about him – he was just 'a common traitor'.[5] Not long afterwards Snow was transferred to Dartmoor and Special Branch instructed to increase surveillance on Lily and a house in Addlestone where she was living with the child.

Snow's son Robert was also interned for the remainder of the war at Peveril Internment Camp, a group of requisitioned guest houses at the end of the promenade at Peel on the Isle of Man. In some cases, husbands and wives were interned together but Snow was refused permission to move to Peveril to be with his son.[6] In January 1943, by which time a large number of detainees had been released back into the community or deported, Snow junior's application for a transfer to Dartmoor so as to be close to his father was rejected by the Home Secretary. A year later both were still interned, the Home Office continuing to regard father and son a security risk especially on the eve of the D-Day landings. 'They have both been in detention for some time and it will not in fact do much harm to them if they remain there a few months longer,' Robertson wrote to the

Director-General, Petrie. The Snows would be among the very last to be freed in August 1944.[7]

Robert Snow would have been conscripted immediately into the armed forces but for the intervention of MI5, which preferred him to be judged unfit for military service rather than run the risk he fell into enemy hands. His father had only £2.10s in cash, no identity card or ration card when he left Dartmoor. But MI5 felt obligated to help rehabilitate its former agent by providing temporary accommodation while he looked for work.

In September 1944, the secretary of the Twenty Committee, John Marriott, was waiting to collect Snow from Dartmoor. During the drive back to London the conversation was muted. Neither had much to say, 'apart from trivialities', Marriott told Robertson later:

> It had occurred to us he would have nowhere to go and in those circumstances you might have thought he would have been grateful for temporary hospitality while casting around for something to do and somewhere to go … but Snow assumed we should be looking after him … and scarcely showed any gratitude for our consideration.

Marriott, who had never liked or trusted the shifty Welshman, refused to discuss Snow junior although fully aware the youngster had already been released from the Isle of Man. Nor did he offer any information about Lily and the child, replying when Snow asked about their whereabouts, 'I have no idea'.[8]

For six months Snow senior lived off handouts from MI5 totalling £215 until Robertson finally lost patience and recommended to the Director-General, Sir David Petrie, that he should be paid off:

> I do not consider that Snow has made any very serious attempt to find himself a job and I am satisfied that so long as he feels, as he does, that we shall look after him he will be content to drift along without making any effort. In fairness to him I think that it ought to be said that, having regard to his age – he is nearly fifty – and to the fact that throughout the war he has had no proper employment, he

>may be for all practical purposes virtually unemployable,
>except in the one job of which he has any recent experi-
>ence, namely as an agent, and for this he is for a variety of
>reasons no longer suitable.[9]

Robertson made one last attempt to find Snow work. Nothing came of
it and Snow was told he could no longer rely on MI5 support – that it
was time he stood on his own feet. Robertson recommended making
him an *ex gratia* payment of £500, equivalent to £13,000 at 2011 prices
but no comparison to the £10,000 he got from Rantzau in Lisbon, and
surrendered to MI5. That was equivalent to £287,000 and little wonder the Abwehr always thought the most likely explanation for Snow's
sudden 'retirement' on his return from Lisbon was not that he had
suffered a breakdown as claimed in his final transmission but that he
had taken the money and ran. Robertson estimated that the Germans
paid Snow a total of about £4,000 (equivalent to more than £100,000)
in return for information during the three years he spied for them.[10]

Whereas MI5 had no authority or procedure for compensat-
ing former agents, Robertson believed Snow should receive £500 as
an 'intelligence dividend' for his very large contribution to British
counter-espionage. Such an unusual payment could only be authorised by the Director-General. If the £10,000 received from Rantzau
was taken into account, Robertson estimated that the Snow case had
been 'on a pure financial basis alone … profitable to us'. The Director-
General agreed. The only problem was the best way to arrange the
pay-off, he said.[11]

Two MI5 agents, Lieutenant Colonel Cussen and Major L. J.
Burt, handed Snow his cheque for £500 in Room 055 Imperial House
on 6 March 1945. Snow was told the time had come when he could
be of no further assistance to MI5 but was reminded of the need for
secrecy in connection with the work he had been doing. Snow seemed
genuinely surprised to receive redundancy pay. He would, he said,
invest it immediately and had no complaints about his treatment.[12]
His very last action was to sign the Official Secrets Act. Before doing
so Snow was reminded by Colonel Cussen of the penalties he faced if
tempted to write about his espionage activities or discuss them with
any unauthorised persons.[13]

Nothing is known of Snow's immediate movements after being paid off by MI5, except that he appears never to have been reunited with Lily and her daughter, Jean Louise. In 1946 Snow met Hilda White and changed his name to White by deed poll. After a son, Graham, was born in London the family moved to Wexford where Snow ran a radio repair shop, and attended the occasional Sinn Féin meeting, otherwise spending a great deal of time in the public house around the corner. Few in the family knew about his secret life until after he died in December 1957 and was buried in an unmarked grave in Crosstown Cemetery. Released from internment in 1944, Snow's son Robert married before returning to South Wales as a steelworks engineer at Port Talbot where he died in 1981. His sister Patricia became a Hollywood movie star in the 1950s, appearing alongside Vincent Price in the science fiction film *The Fly*.

For whatever reason, Snow never retracted his statement that he had confessed to Rantzau to being a controlled British agent, nor did he appeal against his detention in Dartmoor. But Robertson, the head of the Double-Cross System, admitted in January 1944 that MI5 had got it wrong. Information was subsequently received, he said, from other reliable sources that on his last visit to Lisbon Snow did *not* tell Rantzau he was a controlled British agent.[14] In fact, Rantzau was sacked by the Abwehr for losing control of Snow and instead of being offered a plum posting to Brazil was dispatched to North Africa. Towards the end of the war he was sent to Hanover where on the final night of saturation bombing by the RAF he was the commanding officer in charge of the city's anti-aircraft defences. After closely studying radar and ground observation reports Rantzau decided that the small-scale diversionary attacks in other parts of Germany was Britain's main effort that night and therefore gave orders for the defence of Hanover to stand down. Precisely six minutes later 1,500 RAF bombers arrived! Later, as a POW Rantzau was in charge of a squad sweeping out the mess at the Combined Services Detailed Interrogation Centre, Bad Nenndorf, Germany. Under interrogation at Bad Nenndorf, Rantzau claimed that £500 was the largest single payment he ever made to Snow. The £10,000 that the Welshman was carrying when he returned from Lisbon must have been obtained from some other

Abwehr source, possibly in Madrid where Snow was known to have contacts, Rantzen suggested.[15]

So why did Snow invent the story of his confession? Masterman, one of the best brains in MI5, believed the simple explanation was that Snow was looking to escape a situation that had become unsustainable, too complicated for even his inventive mind to handle. Sooner or later the Germans were sure to rumble him. If they did, and he was no use to the British either, then where was he to hide? In Lisbon he spoke about taking Lily and the baby to Germany and a job with Rantzau in military intelligence. For someone like Snow, that would have been an attractive proposition – but only if Hitler was victorious. By February 1941, that was by no means certain. The Battle of Britain was won and a German invasion receding. Perhaps Snow decided that the best place to hide was prison. If the Germans were the victors, he would be released, a hero of the Third Reich. In the meantime he awaited developments, biding his time in Dartmoor, building up his stock with MI5 by squealing on other inmates, never appealing against his detention, not retracting a word of a 'confession' that, paradoxically, became his passport to a safe haven.

GW returned to private detective work but not for long. Eighteen months after he was terminated as an agent by the Double-Cross System he suffered a debilitating illness that left him barely able to sign his name, or leave home except by ambulance for physiotherapy at the local hospital. He died at the Royal Chelsea Hospital in 1949, aged 62, after a prolonged illness, leaving a wife and stepdaughter, but not a word about his audacious excursion into the world of espionage. Like the perfect spy, Williams vanished into the shadows.

The Welsh double agents were hugely valuable to British intelligence in their different ways. Owens was most useful in the period immediately before and after the outbreak of war. A founding member of the Double-Cross System, he was at one and the same time duplicitous and unreliable, extremely difficult to control. But despite his numerous flaws, Owens's aptitude for working on both sides of the espionage divide delivered a mass of intelligence to the British about Nazi operations. The final verdict of John Gwyer, MI5's security analyst was that however 'obscurely Snow wrapped up his information he provided MI5 with an immense amount of detail which subsequent cross-checking has shown to be true'.[16] But on which side he personally stood at any given moment is a secret Snow took to the grave – if, in fact, he ever knew himself!

Williams's contribution to strategic deception was that of an ordinary man who did an extraordinary job for his country, one that could have been even more productive but for the shadow cast over his operations by Calvo's arrest. Not for a moment did Rantzau seem to suspect Williams was anything other than the fanatical Welsh nationalist collaborator he pretended to be. After Owens's termination Williams was regarded by the Abwehr as its last man standing in Britain. For their part, Masterman and Robertson saw his loss as a great disaster putting at risk the entire Double-Cross System.

CONCLUSION

BY MASQUERADING AS WELSH NATIONALIST collaborators, Gwilym Williams and Arthur Owens helped win the war of strategic deception for Britain. But were others playing a more deadly game?

Pacifist nationalism was always going to be open to exploitation by Nazi Germany as well as a British security service eager to seize every chance to penetrate German military intelligence. But did a spurious offer of Welsh independence persuade some disaffected nationalists to collaborate, believing, as did some members of the IRA, that England's problems was Wales's opportunity? Did Welsh resistance, albeit limited, to conscription into an English war gain sufficient traction to turn a handful into Nazi collaborators?[1]

Accounts of potential collaborators lurking in the Welsh shadows were, on the balance of currently available evidence, the invention of a security apparatus sensitive to the necessity for constant vigilance. The perceived nationalist 'threat' was not very different to Home Office warnings that 'Walls Have Ears' for which a Blaenclydach man of Russian descent was jailed at Glamorgan Assizes for twelve months after a bar-room argument during which all he said was 'The British took Palestine from the Jews and Hitler will take England from the English'.[2]

Until more secrets from the Second World War are in the public domain it will be impossible to say with absolute certainty whether there were others or, more likely, how closely some may have flirted with the idea of collaboration. Judging from the Williams/Owens files, three dossiers entitled 'WNP', 'WW' and 'The Welsh Agent' remain to be declassified – if not already destroyed as part of what is euphemistically described by government departments as 'periodic housekeeping'.

The subjugation of much of mainland Europe by Nazi Germany provided the opportunity for collaboration on a scale unprecedented since the Napoleonic Wars. The true extent, however, has not been fully documented partly because of the sensitivity of the subject for historians exposing what happened in their own country. Individual motives for collaboration are also complex, and not always in direct response to the ideological and social conflicts arising in a defeated country from the sanctions of the victorious power.[3] Of the individuals who form the subject of this work, it has to be said that Owens's principal motivation was money, his professed nationalism a smokescreen for what certainly began as a mercenary enterprise.

In any discussion of Welsh nationalism immediately prior to and during the Second World War it is important to distinguish between the mainstream as represented by Plaid Cymru and a minority of disaffected nationalists impatient with the party's cultural/pacifist stance in the struggle for greater self-determination. Since the party was founded in 1925 its only act of violent defiance against an English conquest that occurred eight hundred years before the rise of Nazi Germany was the burning down of the RAF bombing school on the Llŷn Peninsula by Saunders Lewis and others in 1936. This wholly cultural protest in defence of the language defined Plaid Cymru until Tryweryn in 1966. The bombing of water pipelines and government buildings that followed, and the arson attacks on holiday homes, was the work of those generally regarded as renegades. To what extent, if at all, their violent, direct action influenced the pace of devolution in Wales from a Government that had already begun the process by establishing a Welsh Office will never be admitted even though the pages of history are littered with the effectiveness of violent direct action in support of self-determination.

Pacifism has always been at the heart of Plaid Cymru's nationalist philosophy, no more so than prior to the outbreak of war. The party, however, has also stood accused of being imprecise, even indifferent about that other pole around which nationalists gather – self-government. But what was even more unusual about 1940s Wales was that nationalism, pacifism and neutrality were bedfellows. Patriotic Germans were nationalists following the humiliating reparations of the Versailles Treaty after the First World War; in Italy, the idea of restoring the Roman Empire was a nationalist dream, while Japan's nationalism was born out of a sense of duty and honour. Few, if any, saw pacifism as a means of resolving their supposed grievances.

The Welsh nationalism of Saunders Lewis was the product of the continuing threat to his nation's language and culture. For Lewis, Plaid Cymru aimed to 'take away from the Welsh their sense of inferiority ... to remove from our beloved country the mark and shame of conquest'.[4] But when speaking of revolution to restore this to its proper place in Welsh life he never advocated violence against the British state. By recognising a common heritage, language, and culture Welsh nationalism was no more racist than any nation believing in the integrity of its ethnicity, and the tension created by national rivalry never synonymous with the racist sentiments of Nazi Germany.

How Plaid's ambitions were to be realised might not always have been clear, but fighting a war against the English, in whatever form, never figured in the party's development, in addition to which by the 1940s the majority of Welsh thought themselves ethnically indistinguishable from the English. Second class citizens maybe in the social and economic context but, nevertheless, still citizens of a United Kingdom. Even the violent direct action perpetrated by so-called renegade nationalists between the 1960s and 1980s had a cultural dimension by focussing on the part bricks and mortar played in the decline of Welsh communities. But it was not racist, the arsonists indifferent to the nationality of holiday-home owners while taking care that no person was harmed during more than 200 attacks on property.[5]

In a country with a long tradition of liberal pacifism, Saunders Lewis was an enthusiastic supporter of the non-Governmental Peace Pledge Union, which by 1940 had almost 136,000 members.[6] Prominent in its Welsh equivalent, Heddychwyr Cymru, was Gwynfor Evans, Lewis's successor in 1945 and one of the men credited with guiding the party through the lean years of the war. Evans's conscientious objection was rooted in Christianity, and so was his nationalism, his face set against the use of violence to procure a non-belligerent Wales as a member of the community of nations.

But in the febrile atmosphere swirling around appeasement in pre-war Britain it was perhaps inevitable that Plaid's unfamiliar brand of neutral nationalist pacifism was misconstrued as racist by critics for whom it jarred with preconceptions.

Despite Plaid Cymru's declared neutrality only fourteen nation-alists are believed to have sought conscientious objection on politi-cal grounds out of a total of 60,000 registered for military service exemption across the British Isles (four times as many as in the First World War), the clearest evidence the majority of nationalists sup-ported the war effort.[7] The ostracism of fellow citizens and the fear of losing their jobs weighed as heavily on the decisions of conscien-tious objectors as appearing before the Government appeal tribunals, which were generally regarded as fair and sympathetic.

That a party led by Lewis and the devout pacifist Evans should somehow be the unintentional inspiration for a nest of Nazi col-laborators defies belief. But not everyone saw it this way. Pacifism, in whatever guise, according to the author and journalist George Orwell, was naturally pro-fascist:

> If you hamper the war effort on one side you automatically help that of the other ... In so far as it takes effect at all, paci-fist propaganda can only be effective against those countries where a certain amount of freedom of speech is still permit-ted; in other words it is helpful to totalitarianism.[8]

That Lewis used extravagant language when discussing the impact of the war on Welsh communities is undeniable. Even his left-lean-ing colleagues thought his views 'elitist' and his attitude towards the socialist, working-class pacifist tradition of the valleys 'condescend-ing'.[9] During the turmoil surrounding the burning down of the RAF bombing school on the Llŷn Peninsula he praised Hitler for fulfill-ing his promise 'to completely abolish the financial strength of the Jews in the economic life of Germany', a comment that haunts his legacy to this day although favourable remarks about fascist leaders were also made by Winston Churchill and Lloyd George during the 1930s.[10] Nor was the Plaid leadership united in adopting a neutral-ist stance. Ambrose Bebb, a lecturer at Bangor Normal College, was outspoken in support of the war, believing that a party that relied solely upon pacifism bred apathy.[11]

Mindful of England's war in Ireland, Chamberlain's policy of appeasement, and the initial opposition of Lloyd George and other leading politicians to a military solution, Hitler was encouraged to believe there was something to play for in a pacifist, nationalist Wales. During the Phoney War Germany had supported regional movements in France, Belgium, the Netherlands and Norway as a means of undermining their governments. Breton nationalists were persuaded that with the fall of France independence would be theirs, their language and culture reinstated after many years of suppression. The most extreme Breton nationalists claimed descent from a race of pure Celts, and had links with Nazi Germany long before the outbreak of war. The Breton National Party also declared itself neutral but Breton nationalism was influenced by German racism and other varieties of European fascism. A breakaway faction, the Bezen Perrot, collaborated with the SS in hunting down and executing French resistance fighters and then fought alongside their German comrades on the Eastern Front.[12]

Nazi Germany would discover that the cultural nationalism of Wales was markedly different from what it knew in Brittany and Eastern Europe where the racist inclinations of regional movements could be manipulated to support German ambitions.[13] Nor were the Irish what was expected, the vast majority backing England to win the war, and the Garda rounding up German agents the moment they landed. Occasionally, a German U-boat picked up provisions at some secluded bay on Ireland's west coast, but even that facility ceased once de Valera discovered the German High Command planned to land troops in Ireland as a backdoor into Britain. As for the IRA, it diverted whatever it could squeeze out of the Abwehr to fund its own war with England until Hitler finally abandoned efforts to subsume Ireland into the Axis camp.

After the First World War, peace movements had flourished in a moderately secure Britain, strategically well-positioned, with a tolerant, pluralistic, liberal culture. The British peace movement became the most influential in Europe, drawing considerable support from the Liberal Party and nascent Labour Party. But after Czechoslovakia was invaded the number of conscientious objectors declined, some recanted, while others felt considerable unease about their stance.[14] At the same time, the implementation of Regulation 18B, and the internment of aliens as well as the leadership of Sir Oswald Mosley's British Union of Fascists, denied Nazi Germany its Fifth Column and a pool of potential collaborators.

In the absence of a real Fifth Column MI5 turned to Wales. At first the security service seems to have shared Hitler's belief in the existence of nationalist subversives, otherwise why should it have instructed the mysterious 'WW', the Immigration Officer from Swansea, to infiltrate the movement. When none were found, MI5 invented Gwilym Williams, while exploiting Arthur Owens's antagonism towards the English to build a bridgehead inside German military intelligence.

By focusing German intelligence activity on a bunch of saboteurs, Williams and Owens deflected the threat of espionage and sabotage from one of the most vulnerable parts of Britain. As far as can be seen no Abwehr agent landed in Wales undetected, nor was there a single act of sabotage. Paradoxically, however, the invention of Gwilym Williams and his indisputable success in convincing Nazi Germany he was at least for a time its British master spy – and certainly the only agent it ever needed in Wales – is probably largely responsible for the enduring shadow cast over post-war nationalism.

NOTES

INTRODUCTION

1. David Kahn, *Hitler's Spies: German Military Intelligence in World War II* (London: Macmillan, 1978), p. 273.

2. John Davies, *A History of Wales* (London: Penguin, 1994), p. 592; R. Merfyn Jones, 'Wales and British Politics 1900–1939', in Chris Wrigley (ed.), *A Companion to Early Twentieth Century Britain* (London: Blackwell Publishing, 2002), Chapter 6.

3. John Davies, *A History of Wales*, 1994, pp. 592–3, 598–9, 610–11.

4. Ibid, pp. 574, 581–2; *Western Mail*, Saunders Lewis speech at Bangor, 'Welsh "Revolution" aims, defined by leader of Nationalists', 5 August 1939, p. 8.

5. The National Archives (TNA), HO 382, 396, 405 (alien Papers and index cards): P. Kershan and M. Pearsall, *Immigrants and Aliens* (TNA: Second Edition, 2004); TNA, LAB6 (conscientious objectors files).

6. TNA, CAB 66/23/3, folio 29, Attlee memorandum to Secretary of State for Dominion Affairs, entitled 'War Cabinet: Welsh Representation', 14 March 1942.

7. *Western Mail*, 5 August 1940, p. 5.

8. TNA, NF 1/257, C. H. Wilson to Sir Kenneth Clark, Ministry of Information, 1 April 1940.

9. A. Daniel, *Le Mouvement Breton*, pp. 303–6; Daniel Leach, 'Bezen Perrot: The Breton Nationalist Unit of the SS, 1943–5', *Journal of Inderdisciplinary Celtic Studies*, p. 24.

10. *Western Mail*, 9 August 1939, p. 8; *Western Mail,* IRA round-up, 15 August 1939, p. 7; David O'Donoghue, *Hitler's Irish Voices: The Story of German Radio's Wartime Irish Service* (Belfast: Beyond the Pale Publications, 1998), pp. xi–xiv.

11. TNA, KV 2/446, Lord Cottenham note to file, 17 October 1939; TNA, KV 2/446, Snow to Robertson, 22 December 1939.

12. TNA, KV 2/468, Letter from WW to Robertson, 11 October 1939; TNA, KV 2/468, Lord Cottenham report, 354a, on first meeting GW, WW, Snow, 16 October 1939; TNA, KV 2/446, Cottenham report on second meeting with GW, WW, Snow, 17 October 1939.

13. TNA, KV 2/468, Letter from WW to Robertson, 11 October 1939.

14. Ladislas Farago, *The Game of the Foxes* (Toronto, New York, London: Bantam Books, 1973), pp. ix–xiii.

15. Michael Howard, 'Strategic Deception in World War II', in *British Intelligence in the Second World War* (Volume 5), ed. F. H. Hinsley (Cambridge University Press: 1990).

16. Guy Liddell (MI5) to FO, 27 Apr. 1945, N4806/346/G42, FO 371/48032; Sir David Petrie (MI5) to Sargent, 9 Jun. 1945, N6745/346/42G, FO 371/48032.

17. R. Aldrich, 'Policing the Past: Official History, Secrecy and British Intelligence since 1945', *The English Historical Review* (2004), pp. 922–53.

ONE OPERATION CROWHURST

1. The National Archives (TNA), KV 2/468, 'WW' recommends Gwilym Williams as replacement for Brussels mission.

2. TNA, KV 2/468, folio 1f, Cottenham account of Williams's briefing for Operation Crowhurst.

3. West Glamorgan Archives, Gwilym Williams's service record in Glamorgan Constabulary.

4. Ibid.

5. A. J. Sylvester, *The Real Lloyd George* (London: 1947), p. 202; see also Peter Rowland, *Lloyd George* (London: Barrie and Jenkins Ltd., 1975), pp. 735–7.

6. *Daily Express*, British Newspaper Library (BNL), 17 September 1936.

7. *News Chronicle*, BNL, 21 September 1936.

8. National Library of Wales (NLW), Lloyd George Papers, 20475C (3151).

9. Richard Deacon, *British Secret Service: the Classic History – Thoroughly Revised and Updated* (London: Grafton Books, 1991), pp. 273–6.

10. TNA, KV 2/468, report, Gwilym Williams (GW) to Major T. A. Robertson, 30 October 1939, on Abwehr meeting in Antwerp.

11. Federal Bureau of Investigation, trial of 'Frederick Joubert Duquesne *et al.*, Espionage', Norden Bombsight, pp. 21–2, declassified 5 May 1953.

12. TNA, KV 2/451, folio 1472k, undated description given to MI5 by Owens (Snow) of Ritter and his accomplices; TNA, KV 2/468, folio 365a, Cottenham instructions to Gwilym Williams, 19 October 1939.

13. TNA, KV 2/451, Snow profile drafted for file by Captain J. M. A. Gwyer, MI5 (B1), 10 August 1943; see also, TNA, KV 2/451, folio 1798a.

14. TNA, KV 2/451, folio 1798a; Ladislas Farago, *The Game of the Foxes* (New York: Bantam Books, 1973), p. 327.

15. TNA, KV 2/444 for further description of Snow; see also TNA, KV 2/451, folio 1798a, information supplied by British agent 'PW' (Wichman) from inside Hamburg *Ast*.

16. Michael Hopkinson, *The Irish War of Independence* (Montreal, Quebec, Ontario: McGill-Queen's University Press, 2004), p. 91.

17. TNA, KV 2/446, folio 275a; also Farago, *The Game of the Foxes*, p. 189, 195.

18. Farago, *The Game of the Foxes*, p. 190.

19. David Kahn, *Hitler's Spies: German Military Intelligence in World War II* (New York: De Capo Press, 2000), pp. 296, 302, pp. 355–6.

20. Kahn, *Hitler's Spies*, p. 306.

21. TNA, KV 2/451, folio 13606, translation, Major Nikolaus Ritter's report on the Snow case, dated Berlin, 31 July 1941; also TNA, KV 2/468, 28 October 1939.

22. Kahn, *Hitler's Spies*, p. 273, 304.

23. Kahn, *Hitler's Spies*, p. 357. Author's note: Kahn attributes his claim that the German agent Cato (later 'Garbo' when 'turned' by MI5 into a British double agent) ran a Swansea espionage cell led by a retired merchant seaman to John Masterman's *The Double-Cross System*, p. 143. However, Masterman, chairman of the committee that ran the double agents, says clearly that apart from Cato/Garbo himself all his agents were fictional; see TNA, KV 2/451, folio 1472k for account of activities of German agent Walter Simon.

24. TNA, KV 2/451, translation, Major Nikolaus Ritter's report on the Snow case, Berlin, 31 July 1941.

25. TNA, KV 2/446, Myner statement to Special Branch, 6 September 1939, regarding Hamburg visit with Snow, Lily.

26. Ibid.

27. TNA, KV 4/188, Volume 4, Part 1, Guy Liddell Diaries, pp. 7, 13, 15–17, 19, 112, 119; also KV 4/191, GLD, secret inks, Volume 7, Part 1, p. 17.

28. Deakin, *British Secret Service*, p. 256.

29. TNA, KV 4/188, Volume 4, Part 1, p. 999.

30. TNA, KV 4/187, GLD, Volume 3, Part 2, p. 854.

31. Kahn, *Hitler's Spies*, pp. 293–5; also TNA, KV 2/468, folio 172b.

32. TNA, KV 2/451, translation, Major Nikolaus Ritter's report on the Snow case, Berlin, 31 July 1941.

33. TNA, KV 2/446, Mrs Owens's statements to Special Branch, 18, 24 August 1939, informing on Snow.

34. Kahn, *Hitler's Spies*, interview 1970 with Hans Speidal, Abwehr Section Head (Foreign Armies), pp. 292–3.

35. TNA, KV 4/187, Guy Liddell Diaries, Volume 3, Part 1, p. 643.

36. Farago, *The Game of the Foxes*, pp. 226–8.

37. Ibid.

38. TNA, KV 2/446, Myner statement to Special Branch, 6 September 1939.

39. TNA, KV 2/446, Special Branch report, undated, following Snow arrest.

40. TNA, KV 2/446, account, Major Robertson of Snow radio transmissions from cell at Wandsworth Prison, 8 September 1939.

41. Ibid.

42. TNA, KV 2/450, folios 1090a, 1103b, and 1330c.

43. TNA, KV 2/446, logs (folio 335a) of messages sent by Snow, 7 October 1939, using five-letter code.

44. TNA, KV 2/466, Hinchley-Cooke account 18 October 1939 of conversation with Snow.

TWO WALES READY!

1. TNA, KV 2/446, folio 311a, 'The Welsh Agent: WW folder', 22 September 1939.

2. TNA, KV 4/188, GLD, Volume 4, Part 2, pp. 79–81, list and mode of travel of German agents (saboteurs underlined in red).

3. TNA, KV 2/446, folio 311a, 22 September 1939.

4. TNA, KV 2/446, WW pulled from Operation Crowhurst, suspicious bookseller, 28–30 September 1939.

5. TNA, KV 2/468, letter, 11 October 1939, WW recommends GW as replacement for Brussels assignment.

6. TNA, KV 2/446, Robertson on purpose of GW/Snow mission, undated note to file.
7. TNA, KV 2/446, Robertson note to file, 26 September 1939, regarding Snow, WW.
8. TNA, KV 2/468, Cottenham report, 16 October 1939, of briefing GW, Snow for Operation Crowhurst.
9. Ibid.
10. TNA, KV 2/446, GW report, 17 October 1939, to Cottenham/Robertson on evening with Snow, WW and Lily, on eve of Operation Crowhurst.
11. Ibid.
12. TNA, KV 2/468, Cottenham note to file, 16 October 1939, on cover story for GW, Snow for Operation Crowhurst.

THREE THE INTERROGATION

1. TNA, KV 2/468, GW report to Robertson, controller Double-Cross System, after Antwerp meeting with Rantzau, 28 October 1939; TNA, KV 2/446, Snow report to Robertson after Antwerp meeting for comparison purposes, 29 October 1939.
2. TNA, KV 2/450, folio 1097a, J. Marriott note on Snow's mental health, 3 April 1941, after Snow interrogation following his 'confession' in Lisbon.
3. Rudi Van Doorslaer, *Docile Belgium* (Brussels: Centre for Historical Research and Documentation on War and Contemporary Society, 2007), commissioned by Belgian Senate on the rounding up, segregation and dispossession of Jews before and during the Second World War.
4. Farago, *The Game of the Foxes*, p. 225.
5–9. TNA, KV 2/468, GW report to Robertson after Antwerp meeting with Rantzau, 28 October 1939; see also KV 2/446, folio 492 for details of Kruger activities at Farnborough.
10. TNA, KV 2/468, GW report to Robertson, after Antwerp meeting with Rantzau, 28 October 1939.
11. Ibid.
12. Ibid.
13. Ibid.
14. Ibid.
15. TNA, KV 2/468, file marked 'Not to be opened' for photographic copies of stamps sent to GW by de Ridder.

16. TNA, KV 2/446, account by 'Charlie' of meeting with 'Mr and Mrs Graham', 24 November 1939; see also TNA, KV 2/446, folio 138a (also in PF 48283), 16 November 1939, for Snow statement concerning Abwehr instructions to Charlie.

17. Ibid.

18. TNA, KV 2/468, GW report to Robertson after Antwerp meeting, 28 October 1939.

19. TNA, KV 2/185, GLD, 31 October 1939, Volume 1, Part 1, p. 129.

20. TNA, KV 4/185, GLD, 26 October 1939, Volume 1, Part 1, pp. 118–19.

21. TNA, KV 2/450, folio 1264c, for details of case against Mathilde Kraft; TNA, KV 4/465, 1942–5 for details of fraudulent sterling notes paid to double agents by the Abwehr.

22. National Archives, Washington DC, Abwehr Diaries, extracts from Page 12 of 'the Logbook of Counter-Intelligence (Section II) relating to operations against England undertaken by the Section in Association with members of the Irish Republican Army, the IRA'.

FOUR IF THE INVADER COMES!

1. Walter Warliamont, *Inside Hitler's Headquarters* (London: Wiedenfeld, 1964), p. 106; TNA, KV 4/186, GLD, Volume 2, Part 1, p. 527; TNA, NF 1/257; TNA, KV 6/50 'Fifth Column Activities'.

2. TNA, KV 4/186, Guy Liddell Diaries, Volume 2, Part 1, pp. 436, 466–8; KV 4/186, GLD, Volume 2, Part 1, pp. 471–3; KV 4/186, GLD, Volume 2, Part 1, p.513; KV 4/187, GLD, Volume 3, Part 1, p.670.

3. Ibid.

4. TNA, KV 4/186, GLD, Volume 2, Part 1, pp. 518–19; *Western Mail*, 'Little Berlin', 14 May 1940, p. 5; *Western Mail*, arrest of Italians (70 Cardiff City, 160 Glamorgan County, 17 Newport Borough, 13 Merthyr Borough, 2 Neath Borough), 12 June 1940, p. 5; *Western Mail*, surrender of documents by enemy aliens, 13 May 1940, p. 3.

5. *Western Mail*, country rotten with Fifth Columnists, 9 July 1940, p. 3; TNA, KV 4/186, Churchill's 'bow and arrow' scare, GLD, Volume 2, Part 2, pp. 527–8.

6. TNA, KV 4/186, GLD, Volume 2, Part 1, pp. 503, 512–13.

7. TNA, KV 4/186, GLD, Volume 2, Part 1, pp. 401–2.

8. TNA, KV 4/186, GLD, Volume 2, Part 2, pp. 486, 492, 588.

9. Richard Deacon, *British Secret Service: The Classic History – Thoroughly Revised and Up-dated* (London: Frederick Muller, 1979), pp. 272–7; Norman Longmate, I*sland Fortress: the Defence of Great Britain* (London: Hutchinson, 1991), p. 467–9, pp. 476–7, pp. 576–8.

10. *Western Mail*, evacuees arrive in Wales, 18 May 1940, p. 3; *Western Mail*, Dunkirk troop trains at Cardiff, 3 June 1940, p. 3; *Western Mail*, Welsh evacuees for Canada scheme, 26 June 1940, p. 3; *Western Mail*, 1 August 1940, p. 3; TNA, KV 4/188, GLD, Volume 4, Part 2, p. 186.

11. Longmate, *Island Fortress*, pp. 474–5.

12. Longmate, *Island Fortress*, p. 476.

13. TNA, KV 4/188, GLD, Volume 4, Part 2, p. 185.

14. Longmate, *Island Fortress*, p. 478.

15. TNA, NF 1/257; also KV 6/50 'Fifth Column Activities'.

16. TNA, KV 4/185, GLD, Volume 1, Part 2, pp. 284–5; TNA, KV 4/186, GLD, Volume 2, Part 1, pp. 369–70; *Western Mail*, 'Conchies Schooled for the Tribunals', 13 May 1940, p. 4; *Western Mail*, 'A Conchie's Appeal', editorial, 22 July 1940, p. 4; *Western Mail*, Williams tribunal hearing, 17 May 1940, p. 4; *Western Mail*, Revd Dr E. Griffith-Jones, 31 May 1940, p. 6; *Western Mail*, 'Welsh Pulpit and the War', 20 June 1940, p. 4; *Western Mail*, Revd J. D. Jones, 'Welsh Pulpit and the War', 20 June 1940, p. 4; *Western Mail*, 'Welsh nationalists before conscientious objectors tribunal', 14 June 1940, p. 3; *Western Mail*, 'London Appeals Tribunal dismiss Welsh Nationalist appeal', 22 July 1940, p. 1; *Western Mail*, William George tribunal hearing, 10 July 1940, p. 2; *Western Mail*, 'A conchies appeal', 22 July 1940, p. 4.

17. TNA, KV 4/190, GLD, Volume 6, Part 2, pp. 786–8.

18. TNA, KV 4/186, GLD, Volume 2, Part 1, p. 536.

19. TNA, KV 4/186, GLD, Volume 2, Part 1, pp. 517–18.

20. TNA, KV 4/186, GLD, Volume Volume 2, Part 1, pp. 471, 491.

21. TNA, KV 4/186, GLD, Volume 2, Part 1, pp. 489–90.   .

22. TNA, NF 1/257; KV 6/50, 'Fifth Column Activities'.

23. Ibid.

24. TNA, NF 1/257, memoradnadum C. H. Wilson to Sir Kenneth Clark, Ministry of Information.

25. TNA, NF 1/257; KV 6/50 'Fifth Column Activities'.

26. Ibid.

27. TNA, KV 6/50 'Fifth Column Activities'.

28. Ibid.

29. TNA, KV 6/50 'Fifth Column Activities', memorandum R. L. Hughes (B.3.B) to B. Machell (B.3.A), Box 500, Parliament Street, SW1, 11 November, 1941.

30. TNA, KV 6/50 'Fifth Column Activities', Albert Foyer, Code Section, to Fl. Lt. R. M. Walker.

31. *The Times*, British Newspaper Library, Petrie obituary, 8 August 1961.

32. TNA, KV 4/186, GLD, Volume 2, Part 1, p. 510.

FIVE DOUBLE-CROSS, PHILATELY AND SUBMARINES

1. TNA, KV 2/446, folio 138a, Robertson note to Snow file, 16 November 1939.

2. TNA, KV 2/468, report, Cottenham to Robertson after debriefing GW, 28 October 1939.

3. Lord Rothschild, *The File is Never Closed* (London: Random Variables), pp. 203–4.

4. J. Colville, *The Fringes of Power: Downing Street Diaries 1939–1955* (London: Hodder and Stoughton, 1985), p. 471.

5. TNA, KV 2/468, photographic copy of stamps from de Ridder to GW, 27 October 1939; TNA, KV 2/468, letter, GW to Rothschild enclosing draft paragraph for inclusion in reply to de Ridder, 6 November 1939.

6. TNA, KV 2/468, extract from B.3 note, Snow file, Vol. 10, 438a, 18 November 1939.

7. TNA, KV 2/468, letter, Robertson to GW, 19 November 1939.

8. *Western Mail*, 23 August 1940, p. 2.

9. TNA, KV 2/468, letter, GW to Lord Rothschild, 27 December 1939.

10. TNA, KV 2/468, letter, GW to de Ridder, 29 February 1940.

11. TNA, KV 2/468, letter, de Ridder to GW reopening channel, 15 April 1940.

12. TNA, KV 2/468, letter, Louis Mercader to GW, 7 May 1940.

13. TNA, KV 2/468, letter, undated, from British Censor's Office to GW quoting regulation P.C.82 stating that 'postage by individuals of Christmas Cards, Greeting cards of all kinds, Calendars, printed matter, literature for the blind, used or unused postage stamps addressed to certain Neutral Countries is forbidden'.

14. TNA, KV 2/468, letter, Robertson to GW, 20 June 1940.

15. TNA, KV 2/468, report, GW to Robertson on Snow/Biscuit visit to South Wales, 17 July 1940.

16. TNA, KV 4/185, GLD, Volume 1, Part 1, pp. 28–9, 75; TNA, KV 4/189, GLD, Volume 5, Part 1, p. 332.

17. TNA, KV 4/189, GLD, Volume 5, Part 2, pp. 540–1.

18. Masterman, *The Double-Cross System*, pp.4–16; TNA, KV 4/186, GLD, Volume 2, Part 2, p. 603; TNA, KV 4/190, GLD, Hart Report for MI5, Volume 6, Part 2, pp. 825–7.

19. Masterman, *The Double-Cross System*, pp.4–16.

SIX THE CUBAN CONNECTION

1. TNA, KV 4/186, GLD. Volume 2, Part 2, pp. 619–20.

2. Ladislas Farago, *The Game of the Foxes* (New York: Bantam Books, 1971), pp. 353–4.

3. TNA, KV 2/468, report on Snow case, original Snow file, Vol. 19, 902X, 902 a.

4. TNA, KV 4/186, GLD. Volume 2, Part 1, pp. 523–4.

5. TNA, KV 4/187, GLD, Volume 3, Part 2, pp. 841–2.

6. Masterman, *The Double-Cross System*, pp. 50–2; Farago, *The Game of the Foxes*, p. 324, 329, 333, 336.

7. TNA, KV 2/546, 'A Chronological Survey of the Case of Silvio Ruiz Robles', pp. 26–30.

8. TNA, KV 2/546, 'Summary of the set-up and functions of the *Abwehrstelle* at Brest by which expedition was arranged', Part 1, pp. 2–3.

9. Ibid, p. 3.

10. TNA, KV 2/546, 'Summary of the set-up and functions of the *Abwehrstelle* at Brest by which expedition was arranged', Part II, p. 1.

11. TNA, KV 2/546, 'A Chronological Survey of the Case of Silvio Ruiz Robles', pp. 27–8.

12. TNA, KV 2/546, 'Summary of the set-up and functions of the *Abwehrstelle* at Brest by which expedition was arranged', Part 1, p. 3.

13. TNA,KV 2/546, 'The Voyage of the *Josephine*', Part II, pp. 4–6.

14. TNA, KV 2/546, 'The fishing smack *Josephine*', report to MI5 (B2) 15 November 1940; TNA, KV 2/546, folio 69a, report from J. R. E. Guild, Security Control Officer, Milford Haven, 19 February 1941 to MI5 giving details of what was found aboard the *Josephine*.

15. TNA, KV 2/546, 'Camp 020: report on the case of Cornelius Evertson and the *Josephine* expedition', November 1940.

16. TNA, KV 2/546, 'The Voyage of the *Josephine*', Part II, pp. 4–6.

17. Masterman, *The Double-Cross System*, Chapter 3, pp. 46–59.
18. TNA, KV 2/546, J. M. A. Gwyer minute (172) for Colonel T. A. Robertson, 27 November 1945.

SEVEN KEY TO THE DIPLOMATIC BAG

1. TNA, KV 4/186, Guy Liddell Diaries, Volume 2, Part 2, pp. 627–8, security chiefs' meeting, 1 October 1940; TNA, KV 4/188, GLD, Volume 4, Part 2, pp. 201–7, Liddell lecture to Regional Security Liaison Officers (RSLOs), 24 November 1941.
2. TNA, KV 4/186, GLD, Volume 2, Part 2, pp. 364–5.
3. TNA, KV 4/187, GLD, Volume 3, Part 1, pp. 640–1.
4. TNA, KV 4/188, GLD, Volume 4, Part 1, p. 40.
5. TNA, KV 4/187, GLD, Volume 3, Part 1, pp. 636–7.
6. Towards the end of his life, Goronwy Rees, the Welsh journalist and academic, admitted to spying for the USSR and also accused Liddell of being the fifth man in the Cambridge spy ring. Although this might well have cost Liddell promotion to Director-General of MI5 after the war, there is no evidence the allegation was true but Liddell was damaged because of his professional association with Burgess, Blunt and Philby while working for the security services during the Second World War.
7. TNA, KV 2/468, folio 302, letter from GW to Robertson, 11 October 1940; TNA, KV 4/187, GLD, Volume 3, Part 1, pp. 644–5.
8. TNA, KV 2/468, GW report to Robertson after meeting with del Pozo, 15 October 1940.
9. TNA, KV 2/468, folio 1B, Welsh Activity Report, 15 October 1940.
10. TNA, KV 2/468, folio 3Q, GW to Robertson, 11 October 1940.
11. TNA, KV 2/468, folio 3T, GW to Robertson, 21 October 1940.
12. TNA, KV 4/187, GLD, Volume 3, Part 1, Joint Intelligence Committee assessment, pp. 656–60.
13. TNA, KV 2/468, folio 3T, GW to del Pozo, military installations report, 15 October 1940.
14. TNA, KV 2/468, folio 3W, Robertson to GW, 26 October 1940.
15. TNA, KV 2/468, folio 3T, GW to del Pozo, military installations report, 15 October 1940.
16. TNA, KV 4/187, GLD, 'Mrs Harris', Volume 3, Part 1, pp. 656–7.
17. TNA, KV 2/468, folio 4W, GW to Robertson, report, meeting with del Pozo, 9 November 1940; TNA, KV 4/187, GLD, Volume 3, Part 1, p. 673.

18. TNA, KV/468, folio 4W, GW to Robertson, report, meeting with del Pozo, 9 November 1940.
19. TNA, KV 2/468, folio 5A, GW to Robertson, report, meeting with del Pozo, 1 December 1940.
20. Ibid.
21. TNA, KV 4/187, GLD, Volume 3, Part 1, pp. 672, 685.
22. TNA, KV 4/187, GLD, Volume 3, Part 1, pp. 674, 681.
23. *Western Mail*, Lloyd George speech to House of Commons, 10 May 1940, p. 5.
24. British Library, Lloyd George Papers, G/3/4/9.
25. TNA, KV 4/187, GLD, Volume 3, Part 2, pp. 845, 883.
26. Peter Rowland, *Lloyd George*, 1975 (London: Barrie and Jenkins), pp. 786–7.
27. Ibid.
28. TNA, KV 4/187, GLD, Volume 3, Part 1, pp. 679, 680, 682, 685.
29. TNA, KV 4/187, GLD, Volume 3, Part 1, p. 186.
30. TNA, KV 2/468, GW to Robertson, report, meeting with del Pozo, 13 December 1940.
31. TNA, KV 2/468, GW to Robertson, report for approval by the Twenty Committee, 20 December 1940.
32. TNA, KV 2/468, folio 7A, GW to Robertson, report, 20 December 1940.
33. TNA, KV 2/468, folio 11A, GW to Robertson, report, del Pozo meeting, 9 January 1941.
34. TNA, KV 2/468, folios 13A, 21B, poisoning Cray Reservoir, GW to Rothschild; TNA, KV 2/468, del Pozo followed.
35. TNA, KV 2/468, folio 28A, del Pozo arrest, escape, telegram, 3 March 1941.
36. TNA, KV 2/468, Swansea Blitz, folios 20A, 22G, GW to Robertson, 27 February 1941, 13 March 1941.
37. TNA, KV 2/468, folio 31A, Plaid Cymru meeting, 17 March 1941.

EIGHT THE CONFESSION

1. TNA, KV 2/451, final report by John Gwyer for MI5 on 'Snow, Biscuit, Celery, GW, Charlie, and Summer' cases, 23 April 1946.
2. Ibid.
3. TNA, KV 4/187, GLD, Volume 3, Part 1, pp. 741–4, 751–2, 759–60, 763, 767–70; TNA, KV 2/451, 1483a, J. M. A. Gwyer to Lord Rothschild, 25 May 1942.

4. Masterman, *The Double-Cross System*, p. 92.
5. TNA, KV 2/451, folio 1360b, Dr Rantzau meeting with Snow and Celery in Lisbon, J. H. Marriott and J. M. A. Gwyer report, 17 November 1941; TNA, KV 2/451, Major Ritter's [Rantzau] final report on the Johnny [Snow] case (translation), 31 July 1941.
6. TNA, KV 2/450, folio 1109a, Snow statement to MI5, 7 April 1941, pp. 1–2.
7. Ibid, p. 2.
8. Ibid, pp. 1–6.
9. Ibid, p. 2.
10. Ibid, p. 3, 5
11. TNA, KV 4/187, GLD, Volume 3, Part 1, 22 March 1941, pp. 815–6.
12. TNA, KV 2/450, folio 1109a, Snow statement to MI5, 7 April 1941, pp. 1–6. 4
13. Ibid, pp. 4–5.
14. TNA, KV 2/451, folio 1360b, Rantzau meeting with Snow and Celery in Lisbon, J. H. Marriott and J. M. A. Gwyer report, 17 November 1941, pp. 1–6.
15. TNA, folio 1109a, Snow statement to MI5, 7 April 1941, pp. 1–16.
16. Ibid.
17. Ibid.
18. TNA, folio 1109a, Snow statement to MI5, 7 April 1941, p. 9.
19. TNA, KV 2/450, transcript of Snow interrogation, 13 April 1941; TNA, KV 2/451, folio 1360b, Marriott, Gwyer report on Lisbon meeting, 17 November 1941.
20. TNA, KV 2/451, Major Ritter's [Rantzau] final report on the Johnny [Snow] case (translation), 31 July 1941.
21. Masterman, *The Double Cross-System*, p. 93; Snow payments to Tate, pp. 160–1.
22. TNA, KV 2/450, folio 1097a, note on Snow interrogation, Marriott, 3 April 1941.
23. TNA, KV 2/450, folio 1093, 'Snow', transcript of interrogation by Marriott, 1 April 1941.
24. TNA, KV 2/450, folio 1090a, Marriott on Snow, undated.
25. TNA, KV 2/450, folio 1110a, transcript Snow/Celery interrogation, Part 111, pp. 1–45.
26. TNA, KV 2/674, Celery to Robertson, 29 March 1941; TNA, KV 2/450, folio 1110a, transcript Snow and Celery interrogation by Dick White, Part 111, undated.

27. TNA, KV 2/450, Snow consultation with Harley Street specialist, 4 April 1941, reports, Masterman to Robertson, 5, 18 April 1941.
28. Ibid.
29. Ibid.
30. TNA, KV 4/187, GLD, Volume 3, Part 2, MI5 discussion of Snow options, pp. 851–4; TNA, KV 2/450, interrogation of Snow by Masterman, Robertson, case closed, 10 April 1941; Marriott, KV 2/450, folio 1092, 31 March 1941, also folio 1109A, 7 April 1941.
31. TNA, KV 2/451, folio 1360b, Major Ritter's final report on Snow Case (translation), 31 July 1941.
32. Ibid.
33. Ibid; Masterman note on the memorandum, 'Dr Ritter's meeting with Snow and Celery in Lisbon,' 26 November 1941.
34. TNA, KV 2/450, folios 1090a, 1097a Marriott on Snow, undated.
35. Masterman, *The Double-Cross System*, pp. 36–45.
36. Farago, *The Game of the Foxes*, pp. 226–8.
37. TNA, KV 2/450, Petrie to Marriott, instruction 3 April 1941, Snow family.
38. TNA, KV 2/451, folio 1230a, Robert Snow confession, 7 August 1941; KV 2/451, folio 1231x, Masterman note to file.
39. Ibid.
40. TNA, KV 2/451, letter, Snow Junior to Home Secretary Mr H. Morrison, 21 January 1943.
41. TNA, KV 4/188, GLD, Volume 4, Part 1, pp. 938, 996; TNA, KV 4/188, GLD, Volume 4, Part 2, p. 29; Masterman, *The Double-Cross System*, pp. 92–3.

NINE INSIDE ALCAZAR'S SPANISH SPY RING

1. TNA, KV 4/188, Guy Liddell Diaries, Liddell lecture to regional liaison officers, 25 November 1941, pp. 201–7.
2. TNA, KV 2/468, folio 63a, GW to Robertson, undated; also see TNA, KV 4/191, GLD, 'Antaza [Parsley] Spanish consul in Cardiff', Volume 7, Part 2, pp. 304–5.
3. TNA, KV 4/188, GLD, Volume 4, Part 1, pp. 983–4, 995.
4. TNA, KV 2/468, folio 47a, GW letter to Calvo, 24 May 1941; TNA, KV 2/468, folio 47b, Calvo letter to GW [to cover address 'Thomas', GW's father-in-law] arranging first meeting, 17 July 1941.
5. TNA, KV 2/468, folio 52a, 'Plan IV'.
6. Ibid.

7. TNA, KV 2/468, folio 52a, 23 June 1941.
8. TNA, KV 2/468, folio 52/2, GPO telephone tap on Sloane 4040, 26 June 1941.
9. TNA, KV 2/468, 53A, report, GW to Robertson, 24 June 1941.
10. TNA, KV 2/468, folio 52b, GW to Robertson, 25 June 1941.
11. TNA, KV 2/468, folio 62a, GW to Robertson, 24 June 1941.
12. Farago, *The Game of the Foxes*, pp. 650, 654–5.
13. TNA, KV 2/468, folio 64a, GW to Robertson, 26 July 1941.
14. Masterman, *The Double-Cross System*, Chapter 4, pp. 60–70.
15. TNA, KV 2/468, folio 66d, 'Future uses of GW', 6 August 1941.
16. Ibid.
17. TNA, KV 2/468, folio 67a, GW to Robertson, 7 August 1941.
18. TNA, KV 2/468, folio 66c, GW to Calvo, 6 August 1941; folio 68A, Robertson memorandum, 7 August 1941.
19. TNA, KV 2/468, folio 71a, GW to Robertson, 7 August 1941.
20. TNA, KV 2/468, folio 85a, GW to Robertson, 28 August 1941.
21. TNA, KV 2/468, folio 88a, GW to Robertson, 2 September 1941,
22. Sharkhunters International Inc., 'Biography of Don Angel Alcazar de Velasco'.

TEN THE MALTA CONVOY AND SINKING OF *ARK ROYAL*

1. TNA, KV 2/468, folio 88a, GW to Robertson, 2 September 1941.
2. TNA, KV 2/468, folio 99a, White memorandum 'Luis Calvo' for Masterman/Robertson, 3 October 1942.
3. TNA, KV 2/468, folio 99a, White memorandum for B Division, Masterman comments attached, 3 October 1941.
4. TNA, KV 4/188, GLD, Volume 4, Part 1, pp. 991–2.
5. Karl Doenitz, *Memoirs: Ten Years and Twenty Days* (Annapolis, Maryland: Da Capo Press edition, 1997), pp. 158–63.
6. TNA, KV 2/468, folio 103a, GW to Robertson, 'Malta Convoy'.
7. Ibid.
8. Masterman, *The Double-Cross System*, p. 93.
9. TNA, KV 2/468, 'Plan Minotaur', meeting, GW, Masterman, Robertson; TNA, KV 2/468, folio 115a, report GW to Robertson, 20 November 1941.
10. Ibid.
11. Ibid.
12. TNA, KV 2/468, folio 121a, Special Branch report for Masterman, RAF officer sighting, 2 December 1941.

13. TNA, KV 2/468, folio 120a, report on Calvo, 10 December 1941; TNA, KV 2/468, folio 124a, GW to Robertson 10 December 1941.

14. TNA, KV 2/468, folio 135a, GW to Robertson, 9 January 1942.

15. Ibid.

16. TNA, KV 2/468, folio 130a,b, GW to Robertson, 29 December 1941.

17. TNA, KV 2/468, folio 138, GW to Robertson, 17 January 1942.

18. TNA, KV 2/468, folio 142, GW to Robertson, 28 January 1942.

19. TNA, KV 2/468, folio 145a, Masterman to Twenty Committee, 7 February 1942.

20. TNA, KV 2/468, folio 153a, 154a, extracts from Calvo confession, Camp 020; TNA, KV 4/189, GLD, Volume 5, Part 1, pp. 364–9, for further details of contents of Diplomatic Bag; Masterman, *The Double-Cross System*, 'Sweet William', pp. 78, 99.

21. *The Times*, 'The truth that Tin-Eye saw', 10 February 2006; also TNA, Oliver Hoare, 'Camp 020: MI5 and the Nazi Spies – the official history of MI5's wartime interrogation centre (2000), ISBN 1-903365-08-2.

22. *The Times*, 'The truth that Tin-Eye saw', 10 February 2006.

23. TNA, KV 2/468, folio 152b, Camp 020 report, R. Stephens to Masterman, 5 March 1942.

24. Ibid.

25. Ibid.

26. TNA, KV 2/40, KV 2/42; also see TNA, Secret History Files, Tomas Harris, 'Summary of the Garbo case, 1941–45' (1999).

27. Ibid.

28. Masterman, *The Double-Cross System*, pp. 78, 99.

29. TNA, KV 2/468, folio 152a, Marriott/Wilson meeting with GW to discuss Camp 020 options, 4 March 1942.

30. Ibid.

31. TNA, KV 2/468, folio 179a, GW draft letter to Mme. de Ridder, undated.

32. TNA, KV 2/468, folio 155a, Wilson note to file on GW visit to Spanish Embassy, 7 March 1942.

33. TNA, KV 2/468, folio 156a, GW to Robertson offering resignation, 19 March 1942.

ELEVEN THE MAN FROM BRAZIL

1. TNA, KV 2/468, folio 164a, 'GW folder', report of Starziczny arrest, April 1942, originals in P.F. 64717, 'Starziczny', 1a, 1b, 2a, 2b.

2. TNA, KV 4/188, Volume 4, Part 1, Guy Liddell Diaries, pp. 7, 13, 15–17, 19, 112, 119.

3. Stanley Hilton, *A Guerra Secreta de Hitler no Brazil* (Brazil: Nova Fronteira, 1983); in English, *Hitler's Secret War in South America* (United States: Louisiana State University Press, 1999).

4. Ibid.

5. Queen Mary.

6. Stanley Hilton, *A Guerra Secreta de Hitler no Brazil* (Sao Paulo, Brazil: Nova Fronteira, 1983).

7. TNA, KV 2/468, folio 164a, 'GW folder', report of Starziczny arrest, April 1942, originals in P.F. 64717, 'Starziczny', 1a, 1b, 2a, 2b.

8. Ibid.

9. TNA, KV 2/468, folio 169a, 19 May 1942.

10. Ibid.

11. Ibid.

12. Ibid.

13. TNA, KV 2/468, folio 163, GW to Robertson, 28 April 1942.

14. Ibid.

15. Ibid.

16. Ibid.

17. TNA, 2/468, folio 172a, b, GW to Robertson, 29 May 1942.

18. TNA, KV 2/468, folio 170a, Robertson note on GW meeting, 23 May 1942.

19. TNA, KV 2/468, folio 173a, GW to Robertson, 2 June 1943.

20. TNA, KV 2/468, folio 172b, SIS (MI6) extracts from report of Starziczny interrogation, 30 May 1942.

21. TNA, KV 2/468, folio 179a, letter, GW to Madam de Ridder, undated.

22. TNA, KV 2/468, folio 181a, Marriott to Robertson, 14 July 1942.

23. TNA, KV 2/468, letter, Robertson to GW, 5 August 1942.

TWELVE THE AFTERMATH

1. TNA, KV 2/451, folio 582a, Marriott to Major W. H. Coles, Home Office, 29 June 1943.

2. TNA, HO 45/25690, Defence Regulations detainee files, 1939–45.

3. TNA, KV 2/450, folio 1116a, Masterman to Governor, Stafford Gaol, 24 April 1941.

4. TNA, KV 2/450, folio 1241a, statement by Dirk Boon, 15 August 1941.

5. TNA, KV 2/450, folio 1233a, Robertson/Masterman interview with Boon, 14 August 1941; TNA, KV 2/450, Robertson note to Snow file concerning escape plan, 18 August 1941.

6. TNA, HO 215/360-2, 'Married couples as detainees', 1941.

7. TNA, KV 2/451, letter from Snow junior to Home Secretary, Herbert Morrison, 21 June 1943.

8. TNA, KV 2/451, folio 1730a, Marriott to Robertson, 1 September 1944, on release of Snow from Dartmoor.

9. TNA, KV 2/451, Robertson to Sir David Petrie, Director-General MI5, recommending payment to Snow, 24 June 1945.

10. Ibid.

11. TNA, KV 2/451, Petrie reply to Robertson, 3 February 1945.

12. TNA, KV 2/451, report to Robertson confirming compensation paid to Snow, 6 March 1945.

13. TNA, KV 2/451, Official Secrets Act certificate signed by Snow, 6 March 1945.

14. TNA, KV 2/451, Robertson to Hale (SLA), confirming Snow never confessed, 13 January 1944; for Snow family details see Nigel West and Madoc Roberts, *Snow: The Double Life of a World War II Spy* (London: Biteback Publishing, 2011), pp. 195, 198–201.

15. TNA, KV 2/451, folio 1804a, Gwyer report on Rantzau interrogation, 15 May 1946.

16. TNA, KV 2/451, folio 1317b, Marriott to Robertson quoting Gwyer verdict on the value of Snow's intelligence gathering, 17 October 1941.

CONCLUSION

1. John Davies, *A History of Wales* (London: Penguin, 1994), pp. 574, 581–2.

2. *Western Mail*, 20 July 1940, p. 2.

3. John A. Armstrong, 'Collaboration in World War II: The integral nationalist variant in Eastern Europe', *Journal of Modern History* (Chicago: University of Chicago Press, 1968), 40/3, 396–410.

4. Davies, *A History of Wales*, p. 591.

5. John Humphries, *Freedom Fighters: Wales's Forgotten War* (Cardiff: University of Wales Press, 2008), pp. 154–71.

6. Martin Ceadel, 'A legitimate peace movement: the case of Britain 1918–1945', report from conference, *Acceptance of peace movements in national societies during the inter-war period 1919–1939:*

a comparative study (Stadtschlaining, Austria, 25–29 September 1991).

7. Davies, *A History of Wales*, p. 599.
8. Sonia Orwell and Ian Angus (eds), *The Collective Essays, Journalism and Letters of George Orwell* (New York: Harcourt Brace Jovanovich: 1968), Volume 2/261.
9. Davies, *A History of Wales*, p. 599.
10. Ibid, p. 591.
11. United Kingdom Parliament: Debate on *Government of Wales Act 1998*, retrieved 31 August 2006; *Western Mail,* Ambrose Bebb at Plaid Cymru Summer School, 4 August 1939, p. 5.
12. Daniel Leach, 'Bezen Perrot: The Breton nationalist unit of the SS, 1943–5', *Journal of Interdisciplinary Celtic Studies*, 24; John Armstrong, 'Collaboration in World War II: The integral nationalist variant in Eastern Europe', pp. 396–410.
13. Michel Nicolas, *Historie du Movement Breton* (Paris: Syros, 1982), p. 102; John Armstrong, 'Collaboration in World War II: The integral nationalist variant in Eastern Europe', pp. 396–410.
14. John Armstrong, 'Collaboration in World War II: The integral nationalist variant in Eastern Europe', pp. 396–410.

SELECT BIBLIOGRAPHY

Aldrich, R. 'Policing the Past: Official History, Secrecy, and British Intelligence since 1945' in *The English Historical Review* (Oxford: 2004), 119, pp. 922–53.

Armstrong, John A., 'Collaboration in World War II: The Integral Nationalist Variant in Eastern Europe', *Journal of Modern History* (Chicago: University of Chicago Press, 1968).

Chapman, T. Robin, *Un Bywyd O Blith Nifer: Cofiant Saunders Lewis* (Llandysul: Gomer, 2006).

Charmley, John, *Chamberlain and the Lost Peace* (London: Hodder and Stoughton, 1989).

Clarke, Peter, *A Question of Leadership: from Gladstone to Thatcher* (London: Hamish Hamilton, 1991).

Davies, John, *A History of Wales* (London: Penguin, 1994).

Deacon, Richard, *British Secret Service: the Classic History* (London: Frederick Muller, 1969).

Farago, Ladislas, *The Game of the Foxes* (New York: Bantam, 1973).

Graves, Robert and Hodge, Alan, *The Long Weekend: a Social History of Great Britain* (London: Sphere Books, 1991).

Hesketh, Roger, *Fortitude: The D-Day Deception Campaign* (New York: Overlook Press, 2000).

Hoare, Oliver, *Camp 020: MI5 and the Nazi Spies – The Official History of MI5's Wartime Interrogation Centre* (London: Pen and Sword, 2001).

Kahn, David, *Hitler's Spies: German Military Intelligence in World War II* (New York: First Da Capo Press, 2000).

Longmate, Norman, *Island Fortress* (London: Huchinson, 1991).

Masterman, J. C., *The Double-Cross System* (Yale: Yale University Press, 1972).

Macintyre, Ben, *Operation Mincemeat* (London: Bloomsbury, 2010).

McLachan, Donald, *Room 39: Naval Intelligence in Action, 1939–45* (London: Weidenfeld and Nicolson, 1968).

Montagu, Ewen, *The Man Who Never Was* (Philadelphia: Lippincott, 1954).

Morgan, Kenneth O., *Rebirth of a Nation: Wales, 1880–1980* (Oxford: Oxford University Press, 1981).

Nicolas, Michel, *Historie du Mouvement Breton* (Paris: Syros, 1982)

O'Donoghue, David, *Hitler's Irish Voices: the Story of German Radio's Wartime Irish Service* (Belfast: Beyond the Pale Publications, 1998).

Orwell, Sonia and Angus, Ian (eds), *The Collective Essays, Journalism and Letters of George Orwell* (New York: Harcourt Brace Jovanovich, 1968)

Ritter, Nikolaus, *Deckname Dr Rantzau: Die Aufzeichnungen des Nikolaus Ritter, offizer im geheimen nachrichtendienst* (Hamburg: Hoffman und Campe, 1972).

Rowland, Peter, *Lloyd George* (London: Barrie and Jenkins, 1975).

Wark, Wesley, 'In Never-Never Land? The British Archives on Intelligence', *Historical Journal*, 35, 1 (1992), 196–203.

Watt, Donald Cameron, *How War Came* (London: Heinemann, 1989).

West, Nigel and Roberts, Madoc, *Snow: The Double Life of a World War II Spy* (London: Biteback Publishing, 2011).

Wilmot, Chester, *The Struggle for Europe* (London: Collins, 1971).

Wilson, Derek, *Rothschild: a Story of Wealth and Power* (London: Andre Deutsch, 1988).

INDEX

Aberaeron 77

Abwehr, the 5, 6, 8, 9, 10, 11, 12, 13, 14, 15, 16, 17, 18, 19, 20–1, 22, 23, 27, 30, 35, 36, 37, 38, 41–2, 44, 45, 47, 53, 62, 71, 73, 76, 77, 78, 79, 80, 81, 82, 83, 84, 86, 87–8, 90, 91, 93, 94, 95, 96, 98, 99, 102, 103, 104, 105, 109, 110, 116, 122, 125, 126, 128, 129, 130, 131, 134, 136, 138, 139–40, 144, 152–3, 154, 157, 164, 165, 166, 168, 169–70, 171–2, 173, 175, 179, 180, 182, 185, 189, 192–3, 194, 196, 197, 198, 199, 200, 202, 203, 205, 207, 208, 209, 210, 214, 216, 217–18, 219, 225, 226

Abwehr *Diaries* 8, 45

Action 48

Addlestone 214

Adelaide 200

Admiralty 16, 19

Aerodromes today – bombing tomorrow 101

Air Intelligence 126

Air Ministry 66, 165

Alcazar de Velasco, Don Angel (Angel; Captain; Guillermo)

94–5, 105, 115, 119, 163, 164, 169–70, 171, 173, 174–5, 176, 177, 179, 180, 186, 187, 193, 194, 203, 207, 209, 210

Aldington 139

Algiers 103

aliens 3, 29, 47, 48–50, 51, 54, 156, 213, 226

Allies, the 5, 7, 16–17, 85, 90, 123, 129, 190, 192

Alsace-Lorraine 103

Amsterdam 80

Anderson, Sir John 48–9, 56

Angel, *see* Alcazar de Velasco, Don Angel

Anglesey 47

Anglo-Irish Trade Agreement (1938) 85

Anglo-Irish war 14

Ankara 79

anti-Semitism 1, 61, 108

Anton, Natasha 165, 169

Antwerp 36–7, 38, 39, 41, 73, 74, 76, 77, 88, 99, 126, 158, 164

ap Owen, Owen 78

Arcadia night club (Lisbon) 136, 137, 142, 143

Ardennes, the 28, 76

Ark Royal 184

Athenaeum Court (London) 94, 95, 96, 97, 98, 106, 115, 116, 119, 167
Attlee, Clement 3
Audierne 89
Australia 49, 104, 200, 205
Austria 3, 5, 15, 35–6
Axis powers 18, 95, 106, 193, 225
Azores, the 120, 167

B Branch (MI5) 9, 19, 21, 44, 69, 80, 82, 83, 140
Bachelors' Club (London) 97, 164, 173, 184, 185, 197, 206, 207
Bade, Jean Louise 130, 131, 134, 135, 158, 159, 218
Bade, Lily 14, 17, 20, 21, 22, 23, 32, 33, 42, 129, 130, 133, 134, 135, 142, 149, 151, 155, 158, 159–60, 208, 214, 215, 217, 218
Baldwin, Stanley 63–4
Balearic Islands 106
Balloon, agent 139
Bangor 2, 116
Bangor Normal College 224
Baptist Church 10
Barcelona 196
Barnegat Bay (New Jersey) 205
Barra, Colonel Alfonso 187–8
Battle of Britain 54, 83, 95, 103, 111, 218
BBC 61, 62, 63, 106
Bebb, Ambrose 224–5
Bedford, duke of 112
Belfast 73, 182, 183
Belgium 9, 14, 15, 27, 28, 32, 33, 35–6, 42, 53, 65, 73, 76, 81, 93, 94, 168, 225
Belgrade 51
Berchtesgaden 11

Berehaven 85
Berlin 4, 20, 33, 36, 48, 104, 129, 137, 142, 177, 184, 196, 199, 201, 214
Berliner Hof Hotel 17
Bevin, Ernest 190
Bezen Perrot 25
BIA, see Double-Cross System, the
Big Ben 96
Biggin Hill 161
Birmingham 5, 107, 110
Biscuit, see McCarthy, Sam
Black Mountains 38
Blackshirts, see British Union of Fascists
Blaenclydach 221
Blenheim Palace 83
Bletchley Park, see Government Code and Cipher School (Bletchley Park)
blitz, the 54, 95–6, 110, 117, 121–2
Blohm and Voss 137
Blue Jackets (BJs) 171
Blue Star Line 205
Blunt, Anthony 51, 72, 82, 83
Bond, James 17, 208
Bonnington Hotel 31, 33
Boon, Johan Dirk 214
Bormann, Martin 177
Borras (Wrexham) 116–17
Boy Scouts 95
Brasser, Major 36, 37, 38, 41
Brazil 91, 177, 199, 200, 201, 202, 203, 208, 217
Brecon 188
Brest 45, 87, 88, 89, 90
Breton language 5, 225
Breton nationalism 5, 69, 225

Bridgend 32, 105, 191
Bristol 14, 38, 52, 89, 105, 110, 128, 129, 141, 194
Bristol Aircraft Factory 105
Bristol Channel 37, 84, 91, 110, 158, 163, 188, 199
Britain 1, 5, 6, 9, 15, 16, 19, 20, 22, 24, 27, 28, 41, 45, 49, 50, 53, 58, 60, 61, 66, 78, 81, 83, 85, 86, 87, 90, 93, 94, 95, 111, 112, 114, 119, 122, 132, 133, 134, 139, 157, 177, 180, 182, 187, 190, 192, 193, 200, 202, 205, 206, 208, 219, 221, 225
British Army 53, 125, 175; *see also* British Expeditionary Force
British Communist Party 16, 48, 69
British Council 95, 98
British Embassy (Belgrade) 51
British Embassy (Lisbon) 131, 136, 141
British Empire 48, 55–6
British Expeditionary Force 24, 40, 52; *see also* British Army
British Intelligence Service 5, 14, 18, 22, 23, 130, 135, 145, 148, 150, 152, 153; *see also* MI5; MI6
British Union of Fascists (BUF) 18, 36, 48, 49, 50, 56, 81, 226
Briton Ferry 24
Brittany 69, 87, 89, 225
Brooman-White, Richard 69, 163, 164, 172, 173
Brugada, embassy official 194, 196
Brussels 10, 13, 15, 17, 24, 28, 31, 35, 36, 41, 42, 44, 65, 71, 76, 83, 94, 96, 158
Buckingham Palace 85, 96
Buenos Aires 179, 201

Burgess, Guy 51, 69, 72, 82, 83
Burt, Major L. J. 216
Burton, Maurice 23, 33
Bute Street (Cardiff) 163

Cabinet Office 50
Caernarfon 59
Cairo Gang 14
Calvo, Luis 163–4, 165–9, 170–1, 172, 173, 174–7, 179–80, 182, 183–4, 186–7, 188, 189–90, 192, 193, 194, 195, 196, 197–8, 203, 207, 209, 210, 219
Camberley 104
Cambridge 86, 87
Cambridge Spy Ring 19, 51, 69
Camp 020 (Ham) 87, 90, 114, 194–6, 197
Can Wales Afford Self-Government? 77
Canada 13, 14, 49, 52, 54, 104, 140, 155, 202
Canadian Star 205, 206
Canaris, Admiral Wilhelm 12, 18, 170
Canon Row Police Station 90
Cape Farewell 206
Cape of Good Hope 182
Capel Celyn 1
Cardiff 13, 52, 57, 58, 74, 104, 110, 163, 185, 210
Cardiff Central Market 57
Cardiff Constabulary 49
Cardiff Rural District Council 52
Cardiganshire 74
Carmarthen 57
Caroli, Goesta (Summer) 86–7, 131
Castle Hill (Milford Haven) 188
Castle Hotel (Richmond) 32

Cato, *see* Pujol, Juan
Celery, *see* Dicketts, Walter
Celtic Movements section 69,
    163–4, 203
Chamberlain, Neville 20, 28, 47,
    53, 54–5, 68, 106, 113, 117, 225
Channel Islands 91, 133, 143, 153
Charlie, *see* Kiener, Charlie
Chesham Street (London) 164,
    166, 173, 185
China 170, 204
Christ College, Oxford 7
Christian Peace Movement 61
Christiansen, Nils Christian,
    see Starziczny, Josef
Churchill, Winston 7, 12, 15, 16,
    50, 53, 54, 60, 63, 66, 68, 72, 82,
    83, 84, 85, 95, 111, 112, 113–14,
    118, 144, 171, 190, 191, 192,
    204, 224
Churchill tanks 175
City of Sydney 80
Clydach 14, 58
Coastal Command 188
Cold War 7
Colwyn Bay 159
Combe Florey 67
Combined Services Detailed
    Interrogation Centre (Bad
    Nenndorf) 217
Communism 11, 18, 78, 106, 179;
    see also British Communist
    Party
Congregational Union of England
    and Wales 55
conscientious objection 1, 3, 55,
    56–9, 74–5, 77, 100, 221, 223,
    224, 226
Conservative Party 204
Cooper, Alfred Duff 7, 60, 63

Copacabana (Rio de Janeiro) 200
Corwen 59
Cottenham, Mark Everard Pepys,
    earl of 30, 31, 32, 71–2
Coventry 110
Cowgill, Felix 82, 127
Craven Hill (Paddington) 127
Cray reservoir 120
Cressado, the 128, 134, 135
Criccieth 113
Croke Park massacre 14
Crosstown Cemetery (Wexford)
    217
Croydon 158
Cumberland Hotel (London) 105,
    106, 128, 167
Cummings, A. J. 11
Curaçao 206
Cussen, Lieutenant Colonel 216
Cuxhaven 21
Czechoslovakia 5, 15, 64, 225–6

Daily Express 11, 106, 108, 114, 120
Daily Telegraph 202
Daily Worker 69
Dale (Pembrokeshire) 188
Daniel, Professor J. E. 4
Dartmoor 49, 156, 160, 161, 210,
    213, 214, 215, 217, 218
Davies, George Maitland Lloyd
    56–7
D-Day 47, 196, 214
de Valera, Eamon 5, 85, 225
Deal 51
Deeker, de, agent 91
Defence Regulation 18B 47, 69,
    74, 153, 156, 213, 226
Defence Regulations 21, 78, 101,
    183
Denbigh 2

Denmark 52
Denton 86
Deutsche Arbeitsfront 12
devolution 222
Dicketts, Kaye 129, 143, 149, 158, 159–60
Dicketts, Walter (Celery; Walter Dunkler) 126–7, 128, 129, 131, 132, 133–8, 141–50, 153, 155–6, 161–2
Director of Naval Intelligence (DNR) 98
Director of RAF Intelligence (DOI) 98
Dobler (Duarte), agent 130, 132, 133, 134, 137, 145, 155
Doctor, the, *see* Rantzau, Dr
Documents on German Foreign Policy 12
Doenitz, Admiral Karl 181–2
Dolphin Square, Pimlico 30, 31, 71
Donaldson, Arthur 69
Dopie, dancer 142
Dorchester Hotel (London) 176
Dot, the 199–200
Double-Cross System, the (BIA) 6–7, 9, 22, 23, 28, 29, 30, 42, 69, 75, 77, 78, 79, 80, 81, 82, 87, 91, 93, 103, 105, 110, 114–15, 116, 122, 123, 126–7, 128, 138, 141, 150, 153, 161, 162, 164, 170, 172, 175, 177, 179, 182, 184, 189, 192, 193, 194, 196, 197–8, 202, 203, 208, 210, 217, 218, 219
Double-Cross System, The (Masterman) 7–8
Douglas-Home, Sir Alec 7–8
Dover 20, 139

Duarte, *see* Dobler
Dublin 14, 73, 85, 90, 214
Dubrovnik 139
Dunkirk 52, 53, 54, 83, 125, 175

Easter Rising (1916) 213
Eden, Anthony 16
Edward VIII 64, 94
EFE 95
Egypt 103
Eire 61–2, 85, 174, 181; *see also* Ireland
Elizabeth, Princess 54, 95
Elizabeth, Queen 54, 95
Emergency Powers (Defence) Act 47
England 3, 4, 12, 38, 40, 48, 50, 56, 59, 60, 75, 84, 86, 89, 99, 100, 101, 117, 118, 122, 136, 137, 144, 168, 174, 221, 225
Enigma machine 6, 79
Erikson, Vera 91
Estoril 132, 145
evacuees 52, 101
Evans, Gwynfor 3, 56, 58, 223, 224
Evans, R. J. 59
Evertsen, Cornelius 87, 89, 90–1

Fairey Engineering 39
Fairwood Common (Swansea) 188
Falangist Party 94, 95, 120, 163, 207
Farago, Ladislas 8
Farnborough 16, 36, 39
Fascism 78, 214, 224
Fastnet Rock 90
FBI 66, 199–200
Fellner, FBI agent 165
Ferrett, Jessie, *see* Owens, Jessie

Fifth Columnists 5, 44, 47, 48, 49, 50, 53, 61, 62, 64–5, 68, 74, 77, 226
Finney, Captain 159, 160
First World War 4, 10, 11, 55, 61, 73, 80, 96, 105, 126, 223, 224
Firth of Forth 51
Fishguard 90, 91, 188
Flemish nationalism 42
Flushing 17, 87
Fly, The 217
Folkestone 33, 35, 44, 139
Forbach 49
Ford, Major 104
Foreign Office 51, 95, 106, 115, 120, 164, 180, 196, 201
Foyer, Alfred 67, 68
France 5, 15, 40, 49, 51, 52, 53, 54, 57, 64, 66, 83, 87, 88, 89, 90, 93, 103–4, 172, 191, 225
Franco, General Francisco 1, 47–8, 69, 88, 95, 106, 163, 170, 175, 186, 193
Frederico, agent 116, 172, 203
Free French Forces 104
French Morocco 103–4

Game of Foxes, The (Farago) 8
Garbo, *see* Pujol, Juan
Garda, the 5, 84, 225
Gartner, Dieter 84–5, 86
general election (1945) 204
General Post Office (GPO) 116
Geneva Convention 195
George VI, King 54, 78, 95
George, William 58
German Embassy (Lisbon) 136, 210
German Embassy (London) 107
German Embassy (Madrid) 121

German High Command 16–17, 47, 53, 60, 78, 79, 123, 182, 183, 196, 225
German Military Intelligence, *see* Abwehr, the
German nationalism 222–3
Germany 3, 4, 5, 6, 7, 9, 11, 14, 15, 16, 21, 37, 38, 40, 41, 52, 53, 54, 56, 58, 59, 60, 64, 68, 85, 89, 94, 99, 103, 104, 108, 110, 111, 112, 128, 133, 134, 135, 136, 137, 142, 144, 145, 147, 148, 155, 159, 161, 168, 175, 200, 203, 218, 221, 222, 225, 226
Gestapo, the 49, 201
'GHQ Corps and Divisional Signs' 175–6
Gibraltar 52, 168, 170, 181, 182, 183, 184
Girl Guides 51
Glamorgan 52
Glamorgan Assizes 221
Glasgow 38, 98
Gloucester 190
Glynneath 188
Glynrhonwy Isaf Slate Quarry 116, 117
Goebbels, Joseph 60, 61, 137
Goering, Hermann 53, 148, 170
Goodrich 5
Government Code and Cipher School (Bletchley Park) 6, 79, 171
Government Communications Headquarters (GCHQ) 79
Gravesend 135
Great Depression 4, 11
Greece 7, 103, 111, 123
Griffith-Jones, Revd Dr E. 55
Griffiths, James 63

Grimsby 125, 126
Grosvenor Court (Morden) 21
Guernsey 39
Guggenberger, Lieutenant 184
Gwyer, John 128, 129, 218–19

Halifax, Lord 106
Hamburg 8, 12, 13, 15, 16, 17,
    19–20, 22, 23, 24–5, 28, 33, 37,
    38, 41, 62, 71, 73, 76, 79, 84, 86,
    126, 127, 129, 132, 134, 136,
    137, 139, 143, 144, 161, 194,
    199, 208
Hampstead 196
Hanover 217
Harley Street (London) 151
Harris, Mrs 105–6
Harris, Tommy (Tomas) 196
Harwich 17
Havana 87
Hawarden 116
Hawkinge 139
Hechevarria, Pedro 87, 88–9, 90,
    91, 93, 98, 122
Heddychwyr Cymru 56, 223
Henderson, W. E. B. 59
Hendon 16, 39
Hess, Rudolf 170–1, 174–5
High Holborn (London) 67
High Wycombe 86
Hinchley-Cooke, Col. Edward
    24–5
Hinxton 87
Hitler, Adolf 1, 2, 11–12, 16–17,
    18, 19, 20, 21, 28, 44, 47, 52, 53,
    54, 55, 56, 60, 64, 65, 95, 96, 99,
    103, 106, 107, 108, 112, 113,
    120, 139, 158, 160, 170, 171,
    172, 177, 181, 185, 196, 218,
    221, 224, 225, 226

Holland 14, 41, 64–5, 66, 67, 81,
    214; see also Netherlands, the
Home Defence (Security)
    Executive 68, 175, 176, 192
Home Guard (Local Defence
    Volunteers) 53, 65, 158
Home Office 24, 161, 196, 214, 221
Home Office Directorate of
    Intelligence 69
Hoover, J. Edgar 139
Hore-Belisha, Leslie 112–13
Horrabin, Frank 112
Horsfall, Jock 128
Hotel Vier Jahreszeiten
    (Hamburg) 15
How Green Was My Valley
    (Llewellyn) 19
Hullavington 104
Hungary 111
Hussein, Obed 84, 86
Hyde Park 95, 95, 167, 169, 175
Hyde Park Hotel (London) 50

If the INVADER comes 65
Ilford 158
Iliffe, Lord 50
Immigration Service 27
Imperial Hotel (Russell Square)
    169, 170
Imperial House 164–5, 174, 187,
    216
internment 3, 31, 47, 48–50, 69,
    88, 114, 135, 153, 156, 160, 161,
    213, 214, 217, 226
IRA 5, 14, 45, 47, 50, 53, 81, 84,
    86, 221, 225
Ireland 5, 11, 14, 18, 47, 50, 84,
    85–6, 90, 103, 114, 119, 193–4,
    206, 208, 213, 214, 225; see also
    Eire

Irish nationalism 5, 11, 14, 47, 77, 102, 225
Ironside, General Sir Edmund 53, 54
Isle of Man 49, 160, 161, 213, 214, 215
Isle of Wight 51, 60, 107, 110
ISOS messages 171–2
Italian nationalism 223
Italy 3, 6, 103, 104, 106, 111, 181

Jackson, William (Sweet William) 29, 197
Jaegar, de, agent 27
Jamaica 49
Japan 95, 163, 171, 190, 191, 204
Japanese Embassy (Madrid) 177
Japanese nationalism 223
Jersey 39
Jews 35–6, 41, 221, 224
Johnny, *see* Owens, Arthur Graham
Joint Intelligence Committee (JIC) 49, 82, 103
Jones, Captain Charles James Whatley 206
Jones, G. 59
Jones, George H. 63
Jones, Revd Iorwerth 77
Jones, Revd J. D. 56
Jones, Sir Thomas Artemus 58
Josephine 87, 89, 90
Joyce, William (Lord Haw-Haw) 60–1

Kell, Admiral Vernon 68
Kiener, 'Charlie' 42, 127, 130, 138, 154, 156, 161
Kiener, Hans 42
Kingston-upon-Thames 23, 28, 32, 75, 83, 126, 131

Kirkness 79
Knightsbridge Underground Station 167
Kraft, Mathilde 44–5
Krag, Peter Marcussen 87
Kriegsmarine 201
Kriegsorganisationen (KO; Madrid) 169–70
Kruger, Lisa 36
Kupferreder (Hamburg) 19–20

Labour Party 4, 63, 83, 121, 203–4, 225
Landore 32, 191
Land's End 119
Langland Bay 77
Latchmere 194–5
Le Touquet 87
Leeds 66
Lehrer, V-Mann 45
Lewis, Saunders 1–3, 4, 12, 100–1, 222, 223, 224
Ley, Dr Robert 12
Liberal Party 225
Liddell, Guy 8, 19, 21, 44, 48, 51, 60, 69, 80, 82, 83, 85, 97–8, 112–13, 114, 127, 132, 140, 152, 153, 163, 164, 194
Linney Head (Castlemartin) 24
Lisbon 27, 126, 127, 128, 129, 130, 131, 133, 134, 136, 139, 140, 141, 142, 143, 145, 148, 150, 153, 155, 158, 161, 179, 185, 202, 208, 209, 210, 216, 217, 218
'Little Berlin' (Whitchurch) 49
Liverpool 1, 38, 40, 42, 90, 110, 119, 167, 205, 206
Llanberis 116
Llandudno Junction 117

Llanstephan 158
Llewellyn, Richard 19
Lloyd George, David 11–12, 41, 58, 111–14, 224, 225
Llŷn Peninsula 1, 12, 101, 222, 224
Local Defence Volunteers, see Home Guard
Logbook of Counter-Intelligence (Section II) 45
London 4, 5, 14, 17, 23, 45, 47, 71, 83, 95–6, 110, 117, 163, 164, 167, 179, 180, 185, 194, 206, 209, 217
London Conscientious Objectors Tribunal 59
London Gazette 206
London Welsh, the 56
Lottie, dancer 142, 143
Lough Swilly 85
Low Countries, the 53
Lowndes Mews (London) 166, 167, 186
Luftwaffe, the 21, 23, 36, 51, 52, 53, 83, 95–6, 104, 105, 110, 111, 117, 121, 139, 165, 170, 189, 205, 206, 213
Luxembourg 53
Lyminge 139

McCarthy, Sam (Biscuit) 77, 86, 125–6, 148, 154, 161
MacDonald, Ramsay 117
Maclean, Donald 51, 72
Madrid 45, 48, 94, 96, 97, 99, 106, 107, 108, 109, 110, 115, 116, 119, 120, 121, 136, 164, 166, 167, 168, 169, 172, 177, 180, 185, 186, 187, 188, 193, 194, 196, 198, 209, 218

Maginot Line 24, 52
Malay Peninsula 190
Malaya 184
Malta 181, 182–3, 184
Malta Convoy operation 179, 181, 182–4
Man Who Never Was, The (Montagu) 7
Manchester 5, 38, 42
Mannesmann Tube Works (Landore) 191
Margaret, Princess 54, 95
Margarete, IRA member 45
Margate 60, 107, 110
Marlborough public house (Kingston-upon-Thames) 126–7
Marriott, John 97, 129, 140, 141–4, 152, 158–9, 210, 211, 215
Mars Italian Restaurant (Soho) 161
Martin, Major William 123
Masterman, John (JC) 7–8, 80–1, 91, 93, 97, 98, 122, 127, 128, 140, 148, 150, 151, 152, 154, 155, 156, 161, 162, 164, 171–3, 180, 184–5, 187, 192, 193, 194, 196, 202, 213, 218, 219
Mauritius 80
Mazzini, Giuseppe 122
Mediterranean, the 52, 181, 182, 183, 184
Mercader, Louis de 76, 83, 94, 209
Merthyr 2, 64, 74, 158
Meteorological Office 104
Metropole Hotel (Brussels) 15
Metropole Hotel (Lisbon) 130, 134
Metropole Hotel (Swansea) 71, 78
Mexico City 199

MI5 5–8, 9–10, 11, 13, 14, 16, 19, 20, 21, 22, 23, 27, 28, 30, 32, 33, 37, 42, 47, 48, 49, 50–1, 53, 56, 60, 61, 62, 64, 65, 66, 67, 68–9, 72, 74, 75, 76, 78–9, 80, 81, 82, 83, 93, 94, 95, 97, 98, 99, 104, 108, 112, 114, 115, 120, 121, 126, 127, 128, 129, 130, 131, 132, 133, 134, 138, 139–40, 141, 144, 148, 150, 151, 153, 155, 156, 159, 160, 161–2, 163, 164, 165, 169, 179, 181, 193, 195, 197, 201, 202–3, 204, 207, 208, 210, 213, 214, 215, 216, 217, 218–9, 226; controller (DG) 98
MI6 6, 8, 15, 19, 53–4, 61, 67, 69, 82, 127, 134, 140, 161–2, 171, 193, 208
Michael, Glyndwr 123
Midland Miners' Association 63
Miel 21
Milford Haven 24, 121, 188, 197
Military Foot Police (Redcaps) 10
Military Intelligence 82
Military Service Act 57, 59
Mills, Cyril B. 66–7
Mills, Mr 160
Milton Airfield (Pembroke Dock) 188
Ministry of Home Security 52
Ministry of Information 7, 60, 62, 63, 64, 65, 111, 114
Minotaur 185
Mola, Emilio 48
Monmouthshire 52
Montagu, Ewen 7
Morrison, Herbert 83–4
Morriston 10
Mosley, Sir Oswald 18, 31, 36, 48, 56, 226

Mount Pleasant (Swansea) 10, 44, 73, 84, 91, 121, 208
Mumbles 14
Munich Agreement (1938) 15
Munro, MI5 officer 71
Mussolini, Benito 1, 19, 59
Myner, R. 17, 21, 42

Naples 206
National Archives (Washington) 157
National Eisteddfod (Denbigh, 1939) 2
National Government 63–4, 111
National Intelligence Division (NID) 82
National Service (Armed Forces) Act (1939) 59
National Socialist Party (Nazis) 1, 2, 5–6, 12, 13, 15, 16, 17, 18, 36, 48–9, 50, 56, 58, 64–5, 71, 81, 94, 139, 179, 203, 204, 221, 222, 223, 226
Natural History (Pliny) 18
Nazis, see National Socialist Party
Netherlands, the 28, 53, 225; see also Holland
neutrality 1, 2, 4, 28, 36, 55, 74, 222, 224
New British Broadcasting Service (NBBS) 60–3, 77
New York 66, 214
New Zealand 104, 205
Newfoundland 49
Newport 27, 74, 110
Newport and South Wales Tube Company 191
Newquay (Cornwall) 66
News Chronicle 11
Newtown 121

Nice 103
Nieuw Amsterdam 33
No More War Movement 56
nonconformity 55–6, 57, 77
Norden Bombsight 12
Norfolk 54
Normandy 17, 123, 139, 196
North Africa 54, 181
North American Welsh
    Societies 52
North Atlantic convoys 19, 52,
    61, 85, 119, 122, 181, 183
Northern Ireland 73
Norway 52, 64, 225
Nuremburg 42

Ocean Valour 205, 206
O'Donovan, Jim 5
Official Secrets Act 6, 216
Oliveira Peixoto, Ondina Batista
    de 200, 201
Operation Barbarossa 160
Operation Crowhurst (Ginger)
    11, 13, 24, 28, 30, 31, 32, 33,
    35, 44
Operation Green 47
Operation Heartbreak (Cooper) 7
Operation Mincemeat 7, 123
Operation Overlord 16–27, 123,
    139, 196
Operation Sea Lion 47, 60, 160
Operational Intelligence Centre
    (Admiralty) 19
'Operations against England . . .'
    45
Orwell, George 224   94, 119
Ostend 35, 44
Owens, Arthur Graham (Snow;
    Johnny; Kettering; Ketroch)
    5, 6, 7, 8, 13–17, 18, 19, 20–5,

27, 28, 30, 31–3, 35–7, 38–9, 41,
    42–3, 44, 45, 47, 68, 71, 73–4,
    75, 77–8, 79, 80, 81, 83, 84,
    86–7, 91, 93, 94, 98, 108, 115,
    119, 125–6, 127, 128–9, 130–8,
    139–58, 159, 160, 161, 162, 164,
    171, 176, 177, 180, 185, 202,
    203, 208, 210, 213–19, 221,
    222, 226
Owens, Jessie (née Ferrett) 14, 17,
    20, 79, 160
Owens, Patricia 14, 20, 217
Owens, Robert 14, 20, 158,
    159–61, 214–15, 217
Owens Battery Equipment 14
Oxford 66
Oxwich Bay 24, 32, 38, 77, 122,
    170, 172

Pablo, agent 116, 172, 193, 203
pacificism 1, 4, 50, 55, 56, 61, 74,
    99, 100, 101, 102, 221, 222,
    223–4, 225
Paddington 165
Palestine 221
Pall Mall 83
Palmer's Dry Dock (Swansea) 192
Paris 88, 142
Parliament, Houses of 96
Parsley, consul 163
Pas de Calais 17, 123, 139, 196
Pasoz-Diaz, Nicholas 87, 88–90,
    91, 93, 98, 122
Peace Pledge Union (PPU) 50, 56,
    57, 58, 62, 75, 223
Pearl Harbor 139, 190
Peel, Col. 14–15
Peel (Isle of Man) 214
Pembrey 105, 188
Pembroke Dock 24, 188

Pembrokeshire 5, 24, 74, 90, 188
Penarth 57
Penmaen (Oxwich Bay) 24, 77
Penrhos airfield 116, 117
Penyberth, RAF Bombing School
    1, 12, 100, 101, 222, 224
People's War, the 4, 55, 63, 64;
    see also Second World War
Peppermint, agent 29
Pétain, Marshal Philipe 114
Petrie, Sir David 68–9, 82, 114,
    159–60, 172, 194, 214–15, 216
Peveril Internment Camp 214
Philby, Kim 19, 51, 69, 72
Phoney War 47, 52, 56, 225
Pieper, Conrad 15
Plaid Cymru 1, 2–4, 9, 27, 28, 29,
    30, 37, 55, 56, 58, 74, 75, 77, 78,
    97, 99–100, 101–2, 118, 122,
    169, 222, 223, 224–5
Plain English Code Section 67
Plan IV 164, 165, 168–9, 170
Pliny the Elder 18
Poland 28, 42, 64, 111
Police Pensions Act (1921) 74
Pontardawe 13, 77
Popov, Dusko (Tricycle) 29, 139,
    180, 194
Port Talbot 217
Port Tennant (Swansea) 188
Portsmouth 158
Portugal 10, 27, 69, 94, 110, 120,
    126, 128, 142, 147, 170, 202
Powell Duffryn Steel and Iron
    Company 158
Pozo, Miguel Piernavieja del 94,
    95, 96–7, 98, 102, 104, 105–8,
    109–10, 111, 114–16, 119,
    120–1, 122, 164, 166–8, 169,
    207, 209, 210

Price, Vincent 217
Prison Act 78
Pugh, Sir Arthur 59
Pujol, Juan (Cato; Garbo) 16–17,
    29, 196, 205

Quantocks, the 84
Queen Mary 200–1
Queenie, cafe owner 163
Queen's Hotel (Manchester) 42
Queenstown 85

radar 16, 139, 157, 217
Radio Caledonia 61
Radio National 61
Radio Security Service 69, 79, 177
RAF 39, 50, 66, 79, 86, 95, 104,
    111, 127, 135, 136, 138, 139,
    157, 158, 182–3, 204, 217
RAF Valley 116
Rainbow, agent 180
Rantzau, Dr (Nikolaus Ritter) 8,
    12–13, 15–16, 17, 18, 20, 21,
    22, 24, 27, 28, 30, 31, 32, 36, 37,
    38, 39, 42, 44, 45, 71, 73, 75, 76,
    77, 81, 86, 87, 91, 94, 96, 98, 99,
    105, 125, 126, 127, 128, 129,
    130–2, 133, 134–5, 136, 137,
    138, 139, 140, 141, 142, 143,
    144, 145, 146, 147, 148, 149,
    150, 152–3, 154, 155–6, 157,
    158, 164, 172, 180, 185, 202,
    207, 208, 216, 217–18, 219
Rantzau, Frau 13, 130
Reali, Elpidio 200–1
Reed, MI5 officer 159
Reform Club 83
Reynard, Paul 114
Rhineland, the 15
Rhondda, the 117

Rhosneigr 116
Ribbentrop, Joachim von 12
Richard Thomas and Baldwins 121
Ridder, Frau de 42, 72, 73, 74, 75–6, 93, 122, 198, 207, 208–10, 211
Rio de Janeiro 161, 199, 200
Ritter, Nikolaus, *see* Rantzau, Dr
Ritz Hotel (London) 186
Robertson, Major T. A. (TAR) 6, 22, 28–9, 31, 42, 71, 72, 73, 77, 80, 81, 84, 93, 94, 97, 98, 102–3, 104–5, 108, 117, 121, 122, 125, 127, 128, 129, 133, 138, 139, 140, 141, 148, 151, 152, 153–4, 155, 160–1, 164, 165, 170, 172, 173, 179, 180, 184, 185, 187, 192, 196, 197, 198, 202–3, 204, 206–7, 208, 210, 211, 213, 214–16, 217, 219
Robles, Silvio Ruiz 87, 88–9, 90, 91, 93, 98, 122
Roch (Pembrokeshire) 188
Rockefeller Center (New York) 194
Rolf, W. N. 126
Romania 103
Rommel, Field Marshal Erwin 181
Roosevelt, President F. D. 192
Rothschild, Victor, Baron (R) 72, 73, 74, 75, 94, 120, 132, 141, 171, 172, 173
Rotterdam 21, 33
Royal Artillery 116, 117
Royal Chelsea Hospital 218
Royal Irish Constabulary 14
Royal Naval Armaments Depot 116
Royal Navy 53, 66, 125, 158, 181

Royal Navy Air Arm 111
Royal Oak 68
Royal Ordnance factories 105, 107, 191
Royal Tank Regiment 175
Royal Woolwich Arsenal 105
Russia 21, 41, 172, 190; *see also* Soviet Union
Ruth, dancer 142–3

Sadie, dancer 142
St Athan 21, 66, 158, 188
St Austell 66
St Brides Bay 90
St James's Park 83
Samuel, Wynne 74, 75, 77, 122
Sandhurst 104
Santiago (Cuba) 87
Santos (Brazil) 199, 200
Sao Paulo (Brazil) 199, 200
Savoy Hotel (Brussels) 30, 35, 36
Savoy Hotel (London) 72, 139
Scapa Flow 68
Scheveningen 67
Schimmler, Leutnant 88
Schmidt, Wulf (Harry Wiliamson; Tate) 29, 138–9, 180, 195, 203
Schneiderwind, Korvettencapitaen 88
Scotland 11, 56, 58, 60, 69, 170, 174–5
Scottish National Party 69
Scottish nationalism 11, 61, 69, 171
Second World War 1–7, 8, 9, 10, 47, 54, 80, 157, 181, 190, 204, 208, 221; *see also* People's War
Section V (MI6) 82
Segundo, porter 99, 106, 107, 115, 164, 167, 186, 196, 198

Selfridges 44–5
Sessler, agent 161
Shanghai 79
Short Bros 39
Sicily 7, 123
Simon, Walter 16
Singapore 190, 191
Sinn Féin 217
Skewen 21, 158
Skibereen 84
Smalls lighthouse 90
Snow, see Owens, Arthur Graham
Societé de Consignation et
    Affrètement 126
Society of Friends 58
Soho 14, 21
Southampton 52, 158, 205, 206
Soviet Union 19, 51, 60, 72, 82,
    160, 164; see also Russia
Spain 18, 19, 27, 52, 69, 88, 94, 95,
    97, 98, 103, 106, 163, 167, 168,
    169, 175, 176, 179, 180, 184,
    193, 209
Spanish Civil War 47–8, 69, 88,
    94, 170
Spanish Club 120, 169
Spanish Diplomatic Bag 99, 108,
    109, 114–15, 116, 121, 122, 156,
    164, 169, 170, 172, 180, 182,
    192–3, 194, 205, 207
Spanish Embassy (London) 94,
    95, 98, 99, 106, 107, 108, 114,
    115, 119, 156, 163, 164, 166,
    167, 170, 173, 176, 179, 186,
    187–8, 193, 194, 196, 197, 198,
    206
Spanish Secret Service (Sirene)
    170
Special Branch 20–1, 22, 50, 84,
    126, 155, 161, 187, 188, 214

Speke 40, 42
Stafford, prison 156, 213, 214
Stalin, Marshal Joseph 189, 192
Stalingrad 189
Starziczny, Josef (Lucas) 91,
    199–203, 208
Steigman, Frances (Miss Angel)
    66–7
Stephens, Lieutenant-Colonel
    Robin 194–5, 196, 197
Stephenson, Captain William 194
Stewart, Samuel 73–4
Stormy Down 188
Stowting 139
Strachey, Oliver 79
Strasburg 157
Sudetenland, the 5, 15, 56
'Sullivan' 165, 168, 175–6, 185,
    186, 187
Sullivan-type documents 171,
    172, 173, 174, 175, 176–7;
    see also Plan IV
Summer, see Caroli, Goesta
Sunbeam Racing Car team 30
Sunday Pictorial 112
Sunderland 64
Sunderland Flying Boat base
    (Pembroke Dock) 188
Suñer, Ramón Serrano 95, 115,
    175
Surbiton 17
Swansea 17, 21, 28, 30, 31, 44, 50,
    71, 74–5, 77, 78, 84, 86, 87, 88,
    91, 93, 98, 108, 110, 120, 121–2,
    176, 179, 185, 187, 197, 199,
    201–2, 204, 206, 210, 226
Swansea Bay 10, 87, 89, 90
Swansea Constabulary 9, 11, 29
Swansea Docks 27, 158, 182, 205,
    206

Swansea Valley 57
Sweden 86, 170
Sweet William, *see* Jackson,
  William
Swinton, Lord 53–4, 68
Switzerland 170

Taranto 111
Tarifa 123
Tate, *see* Schmidt, Wulf
Tate, Harry 139
Tazelaar, Peter (Hans) 67
Thames, the 60, 96
Thomas, Winifred Amelia, *see*
  Williams, Winifred Amelia
Times 64, 96
Timoshenko, Marshal Semyon 189
Tokyo 177
Tolten 205–6
Tonfanau 116, 117
Toronto 14, 33
Tower Bridge 96
Trafalgar Square 30
Trautman, Major Werner 17, 19,
  208
Treachery Act (1940) 79
Treaty Ports 85
Trecwn 116, 117, 188
Treharris 158
Treorchy 56
Tributh, Herbert 84–5, 86
Tricycle, *see* Popov, Dusko
Trinity College, Cambridge 72
Tryweryn 1, 222
Tunisia 103
Turkey 170
Twenty Committee 7, 80, 82, 93,
  102, 103, 104, 109, 156–7, 171–3,
  180, 184, 185, 193, 210, 215
Tŷ'r Werin (Ystalyfera) 77

U-boats 19, 21, 24, 27, 32, 38, 52,
  61, 68, 77, 111, 119, 120, 122,
  125, 170, 181, 183, 184, 188,
  200, 201, 205, 206, 214, 225
Ukraine, the 111
Ultra 6
United States 13, 24, 40, 76, 90,
  99, 139, 155, 161, 163, 180, 182,
  190, 199, 205
University College of Wales,
  Aberystwyth 4, 59
Uppsala 86

Vaida, Ernst 88
Valentine, Revd Lewis 1, 3–4,
  100
Versailles, Treaty of 15, 111,
  222–3
Victoria Coach Station 17
Victoria Railway Station 21, 35,
  44, 74
Vitturo, diplomat 197
Vosges mountains 49

Wales 1, 2–3, 4–5, 6, 8, 11, 12,
  38, 40, 44, 47, 50, 52, 55–6, 58,
  59, 60, 66, 69, 73, 99, 100, 101,
  103, 118, 120, 122, 135, 158,
  184, 186–77, 190–1, 221, 222,
  225, 226
Walker, Flight Lieutenant R. M.
  67–8
Walt, agent 91
Wandsworth 22
War Cabinet 50, 52, 61, 111, 112,
  113, 185, 186
War Department 175
War Office 32, 148
Wardlaw-Milne, John 113
Wash, the 60

Waterloo Station 21
Waunarlwydd (Swansea) 188
'Welsh Activity' reports 99–102,
    108–9, 117–18, 187, 188–9
Welsh Guards 19
Welsh language 1–2, 3, 24, 27, 28,
    29, 59, 75, 223
Welsh Nation, The 75, 169
Welsh nationalist movement
    1, 2–3, 5–6, 12, 27, 37, 39, 40,
    55, 57, 58, 59, 69, 73, 74, 76,
    81, 93, 94, 99–101, 102, 108,
    117–18, 122, 185, 221, 222, 223,
    225, 226; *see also* Plaid Cymru
Welsh Office 222
Welwyn Garden City 67
Welzien, Kuno 134
West Hartlepool 158
Western Area UK Warning and
    Monitoring Organisation
    116–17
Western Mail 2–3, 4, 50, 52, 55–6,
    57, 58, 59–60
Weston-super-Mare 66
Wexford 217
Weybridge 39, 159
Whale, plan 45
Whitchurch (Cardiff) 49
White, Dick 19, 114, 140, 144–5,
    146–50, 152, 153, 180
White, Graham 217
White, Hilda 217
Whiteleys (Bayswater) 127

Wilhelm II, Kaiser 96
Williams, Catherine 10
Williams, D. J. 1, 100
Williams, Dafydd 59
Williams, Gwilym (GW) 6, 7,
    8, 9–11, 17, 27, 28–9, 30–3,
    35–8, 39–45, 47, 69, 71–3, 74,
    75–7, 80, 81, 82, 83, 84, 86, 88,
    91, 93–4, 95, 96–103, 104–10,
    115–19, 120, 121–2, 123, 130,
    132, 138, 139, 148, 150, 154,
    156, 162, 163, 164, 165–9,
    170–1, 172, 173–7, 179, 180,
    181, 182–7, 188–94, 195–6,
    197–8, 199, 201–11, 218, 219,
    221, 226
Williams, Reginald Morgan 58
Williams, Winifred Amelia 10,
    33, 218
Windsor, Edward, duke of,
    see Edward VIII
Windsor Castle 95
Witzke, Leutnant 'Charley' 37, 38,
    39–41, 42–3, 88–9, 90, 91
Woolwich Arsenal 20
Workers' Challenge 61, 62–3
Worm's Head (Rhossili) 24
Wrexham 59, 116
WW (the Welsh Agent) 9–10, 27,
    28–9, 30–1, 32, 33, 176, 179,
    182, 221, 226

Ystalyfera 74, 75, 77